Author's National Edition

THE WRITINGS OF
MARK TWAIN
VOLUME XXII

This is the authorized
Uniform Edition of all
my books.
                    Mark Twain

FROM A PHOTOGRAPH TAKEN IN 1899
By H W. Barnett, London

LITERARY ESSAYS

BY

MARK TWAIN
(SAMUEL L. CLEMENS)

ILLUSTRATED

HARPER & BROTHERS PUBLISHERS
NEW YORK AND LONDON

M—Q

ILLUSTRATIONS

CONTENTS

Acknowledgment is hereby made to Harper & Brothers, The Century Company, The Cosmopolitan, and S. S. McClure & Co., for courtesy shown in allowing the reprint in this volume of a number of their articles.

HOW TO TELL A STORY

AND

OTHER ESSAYS

HOW TO TELL A STORY

The Humorous Story an American Development.— **Its**
Difference from Comic and Witty Stories.

I DO not claim that I can tell a story as it ought to
be told. I only claim to know how a story
ought to be told, for I have been almost daily in the
company of the most expert story-tellers for many
years.

There are several kinds of stories, but only one
difficult kind — the humorous. I will talk mainly
about that one. The humorous story is American,
the comic story is English, the witty story is French.
The humorous story depends for its effect upon the
manner of the telling; the comic story and the witty
story upon the *matter*.

The humorous story may be spun out to great
length, and may wander around as much as it
pleases, and arrive nowhere in particular; but the
comic and witty stories must be brief and end with
a point. The humorous story bubbles gently along,
the others burst.

The humorous story is strictly a work of art —
high and delicate art — and only an artist can tell it;

but no art is necessary in telling the comic and the
witty story; anybody can do it.   The art of telling
a humorous story — understand, I mean by word of
mouth, not print — was created in America, and
has remained at home.

The humorous story is told gravely; the teller
does his best to conceal the fact that he even dimly
suspects that there is anything funny about it; but
the teller of the comic story tells you beforehand
that it is one of the funniest things he has ever
heard, then tells it with eager delight, and is the
first person to laugh when he gets through.   And
sometimes, if he has had good success, he is so glad
and happy that he will repeat the " nub " of it and
glance around from face to face, collecting applause,
and then repeat it again.   It is a pathetic thing to
see.

Very often, of course, the rambling and disjointed
humorous story finishes with a nub, point, snapper,
or whatever you like to call it.   Then the listener
must be alert, for in many cases the teller will divert
attention from that nub by dropping it in a carefully
casual and indifferent way, with the pretence that he
does not know it is a nub.

Artemus Ward used that trick a good deal; then
when the belated audience presently caught the joke
he would look up with innocent surprise, as if
wondering what they had found to laugh at.   Dan
Setchell used it before him, Nye and Riley and
others use it to-day.

But the teller of the comic story does not slur the nub; he shouts it at you — every time. And when he prints it, in England, France, Germany, and Italy, he italicizes it, puts some whooping exclamation-points after it, and sometimes explains it in a parenthesis. All of which is very depressing, and makes one want to renounce joking and lead a better life.

Let me set down an instance of the comic method, using an anecdote which has been popular all over the world for twelve or fifteen hundred years. The teller tells it in this way:

THE WOUNDED SOLDIER.

In the course of a certain battle a soldier whose leg had been shot off appealed to another soldier who was hurrying by to carry him to the rear, informing him at the same time of the loss which he had sustained; whereupon the generous son of Mars, shouldering the unfortunate, proceeded to carry out his desire. The bullets and cannon-balls were flying in all directions, and presently one of the latter took the wounded man's head off — without, however, his deliverer being aware of it. In no long time he was hailed by an officer, who said:

" Where are you going with that carcass?"

" To the rear, sir — he's lost his leg!"

" His leg, forsooth?" responded the astonished officer; " you mean his head, you booby."

Whereupon the soldier dispossessed himself of his

burden, and stood looking down upon it in great perplexity. At length he said:

" It is true, sir, just as you have said." Then after a pause he added, " *But he* TOLD *me* IT WAS HIS LEG! ! ! ! !"

Here the narrator bursts into explosion after explosion of thunderous horse-laughter, repeating that nub from time to time through his gaspings and shriekings and suffocatings.

It takes only a minute and a half to tell that in its comic-story form; and isn't worth the telling, after all. Put into the humorous-story form it takes ten minutes, and is about the funniest thing I have ever listened to — as James Whitcomb Riley tells it.

He tells it in the character of a dull-witted old farmer who has just heard it for the first time, thinks it is unspeakably funny, and is trying to repeat it to a neighbor. But he can't remember it; so he gets all mixed up and wanders helplessly round and round, putting in tedious details that don't belong in the tale and only retard it; taking them out conscientiously and putting in others that are just as useless; making minor mistakes now and then and stopping to correct them and explain how he came to make them; remembering things which he forgot to put in in their proper place and going back to put them in there; stopping his narrative a good while in order to try to recall the name of the soldier that was hurt, and finally remembering that the soldier's name was not mentioned, and remarking

placidly that the name is of no real importance,
anyway — better, of course, if one knew it, but not
essential, after all — and so on, and so on, and so
on.

The teller is innocent and happy and pleased with
himself, and has to stop every little while to hold
himself in and keep from laughing outright; and
does hold in, but his body quakes in a jelly-like
way with interior chuckles; and at the end of the
ten minutes the audience have laughed until they
are exhausted, and the tears are running down their
faces.

The simplicity and innocence and sincerity and
unconsciousness of the old farmer are perfectly
simulated, and the result is a performance which is
thoroughly charming and delicious. This is art —
and fine and beautiful, and only a master can com-
pass it; but a machine could tell the other story.

To string incongruities and absurdities together in
a wandering and sometimes purposeless way, and
seem innocently unaware that they are absurdities, is
the basis of the American art, if my position is
correct. Another feature is the slurring of the
point. A third is the dropping of a studied remark
apparently without knowing it, as if one were thinking aloud. The fourth and last is the pause.

Artemus Ward dealt in numbers three and four a
good deal. He would begin to tell with great animation something which he seemed to think was
wonderful; then lose confidence, and after an

apparently absent-minded pause add an incongru-
ous remark in a soliloquizing way; and that was
the remark intended to explode the mine — and
it did.

For instance, he would say eagerly, excitedly, " I
once knew a man in New Zealand who hadn't a
tooth in his head "— here his animation would die
out; a silent, reflective pause would follow, then he
would say dreamily, and as if to himself, " and yet
that man could beat a drum better than any man I
ever saw."

The pause is an exceedingly important feature in
any kind of story, and a frequently recurring feature,
too.   It is a dainty thing, and delicate, and also uncertain and treacherous; for it must be exactly the
right length — no more and no less — or it fails of
its purpose and makes trouble.   If the pause is too
short the impressive point is passed, and the audience have had time to divine that a surprise is
intended — and then you can't surprise them, of
course.

On the platform I used to tell a negro ghost story
that had a pause in front of the snapper on the end,
and that pause was the most important thing in the
whole story.   If I got it the right length precisely,
I could spring the finishing ejaculation with effect
enough to make some impressible girl deliver a
startled little yelp and jump out of her seat — and
that was what I was after.   This story was called
" The Golden Arm," and was told in this fashion.

You can practise with it yourself — and mind you look out for the pause and get it right.

THE GOLDEN ARM.

Once 'pon a time dey wuz a monsus mean man, en he live 'way out in de prairie all 'lone by hisself, 'cep'n he had a wife. En bimeby she died, en he tuck en toted her way out dah in de prairie en buried her. Well, she had a golden arm — all solid gold, fum de shoulder down. He wuz pow'ful mean — pow'ful; en dat night he couldn't sleep, caze he want dat golden arm so bad.

When it come midnight he couldn't stan' it no mo'; so he git up, he did, en tuck his lantern en shoved out thoo de storm en dug her up en got de golden arm; en he bent his head down 'gin de win', en plowed en plowed en plowed thoo de snow. Den all on a sudden he stop (make a considerable pause here, and look startled, and take a listening attitude) en say: " My *lan'*, what's dat!"

En he listen — en listen — en de win' say (set your teeth together and imitate the wailing and wheezing singsong of the wind), " Bzzz-z-zzz "— en den, way back yonder whah de grave is, he hear a *voice !* — he hear a voice all mix' up in de win' — can't hardly tell 'em 'part — " Bzzz-zzz — W-h-o — g-o-t — m-y — g-o-l-d-e-n *arm?* — zzz — zzz — W-h-o g-o-t m-y g-o-l-d-e-n *arm ?*" (You must begin to shiver violently now.)

En he begin to shiver en shake, en say, " Oh,

2E

my! *Oh*, my lan'!" en de win' blow de lantern
out, en de snow en sleet blow in his face en mos'
choke him, en he start a-plowin' knee-deep towards
home mos' dead, he so sk'yerd — en pooty soon
he hear de voice agin, en (pause) it 'us comin'
after him! " Bzzz — zzz — zzz — W-h-o — g-o-t —
m-y — g-o-l-d-e-n — *arm?* "

When he git to de pasture he hear it agin —
closter now, en a-*comin'!* — a-comin' back dah in
de dark en de storm — (repeat the wind and the
voice). When he git to de house he rush up-stairs
en jump in de bed en kiver up, head and years, en
lay dah shiverin' en shakin' — en den way out dah
he hear it *agin!* — en a-*comin'!* En bimeby he
hear (pause — awed, listening attitude) — pat — pat
— pat —*hit's a-comin' up-stairs!* Den he hear de
latch, en he *know* it's in de room!

Den pooty soon he know it's a-*stannin' by
de bed!* (Pause.) Den — he know it's a-*bendin'
down over him* — en he cain't skasely git his
breath! Den — den — he seem to feel someth'n
c-o-l-d, right down 'most agin his head!
(Pause.)

Den de voice say, *right at his year* — " W-h-o —
g-o-t — m-y — g-o-l-d-e-n *arm?*" (You must wail
it out very plaintively and accusingly; then you
stare steadily and impressively into the face of the
farthest-gone auditor — a girl, preferably — and let
that awe-inspiring pause begin to build itself in the
deep hush. When it has reached exactly the right

length, jump suddenly at that girl and yell, "*You've got it!*"

If you've got the *pause* right, she'll fetch a dear little yelp and spring right out of her shoes. But you *must* get the pause right; and you will find it the most troublesome and aggravating and uncertain thing you ever undertook.)

IN DEFENCE OF HARRIET SHELLEY

I

I HAVE committed sins, of course; but I have not committed enough of them to entitle me to the punishment of reduction to the bread and water of ordinary literature during six years when I might have been living on the fat diet spread for the righteous in Professor Dowden's *Life of Shelley*, if I had been justly dealt with.

During these six years I have been living a life of peaceful ignorance. I was not aware that Shelley's first wife was unfaithful to him, and that that was why he deserted her and wiped the stain from his sensitive honor by entering into soiled relations with Godwin's young daughter. This was all new to me when I heard it lately, and was told that the proofs of it were in this book, and that this book's verdict is accepted in the girls' colleges of America and its view taught in their literary classes.

In each of these six years multitudes of young people in our country have arrived at the Shelley-reading age. Are these six multitudes unacquainted with this life of Shelley? Perhaps they are; indeed,

e may feel pretty sure that the great bulk of them
e.   To these, then, I address myself, in the hope
at some account of this romantic historical fable
d the fabulist's manner of constructing and adorn-
g it may interest them.

First, as to its literary style.   Our negroes in
nerica have several ways of entertaining them-
ves which are not found among the whites any-
ere.   Among these inventions of theirs is one
ich is particularly popular with them.   It is a
mpetition in elegant deportment.   They hire a
ll and bank the spectators' seats in rising tiers
ng the two sides, leaving all the middle stretch of
floor free.   A cake is provided as a prize for
winner in the competition, and a bench of ex-
rts in deportment is appointed to award it.   Some-
es there are as many as fifty contestants, male
l female, and five hundred spectators.   One at a
e the contestants enter, clothed regardless of ex-
se in what each considers the perfection of style
l taste, and walk down the vacant central space
l back again with that multitude of critical eyes
them.   All that the competitor knows of fine airs
l graces he throws into his carriage, all that he
ws of seductive expression he throws into his
ntenance.   He may use all the helps he can
ise: watch-chain to twirl with his fingers, cane
do graceful things with, snowy handkerchief to
rish and get artful effects out of, shiny new
vepipe hat to assist in his courtly bows; and the

2*.*.

colored lady may have a fan to work up *her* effect
with, and smile over and blush behind, and sh
may add other helps, according to her judgmen
When the review by individual detail is over, a gran
review of all the contestants in procession follow
with all the airs and graces and all the bowings an
smirkings on exhibition at once and this enabl
the bench of experts to make the necessary con
parisons and arrive at a verdict. The successf
competitor gets the prize which I have before men
tioned, and an abundance of applause and env
along with it. The negroes have a name for th
grave deportment-tournament; a name taken fro
the prize contended for. They call it a Cak
Walk.

This Shelley biography is a literary cake-wal
The ordinary forms of speech are absent from
All the pages, all the paragraphs, walk by sedatel
elegantly, not to say mincingly, in their Sunda
best, shiny and sleek, perfumed, and with *bouto*
nieres in their button-holes; it is rare to find even
chance sentence that has forgotten to dress. If t
book wishes to tell us that Mary Godwin, child
sixteen, had known afflictions, the fact saunte
forth in this nobby outfit: " Mary was herself n
unlearned in the lore of pain " — meaning by th
that she had not always traveled on asphalt; or,
some authorities would frame it, that she had " be
there herself," a form which, while preferable to t
book's form, is still not to be recommended.   If t

book wishes to tell us that Harriet Shelley hired a wet-nurse, that commonplace fact gets turned into a dancing-master, who does his professional bow before us in pumps and knee-breeches, with his fiddle under one arm and his crush-hat under the other, thus: "The beauty of Harriet's motherly relation to her babe was marred in Shelley's eyes by the introduction into his house of a hireling nurse to whom was delegated the mother's tenderest office."

This is perhaps the strangest book that has seen the light since Frankenstein. Indeed, it is a Frankenstein itself; a Frankenstein with the original infirmity supplemented by a new one; a Frankenstein with the reasoning faculty wanting. Yet it believes it can reason, and is always trying. It is not content to leave a mountain of fact standing in the clear sunshine, where the simplest reader can perceive its form, its details, and its relation to the rest of the landscape, but thinks it must help him examine it and understand it; so its drifting mind settles upon it with that intent, but always with one and the same result: there is a change of temperature and the mountain is hid in a fog. Every time it sets up a premise and starts to reason from it, there is a surprise in store for the reader. It is strangely near-sighted, cross-eyed, and purblind. Sometimes when a mastodon walks across the field of its vision it takes it for a rat; at other times it does not see it at all.

B*₊*₊

The materials of this biographical fable are facts, rumors, and poetry. They are connected together and harmonized by the help of suggestion, conjecture, innuendo, perversion, and semi-suppression.

The fable has a distinct object in view, but this object is not acknowledged in set words. Percy Bysshe Shelley has done something which in the case of other men is called a grave crime; it must be shown that in his case it is not that, because he does not think as other men do about these things.

Ought not that to be enough, if the fabulist is serious? Having proved that a crime is not a crime, was it worth while to go on and fasten the responsibility of a crime which was not a crime upon somebody else? What is the use of hunting down and holding to bitter account people who are responsible for other people's innocent acts?

Still, the fabulist thinks it a good idea to do that. In his view Shelley's first wife, Harriet, free of all offense as far as we have historical facts for guidance, must be held unforgivably responsible for her husband's innocent act in deserting her and taking up with another woman.

Any one will suspect that this task has its difficulties. Any one will divine that nice work is necessary here, cautious work, wily work, and that there is entertainment to be had in watching the magician do it. There is indeed entertainment in watching him. He arranges his facts, his rumors, and his poems on his table in full view of the house, and shows you hat everything is there — no deception, everything air and above board. And this is apparently true, et there is a defect, for some of his best stock is id in an appendix-basket behind the door, and you o not come upon it until the exhibition is over and he enchantment of your mind accomplished — as he magician thinks.

There is an insistent atmosphere of candor and airness about this book which is engaging at first, hen a little burdensome, then a trifle fatiguing, then rogressively suspicious, annoying, irritating, and ppressive. It takes one some little time to find out hat phrases which seem intended to guide the reader right are there to mislead him; that phrases which eem intended to throw light are there to throw darkness; that phrases which seem intended to nterpret a fact are there to misinterpret it; that hrases which seem intended to forestall prejudice re there to create it; that phrases which seem anti-dotes are poisons in disguise. The naked facts rrayed in the book establish Shelley's guilt in that ne episode which disfigures his otherwise super-atively lofty and beautiful life; but the historian's areful and methodical misinterpretation of them ransfers the responsibility to the wife's shoulders — s he persuades himself. The few meagre facts of Harriet Shelley's life, as furnished by the book, cquit her of offense; but by calling in the for-bidden helps of rumor, gossip, conjecture, insinua-ion, and innuendo he destroys her character and rehabilitates Shelley's — as he believes. And in truth his unheroic work has not been barren of the results he aimed at; as witness the assertion made to me that girls in the colleges of America are taught that Harriet Shelley put a stain upon her husband's honor, and that that was what stung him into repurifying himself by deserting her and his child and entering into scandalous relations with a school-girl acquaintance of his.

If that assertion is true, they probably use a reduction of this work in those colleges, maybe only a sketch outlined from it. Such a thing as that could be harmful and misleading. They ought to cast it out and put the whole book in its place. It would not deceive. It would not deceive the janitor.

All of this book is interesting on account of the sorcerer's methods and the attractiveness of some of his characters and the repulsiveness of the rest, but no part of it is so much so as are the chapters wherein he tries to think he thinks he sets forth the causes which led to Shelley's desertion of his wife in 1814.

Harriet Westbrook was a school-girl sixteen years old. Shelley was teeming with advanced thought. He believed that Christianity was a degrading and selfish superstition, and he had a deep and sincere desire to rescue one of his sisters from it. Harriet was impressed by his various philosophies and looked upon him as an intellectual wonder — which indeed he was. He had an idea that she could give im valuable help in his scheme regarding his sister; herefore he asked her to correspond with him. She was quite willing. Shelley was not thinking of love, for he was just getting over a passion for his cousin, Harriet Grove, and just getting well steeped in one for Miss Hitchener, a school-teacher. What might happen to Harriet Westbrook before the letter-writing was ended did not enter his mind. Yet an elder person could have made a good guess at it, for in person Shelley was as beautiful as an angel, he was frank, sweet, winning, unassuming, and so rich in unselfishness, generosities, and magnanimities that he made his whole generation seem poor in these great qualities by comparison. Besides, he was in distress. His college had expelled him for writing an atheistical pamphlet and afflicting the reverend heads of the university with it, his rich father and grandfather had closed their purses against him, his friends were cold. Necessarily, Harriet fell in love with him; and so deeply, indeed, that there was no way for Shelley to save her from suicide but to marry her. He believed himself to blame for this state of things, so the marriage took place. He was pretty fairly in love with Harriet, although he loved Miss Hitchener better. He wrote and explained the case to Miss Hitchener after the wedding, and he could not have been franker or more *naïve* and less stirred up about the circumstance if the matter in issue had been a commercial transaction involving thirty-five dollars.

Shelley was nineteen. He was not a youth, b[
a man. He had never had any youth. He was .
erratic and fantastic child during eighteen year
then he stepped into manhood, as one steps over
door-sill. He was curiously mature at nineteen
his ability to do independent thinking on the dee
questions of life and to arrive at sharply defini
decisions regarding them, and stick to them — sti
to them and stand by them at cost of bread, frien
ships, esteem, respect, and approbation.

For the sake of his opinions he was willing
sacrifice all these valuable things, and did sacrifi
them; and went on doing it, too, when he could
any moment have made himself rich and supplie
himself with friends and esteem by compromisin
with his father, at the moderate expense of throwin
overboard one or two indifferent details of his carg
of principles.

He and Harriet eloped to Scotland and got ma[
ried. They took lodgings in Edinburgh of a so[
answerable to their purse, which was about empty
and there their life was a happy one and grew dail
more so. They had only themselves for company
but they needed no additions to it. They were a
cozy and contented as birds in a nest. Harriet san[
evenings or read aloud; also she studied and trie[
to improve her mind, her husband instructing her i[
Latin. She was very beautiful, she was modest
quiet, genuine, and, according to her husband'[
testimony, she had no fine lady airs or aspiration[

about her. In Matthew Arnold's judgment, she
was " a pleasing figure.''

The pair remained five weeks in Edinburgh, and
then took lodgings in York, where Shelley's college
mate, Hogg, lived. Shelley presently ran down to
London, and Hogg took this opportunity to make
love to the young wife. She repulsed him, and reported the fact to her husband when he got back.
It seems a pity that Shelley did not copy this creditable conduct of hers some time or other when under
temptation, so that we might have seen the author
of his biography hang the miracle in the skies and
squirt rainbows at it.

At the end of the first year of marriage — the
most trying year for any young couple, for then the
mutual failings are coming one by one to light, and
the necessary adjustments are being made in pain
and tribulation — Shelley was able to recognize that
his marriage venture had been a safe one. As we
have seen, his love for his wife had begun in a
rather shallow way and with not much force, but
now it was become deep and strong, which entitles
his wife to a broad credit mark, one may admit.
He addresses a long and loving poem to her, in
which both passion and worship appear:

Exhibit A

" O thou
Whose dear love gleamed upon the gloomy path
Which this lone spirit travelled,

·   ·   ·   ·   ·   ·   ·   ·

. . . wilt thou not turn

> Those spirit-beaming eyes and look on me.
> Until I be assured that Earth is Heaven
> And Heaven is Earth?
>
> .   .   .   .   .   .
>
> Harriet! let death all mortal ties dissolve,
> But ours shall not be mortal."

Shelley also wrote a sonnet to her in August o
this same year in celebration of her birthday:

Exhibit B

> " Ever as now with Love and Virtue's glow
>   May thy unwithering soul not cease to burn,
>   Still may thine heart with those pure thoughts o'erflow
>   Which force from mine such quick and warm return."

Was the girl of seventeen glad and proud an
happy? We may conjecture that she was.

That was the year 1812. Another year passed —
still happily, still successfully — a child was born i
June, 1813, and in September, three months late
Shelley addresses a poem to this child, Ianthe,
which he points out just when the little creature
most particularly dear to him:

Exhibit C

> " Dearest when most thy tender traits express
>   The image of thy mother's loveliness."

Up to this point the fabulist counsel for Shell
and prosecutor of his young wife has had easy sailin
but now his trouble begins, for Shelley is getti
ready to make some unpleasant history for himse
and it will be necessary to put the blame of it on t
wife.

Shelley had made the acquaintance of a charmi

y-haired, young-hearted Mrs. Boinville, whose
e " retained a certain youthful beauty "; she
ed at Bracknell, and had a young daughter named
rnelia Turner, who was equipped with many fasci-
:ions.   Apparently these people were sufficiently
timental.   Hogg says of Mrs. Boinville:

> The greater part of her associates were odious. I generally found
> e two or three sentimental young butchers, an eminently philo-
> ical tinker, and several very unsophisticated medical practitioners or
> ical students, all of low origin and vulgar and offensive manners.
> y sighed, turned up their eyes, retailed philosophy, such as it was,"

Shelley moved to Bracknell, July 27th (this is
1 1813) purposely to be near this unwholesome
irie-dogs' nest. The fabulist says: " It was the
rance into a world more amiable and exquisite
n he had yet known."

" In this acquaintance the attraction was mutual "
and presently it grew to be very mutual indeed,
ween Shelley and Cornelia Turner, when they
t to studying the Italian poets together. Shelley,
esponding like a tremulous instrument to every
ath of passion or of sentiment," had his chance
e.   It took only four days for Cornelia's attrac-
ns to begin to dim Harriet's.   Shelley arrived on
27th of July; on the 31st he wrote a sonnet to
rriet in which " one detects already the little rift
the lover's lute which had seemed to be healed or
ver to have gaped at all when the later and hap-
r sonnet to Ianthe was written " — in September,
remember:

Exhibit D

"EVENING. TO HARRIET

"O thou bright Sun !   Beneath the dark blue line
Of western distance that sublime descendest,
And, gleaming lovelier as thy beams decline,
Thy million hues to every vapor lendest,
And over cobweb, lawn, and grove, and stream
Sheddest the liquid magic of thy light,
Till calm Earth, with the parting splendor bright,
Shows like the vision of a beauteous dream;
What gazer now with astronomic eye
Could coldly count the spots within thy sphere ?
Such were thy lover, Harriet, could he fly
The thoughts of all that makes his passion dear,
And turning senseless from thy warm caress
Pick flaws in our close-woven happiness."

I cannot find the " rift "; still it may be there.
What the poem *seems* to say is, that a person would
be coldly ungrateful who could consent to count and
consider little spots and flaws in such a warm, great
satisfying sun as Harriet is. It is a " little rift
which had seemed to be healed, *or* never to have
gaped at all." That is, " one *detects* " a little rift
which perhaps had never existed. How does one
do that ?   How does one see the invisible? It is the
fabulist's secret; he knows how to detect what does
not exist, he knows how to see what is not seeable;
it is his gift, and he works it many a time to poor
dead Harriet Shelley's deep damage.

" As yet, however, if there was a speck upon
Shelley's happiness it was no more than a speck "
—meaning the one which one detects where " a

ay never have gaped at all " — " nor had Harriet
ause for discontent."

Shelley's Latin instructions to his wife had ceased.
From a teacher he had now become a pupil."
Irs. Boinville and her young married daughter
ornelia were teaching him Italian poetry; a fact
hich warns one to receive with some caution that
her statement that Harriet had no " cause for dis-
ntent."

Shelley had stopped instructing Harriet in Latin,
before mentioned. The biographer thinks that
e busy life in London some time back, and the
trusion of the baby, account for this. These were
ndrances, but were there no others? He is always
erlooking a detail here and there that might be
luable in helping us understand a situation. For
stance, when a man has been hard at work at the
alian poets with a pretty woman, hour after hour,
d responding like a tremulous instrument to every
eath of passion or of sentiment in the meantime,
at man is dog-tired when he gets home, and he
n't teach his wife Latin; it would be unreasonable
expect it.

Up to this time we have submitted to having Mrs.
oinville pushed upon us as ostensibly concerned in
ese Italian lessons, but the biographer drops her
w, of his own accord. Cornelia " perhaps " is
e teacher. Hogg says she was a prey to a kind
sweet melancholy, arising from causes purely
aginary; she required consolation, and found it
3E

in Petrarch. He also says, " Bysshe entered at o
fully into her views and caught the soft infecti
breathing the tenderest and sweetest melancho
as every true poet ought."

Then the author of the book interlards a m
stately and fine compliment to Cornelia, furnis
by a man of approved judgment who knew her v
" in later years." It is a very good complim
indeed, and she no doubt deserved it in her " la
years," when she had for generations ceased to
sentimental and lackadaisical, and was no longer
gaged in enchanting young husbands and sow
sorrow for young wives. But why is that com
ment to that old gentlewoman intruded there? I
to make the reader believe she was well-chosen
safe society for a young, sentimental husband?
biographer's device was not well planned. That
person was not present — it was her other self t
was there, her young, sentimental, melanche
warm-blooded self, in those early sweet times bef
antiquity had cooled her off and mossed her back

" In choosing for friends such women as M
Newton, Mrs. Boinville, and Cornelia Turner, Sl
ley gave good proof of his insight and discri
nation." That is the fabulist's opinion — Har
Shelley's is not reported.

Early in August, Shelley was in London try
to raise money. In September he wrote the po
to the baby, already quoted from. In the first w
of October Shelley and family went to Warw

then to Edinburgh, arriving there about the middle of the month.

" Harriet was happy." Why? The author furnishes a reason, but hides from us whether it is history or conjecture; it is because " *the babe had borne the journey well*." It has all the aspect of one of his artful devices — flung in in his favorite casual way — the way he has when he wants to draw one's attention away from an obvious thing and amuse it with some trifle that is less obvious but more useful — in a history like this. The obvious thing is, that Harriet was happy because there was much territory between her husband and Cornelia Turner now; and because the perilous Italian lessons were taking a rest; and because, if there chanced to be any respondings like a tremulous instrument to every breath of passion or of sentiment in stock in these days, she might hope to get a share of them herself; and because, with her husband liberated, now, from the fetid fascinations of that sentimental retreat so pitilessly described by Hogg, who also dubbed it " Shelley's paradise " later, she might hope to persuade him to stay away from it permanently; and because she might also hope that his brain would cool, now, and his heart become healthy, and both brain and heart consider the situation and resolve that it would be a right and manly thing to stand by this girl-wife and her child and see that they were honorably dealt with, and cherished and protected and loved by the man that had promised these things, and so be made happy and kept so. And because, also — may we conjecture this? — we may hope for the privilege of taking up our cozy Latin lessons again, that used to be so pleasant, and brought us so near together — so near, indeed, that often our heads touched, just as heads do over Italian lessons; and our hands met in casual and unintentional, but still most delicious and thrilling little contacts and momentary clasps, just as they inevitably do over Italian lessons. Suppose one should say to any young wife: " I find that your husband is poring over the Italian poets and being instructed in the beautiful Italian language by the lovely Cornelia Robinson " — would that cozy picture fail to rise before her mind? would its possibilities fail to suggest themselves to her? would there be a pang in her heart and a blush on her face? or, on the contrary, would the remark give her pleasure, make her joyous and gay? Why, one needs only to make the experiment — the result will not be uncertain.

However, we learn — by authority of deeply reasoned and searching conjecture — that the baby bore the journey well, and that that was why the young wife was happy. That accounts for two per cent. of the happiness, but it was not right to imply that it accounted for the other ninety-eight also.

Peacock, a scholar, poet, and friend of the Shelleys, was of their party when they went away. He used to laugh at the Boinville menagerie, and " was

t a favorite." One of the Boinville group, writing
Hogg, said, " The Shelleys have made an addi-
n to their party in the person of a cold scholar,
o, I think, has neither taste nor feeling. This,
elley will perceive sooner or later, for his warm
ure craves sympathy." True, and Shelley will
ht his way back there to get it — there will be no
y to head him off.

Towards the end of November it was necessary
Shelley to pay a business visit to London, and
conceived the project of leaving Harriet and the
oy in Edinburgh with Harriet's sister, Eliza West-
ok, a sensible, practical maiden lady about thirty
rs old, who had spent a great part of her time
h the family since the marriage. She was an
mable woman, and Shelley had had reason to
her, and did like her; but along about this time
feeling towards her changed. Part of Shelley's
n, as he wrote Hogg, was to spend his London
nings with the Newtons — members of the Boin-
e Hysterical Society. But, alas, when he arrived
y in December, that pleasant game was partially
cked, for Eliza and the family arrived *with* him.
are left destitute of conjectures at this point by
biographer, and it is my duty to supply one. I
nce the conjecture that it was Eliza who inter-
d with that game. I think she tried to do what
could towards modifying the Boinville connec-
, in the interest of her young sister's peace and
or.

3*.*.

If it was she who blocked that game, she was ⟨s⟩
strong enough to block the next one. Before ⟨a⟩
month and year were out — no date given, let ⟨us⟩
call it Christmas — Shelley and family were nes⟨t⟩
in a furnished house in Windsor, " at no great ⟨dis⟩
tance from the Boinvilles " — these decoys still ⟨re⟩
siding at Bracknell.

What we need, now, is a misleading conjectu⟨re⟩
We get it with characteristic promptness and ⟨de⟩
pravity:

" But Prince Athanase found not the aged Zonoras, the friend o⟨f his⟩
boyhood, in any wanderings to Windsor. Dr. Lind had died a ⟨year⟩
since, and with his death Windsor must have lost, for Shelley, its ⟨chief⟩
attraction."

Still, not to mention Shelley's wife, there ⟨was⟩
Bracknell, at any rate. While Bracknell remai⟨ns⟩
all solace is not lost. Shelley is represented by ⟨his⟩
biographer as doing a great many careless thin⟨gs⟩
but to my mind this hiring a furnished house ⟨for⟩
three months in order to be with a man who ⟨had⟩
been dead a year, is the carelessest of them ⟨all.⟩
One feels for him — that is but natural, and d⟨oes⟩
us honor besides — yet one is vexed, for all th⟨at.⟩
He could have written and asked about the ag⟨ed⟩
Zonoras before taking the house. He may not h⟨ave⟩
had the address, but that is nothing — any postm⟨an⟩
would know the aged Zonoras; a dead postm⟨an⟩
would remember a name like that.

And yet, why throw a rag like this to us raven⟨ous⟩
wolves? Is it seriously supposable that we will s⟨it⟩

chew it and let our prey escape? No, we are
tting to expect this kind of device, and to give it
erely a sniff for certainty's sake and then walk
ound it and leave it lying. Shelley was not after
e aged Zonoras; he was pointed for Cornelia and
e Italian lessons, for his warm nature was craving
mpathy.

II

THE year 1813 is just ended now, and we step
to 1814.

To recapitulate, how much of Cornelia's society
s Shelley had, thus far? Portions of August and
ptember, and four days of July. That is to say,
has had opportunity to enjoy it, more or less,
ring that brief period. Did he want some more
it? We must fall back upon history, and then
to conjecturing.

" In the early part of the year 1814, Shelley was a frequent visitor at
cknell."

" Frequent " is a cautious word, in this author's
outh; the very cautiousness of it, the vagueness of
provokes suspicion; it makes one suspect that
s frequency was more frequent than the mere
mmon everyday kinds of frequency which one is
the habit of averaging up with the unassuming
m " frequent." I think so because they fixed
a bedroom for him in the Boinville house. One

c*.*.

doesn't need a bedroom if one is only going to
over now and then in a disconnected way to resp
like a tremulous instrument to every breath of p
sion or of sentiment and rub up one's Italian poe
a little.

The young wife was not invited, perhaps. If
was, she most certainly did not come, or she wo
have straightened the room up; the most ignor
of us knows that a wife would not endure a room
the condition in which Hogg found this one wl
he occupied it one night. Shelley was away — w
nobody can divine. Clothes were scattered abc
there were books on every side: "Whereve
book could be laid was an open book turned dc
on its face to keep its place." It seems plain t
the wife was not invited. No, not that; I think
was invited, but said to herself that she could
bear to go there and see another young won
touching heads with her husband over an Ita
book and making thrilling hand-contacts with I
accidentally.

As remarked, he was a frequent visitor th
"where he found an easeful resting-place in
house of Mrs. Boinville — the white-haired Maim
— and of her daughter, Mrs. Turner." The a
Zonoras was deceased, but the white-haired Maim
was still on deck, as we see. "Three charm
ladies entertained the mocker (Hogg) with cup;
tea, late hours, Wieland's Agathon, sighs and smi
and the celestial manna of refined sentimen

5uch," says Hogg, " were the delights of Shel-
's paradise in Bracknell."

The white-haired Maimuna presently writes to
gg:

I will not have you despise home-spun pleasures. Shelley is
ing a trial of them with us—"

A trial of them. It may be called that. It was
rch 11, and he had been in the house a month.
e continues:

1elley "likes them so well that he is resolved to leave off ram-
ḡ—"

But he has *already* left it off. He has been there
1onth.

1d begin a course of them himself."

But he has already begun it. He has been at it a
nth. He likes it so well that he has forgotten all
•ut his wife, as a letter of his reveals.

Seriously, I think his mind and body want rest."

Yet he has been resting both for a month, with
ian, and tea, and manna of sentiment, and late
1rs, and every restful thing a young husband
.1d need for the refreshment of weary limbs and a
e conscience, and a nagging sense of shabbiness
l treachery.

His journeys after what he has never found have racked his purse
his tranquillity. He is resolved to take a little care of the former,
ity to the latter, which I applaud, and shall second with all my
it."

But she does not say whether the young wife, a

stranger and lonely yonder, wants another wom:
and her daughter Cornelia to be lavishing so mu
inflamed interest on her husband or not.   Th
young wife is always silent — we are never allow
to hear from her.   She must have opinions abo
such things, she cannot be indifferent, she must
approving or disapproving, surely she would spe
if she were allowed — even to-day and from h
grave she would, if she could, I think — but w
get only the other side, they keep her silent alwa}

"He has deeply interested us.   In the course of your intimacy
must have made you feel what we now feel for him.   He is seekin
house close to us —"

Ah! he is not close enough yet, it seems —

"and if he succeeds we shall have an additional motive to induce
to come among us in the summer."

The reader would puzzle a long time and r
guess the biographer's comment upon the abc
letter.   It is this:

"These sound like words of a considerate and judicious friend.

That is what he thinks.   That is, it is what
thinks he thinks.   No, that is not quite it: it is wl
he thinks he can stupefy a particularly and unspe
ably dull reader into thinking it is what he thin
He makes that comment with the knowledge t
Shelley is in love with this woman's daughter, a
that it is because of the fascinations of these t
that Shelley has deserted his wife — for this mon
considering all the circumstances, and his new p

ɔn, and his employment of the time, amounted to
sertion; that is its rightful name. We cannot
ow how the wife regarded it and felt about it;
t if she could have read the letter which Shelley
.s writing to Hogg four or five days later, we
uld guess her thought and how she felt. Hear
n:

. . . .

" I have been staying with Mrs. Boinville for the last month; I have
aped, in the society of all that philosophy and friendship combine,
n the dismaying solitude of myself."

It is fair to conjecture that he was feeling ashamed.

" They have revived in my heart the expiring flame of life. I have
myself translated to a paradise which has nothing of mortality but
:ransitoriness; my heart sickens at the view of that necessity which
l quickly divide me from the delightful tranquillity of this happy
ne — for it has become my home.

. . . .

" Eliza is still with us — not here ! — but will be with me when the
nite malice of destiny forces me to depart."

Eliza is she who blocked that game — the game
London — the one where we were purposing to
ie every night with one of the "three charming
lies" who fed tea and manna and late hours to
ɔgg at Bracknell.

Shelley could send Eliza away, of course; could
ve cleared her out long ago if so minded, just
he had previously done with a predecessor of
rs whom he had first worshipped and then turned
ainst; but perhaps she was useful there as a thin
cuse for staying away himself.

" I am now but little inclined to contest this point.   I certainly l
her with all my heart and soul. . . .

" It is a sight which awakens an inexpressible sensation of dis;
and horror, to see her caress my poor little Ianthe, in whom I ı
hereafter find the consolation of sympathy.   I sometimes feel f.
with the fatigue of checking the overflowings of my unbounded
horrence for this miserable wretch.   But she is no more than a b.
and loathsome worm, that cannot see to sting.

" I have begun to learn Italian again. . . . Cornelia assists me
this language.   Did I not once tell you that I thought her cold and
served?   She is the reverse of this, as she is the reverse of everyth
bad.   She inherits all the divinity of her mother. . . . I have so.
times forgotten that I am not an inmate of this delightful home — th
time will come which will cast me again into the boundless ocean
abhorred society.

" I have written nothing but one stanza, which has no meaning,
that I have only written in thought:

> " Thy dewy looks sink in my breast;
>   Thy gentle words stir poison there;
> Thou hast disturbed the only rest
>   That was the portion of despair.
> Subdued to duty's hard control,
>   I could have borne my wayward lot:
> The chains that bind this ruined soul
>   Had cankered then, but crushed it not.

" This is the vision of a delirious and distempered dream, wl
passes away at the cold clear light of morning.   Its surpassing ex
lence and exquisite perfections have no more reality than the color o
autumnal sunset."

Then it did not refer to his wife.   That is pla
otherwise he would have said so.   It is well that
explained that it has no meaning, for if he had ı
done that, the previous soft references to Corne
and the way he has come to feel about her n
would make us think she was the person who l

spired it while teaching him how to read the warm
nd ruddy Italian poets during a month.

The biography observes that portions of this letter
" read like the tired moaning of a wounded crea-
ure." Guesses at the nature of the wound are
ermissible; we will hazard one.

Read by the light of Shelley's previous history,
is letter seems to be the cry of a tortured con-
cience. Until this time it was a conscience that
ad never felt a pang or known a smirch. It was
he conscience of one who, until this time, had never
one a dishonorable thing, or an ungenerous, or
ruel, or treacherous thing, but was now doing all
f these, and was keenly aware of it. Up to this
ime Shelley had been master of his nature, and it
as a nature which was as beautiful and as nearly
erfect as any merely human nature may be. But
e was drunk now, with a debasing passion, and
as not himself. There is nothing in his previous
istory that is in character with the Shelley of this
etter. He had done boyish things, foolish things,
ven crazy things, but never a thing to be ashamed
f. He had done things which one might laugh at,
ut the privilege of laughing was limited always to
he thing itself; you could not laugh at the motive
ack of it — that was high, that was noble. His
most fantastic and quixotic acts had a purpose back
f them which made them fine, often great, and
made the rising laugh seem profanation and quenched
t; quenched it, and changed the impulse to homage.

Up to this time he had been loyalty itself, where his obligations lay — treachery was new to him; he had never done an ignoble thing — baseness was new to him; he had never done an unkind thing — that also was new to him.

This was the author of that letter, this was the man who had deserted his young wife and was lamenting, bcause he must leave another woman's house which had become a "home" to him, and go away. Is he lamenting *mainly* because he must go back to his wife and child? No, the lament is mainly for what he is to leave behind him. The physical comforts of the house? No, in his life he had never attached importance to such things. Then the thing which he grieves to leave is narrowed down to a person — to the person whose "dewy looks" had sunk into his breast, and whose seducing words had "stirred poison there."

He was ashamed of himself, his conscience was upbraiding him. He was the slave of a degrading love; he was drunk with his passion, the real Shelley was in temporary eclipse. This is the verdict which his previous history must certainly deliver upon this episode, I think.

One must be allowed to assist himself with conjectures like these when trying to find his way through a literary swamp which has so many misleading finger-boards up as this book is furnished with.

We have now arrived at a part of the swamp where the difficulties and perplexities are going to

: greater than any we have yet met with — where,
deed, the finger-boards are multitudinous, and the
ost of them pointing diligently in the wrong direc-
on.   We are to be told by the biography why
helley deserted his wife and child and took up with
ornelia Turner and Italian.   It was not on account
: Cornelia's sighs and sentimentalities and tea and
anna and late hours and soft and sweet and indus-
ious enticements; no, it was because " his happi-
ess in his home had been wounded and bruised
most to death."

It had been wounded and bruised almost to death
this way:

1st. Harriet persuaded him to set up a carriage.

2d. After the intrusion of the baby, Harriet
opped reading aloud and studying.

3d. Harriet's walks with Hogg " commonly con-
ucted us to some fashionable bonnet-shop."

4th. Harriet hired a wet-nurse.

5th. When an operation was being performed
pon the baby, " Harriet stood by, narrowly ob-
erving all that was done, but, to the astonishment
f the operator, betraying not the smallest sign of
notion."

6th. Eliza Westbrook, sister-in-law, was still of
e household.

The evidence against Harriet Shelley is all in;
ere is no more.   Upon these six counts she stands
dicted of the crime of driving her husband into
at sty at Bracknell; and this crime, by these helps,

the biographical prosecuting attorney has set himself the task of proving upon her.

Does the biographer *call* himself the attorney for the prosecution? No, only to himself, privately; publicly he is the passionless, disinterested, impartial judge on the bench. He holds up his judicial scales before the world, that all may see; and it all tries to look so fair that a blind person would sometimes fail to see him slip the false weights in.

Shelley's happiness in his home had been wounded and bruised almost to death, first, because Harriet had persuaded him to set up a carriage. I cannot discover that any evidence is offered that she asked him to set up a carriage. Still, if she did, was it a heavy offence? Was it unique? Other young wives had committed it before, others have committed it since. Shelley had dearly loved her in those London days; possibly he set up the carriage gladly to please her; affectionate young husbands do such things. When Shelley ran away with another girl, by-and-by, this girl persuaded him to pour the price of many carriages and many horses down the bottomless well of her father's debts, but this impartial judge finds no fault with that. Once she appeals to Shelley to raise money — necessarily by borrowing, there was no other way — to pay her father's debts with at a time when Shelley was in danger of being arrested and imprisoned for his own debts; yet the good judge finds no fault with her even for this.

First and last, Shelley emptied into that rapacious
mendicant's lap a sum which cost him — for he
borrowed it at ruinous rates — from eighty to one
hundred thousand dollars. But it was Mary Godwin's papa, the supplications were often sent through
Mary, the good judge is Mary's strenuous friend, so
Mary gets no censures. On the Continent *Mary
ode in her private carriage*, built, as Shelley boasts,
" by one of the best makers in Bond Street," yet
the good judge makes not even a passing comment
on this iniquity. Let us throw out Count No. 1
against Harriet Shelley as being far-fetched and
frivolous.

Shelley's happiness in his home had been wounded
and bruised almost to death, secondly, because Har-
iet's studies " had dwindled away to nothing,
byshe had ceased to express any interest in them."
At what time was this? It was when Harriet " had
ally recovered from the fatigue of her first effort of
maternity,. . . and was now in full force, vigor,
and effect." Very well, the baby was born two
ays before the close of June. It took the mother
month to get back her full force, vigor, and effect;
this brings us to July 27th and the deadly Cornelia.
If a wife of eighteen is studying with her husband
and he gets smitten with another woman, isn't he
likely to lose interest in his wife's studies for *that*
eason, and is not his wife's interest in her studies
likely to languish for the *same* reason? Would not
the mere sight of those books of hers sharpen the

4E

pain that is in her heart? This sudden breaki
down of a mutual intellectual interest of two year
standing is coincident with Shelley's re-encount
with Cornelia; and we are allowed to gather fro
that time forth for nearly two months he did all h
studying in that person's society. We feel
liberty to rule out Count No. 2 from the indictme
against Harriet.

Shelley's happiness in his home had been wound
and bruised almost to death, thirdly, because Ha
riet's walks with Hogg commonly led to son
fashionable bonnet-shop. I offer no palliation;
only ask why the dispassionate, impartial judge d
not offer one himself — merely, I mean, to offset h
leniency in a similar case or two where the girl wh
ran away with Harriet's husband was the shoppe
There are several occasions where she interest
herself with shopping — among them being wal
which ended at the bonnet-shop — yet in none
these cases does she get a word of blame from th
good judge, while in one of them he covers the de
with a justifying remark, she doing the shoppi
that time to find easement for her mind, her chi
having died.

Shelley's happiness in his home had been wound
and bruised almost to death, fourthly, by the intr
duction there of a wet-nurse. The wet-nurse w
introduced at the time of the Edinburgh sojour
immediately after Shelley had been enjoying the tw
months of study with Cornelia which broke up h

ife's studies and destroyed his personal interest in
em. Why, by this time, nothing that Shelley's
ife could do would have been satisfactory to him,
r he was in love with another woman, and was
ever going to be contented again until he got back
her. If he had been still in love with his wife it
not easily conceivable that he would care much
ho nursed the baby, provided the baby was well
irsed. Harriet's jealousy was assuredly voicing
self now, Shelley's conscience was assuredly nag-
ng him, pestering him, persecuting him. Shelley
eded excuses for his altered attitude towards his
ife; Providence pitied him and sent the wet-nurse.
Providence had sent him a cotton doughnut it
ould have answered just as well; all he wanted
as something to find fault with.

Shelley's happiness in his home had been wounded
d bruised almost to death, fifthly, because Harriet
arrowly watched a surgical operation which was
ing performed upon her child, and, " to the
tonishment of the operator," who was watching
arriet instead of attending to his operation, she
trayed " not the smallest sign of emotion." The
thor of this biography was not ashamed to set
wn that exultant slander. He was apparently not
vare that it was a small business to bring into his
urt a witness whose name he does not know, and
hose character and veracity there is none to
uch for, and allow him to strike this blow at the
other-heart of this friendless girl. The biographer

says, " We may not infer from this that Harriet did
not feel " — why put it in, then? — " but we learn
that those about her could believe her to be hard
and insensible." Who were those who were about
her? Her husband? He hated her now, because he
was in love elsewhere. Her sister? Of course that
is not charged. Peacock? Peacock does not testify.
The wet-nurse? She does not testify. If any others
were there we have no mention of them. " Those
about her " are reduced to one person — her husband. Who reports the circumstance? It is Hogg.
Perhaps he was there — we do not know. But if he
was, he still got his information at second-hand, as
it was the operator who noticed Harriet's lack of
emotion, not himself. Hogg is not given to saying
kind things when Harriet is his subject. He may
have said them the time that he tried to tempt her
to soil her honor, but after that he mentions her
usually with a sneer. " Among those who were
about her " was one witness well equipped to
silence all tongues, abolish all doubts, set our minds at
rest; one witness, not called, and not callable, whose
evidence, if we could but get it, would outweigh
the oaths of whole battalions of hostile Hoggs and
nameless surgeons — the baby. I wish we had the
baby's testimony; and yet if we had it it would not
do us any good — a furtive conjecture, a sly insinua-
tion, a pious " if " or two, would be smuggled in
here and there, with a solemn air of judicial investi-
gation, and its positiveness would wilt into dubiety.

The biographer says of Harriet, " If words of
ider affection and motherly pride proved the
ality of love, then undoubtedly she loved her first-
rn child." That is, if mere empty words can
ove it, it stands proved — and in this way, with-
t committing himself, he gives the reader a chance
 infer that there isn't any extant evidence but
rds, and that he doesn't take much stock in them.
ow seldom he shows his hand ! He is always lurk-
g behind a non-committal "if " or something of
it kind; always gliding and dodging around, dis-
outing colorless poison here and there and every-
ere, but always leaving himself in a position to
y that his language will be found innocuous if
en to pieces and examined. He clearly exhibits
teady and never-relaxing purpose to make Harriet
: scapegoat for her husband's first great sin — but
is in the general view that this is revealed, not in
: details. His insidious literature is like blue
ter; you know what it is that makes it blue, but
u cannot produce and verify any detail of the
ud of microscopic dust in it that does it. Your
versary can dip up a glassful and show you that
s pure white and you cannot deny it; and he can
> the lake dry, glass by glass, and show that
:ry glassful is white, and prove it to any one's
: — and yet that lake *was* blue and you can swear
 This book is blue — with slander in solution.
Let the reader examine, for example, the para-
aph of comment which immediately follows the
   4*.*.

letter containing Shelley's self-exposure which we
have been considering. This is it. One should in-
spect the individual sentences as they go by, the
pass them in procession and review the cake-walk a
a whole:

"Shelley's happiness in his home, as is evident from this pathe
letter, had been fatally stricken; it is evident, also, that he knew whe
duty lay; he felt that his part was to take up his burden, silently a
sorrowfully, and to bear it henceforth with the quietness of despa
But we can perceive that he scarcely possessed the strength and fortitu
needful for success in such an attempt. And clearly Shelley himself w
aware how perilous it was to accept that respite of blissful ease whi
he enjoyed in the Boinville household; for gentle voices and dewy loo
and words of sympathy could not fail to remind him of an ideal
tranquillity or of joy which could never be his, and which he mu
henceforth sternly exclude from his imagination."

That paragraph commits the author in no way
Taken sentence by sentence it *asserts* nothing again
anybody or in favor of anybody, pleads for nobody
accuses nobody. Taken detail by detail, it is a
innocent as moonshine. And yet, taken as a whole
it is a design against the reader; its intent is to re
move the feeling which the letter must leave wit
him if let alone, and put a different one in its plac
— to remove a feeling justified by the letter an
substitute one not justified by it. The letter itse
gives you no uncertain picture — no lecturer
needed to stand by with a stick and point out i
details and let on to explain what they mean. Th
picture is the very clear and remorsefully faithf
picture of a fallen and fettered angel who is ashame
of himself; an angel who beats his soiled wings an

ies, who complains to the woman who enticed him
at he *could* have borne his wayward lot, he *could*
ave stood by his duty if it had not been for her
eguilements; an angel who rails at the " boundless
cean of abhorred society," and rages at his poor
dicious sister-in-law. If there is any dignity about
is spectacle it will escape most people.

Yet when the paragraph of comment is taken as a
hole, the picture is full of dignity and pathos; we
ave before us a blameless and noble spirit stricken
 the earth by malign powers, but not conquered;
mpted, but grandly putting the temptation away;
imeshed by subtle coils, but sternly resolved to
nd them and march forth victorious, at any peril
f life or limb.   Curtain — slow music.

Was it the purpose of the paragraph to take the
ad taste of Shelley's letter out of the reader's
iouth?   If that was not it, good ink was wasted;
ithout that, it has no relevancy — the multiplica-
on table would have padded the space as rationally.

We have inspected the six reasons which we are
sked to believe drove a man of conspicuous
atience, honor, justice, fairness, kindliness, and
on firmness, resolution, and steadfastness, from
ie wife whom he loved and who loved him, to a
efuge in the mephitic paradise of Bracknell. These
re six infinitely little reasons; but there were six
olossal ones, and these the counsel for the destruc-
on of Harriet Shelley persists in not considering
ery important.

D*₊*₊

Moreover, the colossal six preceded the little si
and had done the mischief before they were bor
Let us double-column the twelve; then we shall s
at a glance that each little reason is in turn answer
by a retorting reason of a size to overshadow it a
make it insignificant:

1. Harriet sets up carriage.	1. CORNELIA TURNER.
2. Harriet stops studying.	2. CORNELIA TURNER.
3. Harriet goes to bonnet-shop.	3. CORNELIA TURNER.
4. Harriet takes a wet-nurse.	4. CORNELIA TURNER.
5. Harriet has too much nerve.	5. CORNELIA TURNER.
6. Detested sister-in-law.	6. CORNELIA TURNER.

As soon as we comprehend that Cornelia Turr
and the Italian lessons happened *before* the little s
had been discovered to be grievances, we understa
why Shelley's happiness in his home had be
wounded and bruised almost to death, and no o
can persuade us into laying it on Harriet.   Shell
and Cornelia are the responsible persons, and
cannot in honor and decency allow the cruelt
which they practised upon the unoffending wife
be pushed aside in order to give us a chance to wa
time and tears over six sentimental justifications
an offence which the six can't justify, nor even
spectably assist in justifying.

Six?   There were seven; but in charity to
biographer the seventh ought not to be expose
Still, he hung it out himself, and not only hung
out, but thought it was a good point in Shelle
favor.   For two years Shelley found sympathy a
intellectual food and all that at home; there v

ough for spiritual and mental support, but not
ough for luxury; and so, at the end of the con-
ted two years, this latter detail justifies him in
ng bag and baggage over to Cornelia Turner and
pplying the rest of his need in the way of surplus
npathy and intellectual pie unlawfully.   By the
ne reasoning a man in merely comfortable circum-
nces may rob a bank without sin.

III

IT is 1814, it is the 16th of March, Shelley has
tten his letter, he has been in the Boinville
adise a month, his deserted wife is in her hus-
dless home.   Mischief had been wrought.   It is
biographer who concedes this.   We greatly need
ne light on Harriet's side of the case now; we
d to know how she enjoyed the month, but there
o way to inform ourselves; there seems to be a
ange absence of documents and letters and diaries
that side.   Shelley kept a diary, the approaching
ry Godwin kept a diary, her father kept one, her
f-sister by marriage, adoption, and the dispensa-
n of God kept one, and the entire tribe and all its
nds wrote and received letters, and the letters
re kept and are producible when this biography
ds them; but there are only three or four scraps
Harriet's writing, and no diary.   Harriet wrote
nty of letters to her husband — nobody knows

where they are, I suppose; she wrote plenty o
letters to other people — apparently they have di
appeared, too. Peacock says she wrote good letter
but apparently interested people had sagacity enoug
to mislay them in time. After all her industry sh
went down into her grave and lies silent there—
silent, when she has so much need to speak. W
can only wonder at this mystery, not account for i

No, there is no way of finding out what Harriet
state of feeling was during the month that Shelle
was disporting himself in the Bracknell paradis
We have to fall back upon conjecture, as our fab
list does when he has nothing more substantial t
work with. Then we easily conjecture that as th
days dragged by Harriet's heart grew heavier an
heavier under its two burdens — shame and resen
ment: the shame of being pointed at and gossipe
about as a deserted wife, and resentment against th
woman who had beguiled her husband from her an
now kept him in a disreputable captivity. Deserte
wives — deserted whether for cause or without cau
— find small charity among the virtuous and the di
creet. We conjecture that one after another th
neighbors ceased to call; that one after anoth
they got to being " engaged " when Harriet calle
that finally they one after the other cut her dead o
the street; that after that she stayed in the hou
daytimes, and brooded over her sorrows, and nigh
times did the same, there being nothing else to d
with the heavy hours and the silence and solitu

and the dreary intervals which sleep should have charitably bridged, but didn't.

Yes, mischief had been wrought. The biographer arrives at this conclusion, and it is a most just one. Then, just as you begin to half hope he is going to discover the cause of it and launch hot bolts of wrath at the guilty manufacturers of it, you have to turn away disappointed. You are disappointed, and you sigh. This is what he says — the italics are mine:

"However the mischief may have been wrought — *and at this day no one can wish to heap blame on any buried head —*"

So it is poor Harriet, after all. Stern justice must take its course — justice tempered with delicacy, justice tempered with compassion, justice that pities a forlorn dead girl and refuses to strike her. Except in the back. Will not be ignoble and *say* the harsh thing, but only insinuate it. Stern justice knows about the carriage and the wet-nurse and the bonnet-shop and the other dark things that caused his sad mischief, and may not, *must* not blink them; so it delivers judgment where judgment belongs, but softens the blow by not seeming to deliver judgment at all. To resume — the italics are mine:

"However the mischief may have been wrought — and at this day no one can wish to heap blame on any buried head — *it is certain that one cause or causes of deep division between Shelley and his wife were in operation during the early part of the year 1814.*"

This shows penetration. No deduction could be more accurate than this. There were indeed some

causes of deep division.   But next comes anoth
disappointing sentence:

"To guess at the precise nature of these causes, in the absence
definite statement, were useless."

Why, he has already been guessing at them f
several pages, and we have been trying to outgue
him, and now all of a sudden he is tired of it a
won't play any more.   It is not quite fair to u
However, he will get over this by-and-by, wh
Shelley commits his next indiscretion and has to
guessed out of it at Harriet's expense.

"We may rest content with Shelley's ov
words " — in a Chancery paper drawn up by h
three years later.   They were these: "Delica
forbids me to say more than that we were disunit
by incurable dissensions."

As for me, I do not quite see why we should re
content with anything of the sort.   It is not a ve
definite statement.   It does not necessarily me
anything more than that he did not wish to go in
the tedious details of those family quarrels.   De
cacy could quite properly excuse him from sayin
" I was in love with Cornelia all that time; my w
kept crying and worrying about it and upbraidi
me and begging me to cut myself free from a co
nection which was wronging her and disgracing
both; and I being stung by these reproaches r
torted with fierce and bitter speeches — for it is r
nature to do that when I am stirred, especially
the target of them is a person whom I had grea

ved and respected before, as witness my various
titudes towards Miss Hitchener, the Gisbornes,
arriet's sister, and others — and finally I did not
prove this state of things when I deserted my wife
d spent a whole month with the woman who had
fatuated me.''

No, he could not go into those details, and we
cuse him; but, nevertheless, we do not rest con-
nt with this bland proposition to puff away that
hole long disreputable episode with a single mean-
gless remark of Shelley's.

We do admit that '' it is certain that some cause
causes of deep division were in operation.'' We
ould admit it just the same if the grammar of the
atement were as straight as a string, for we drift
to pretty indifferent grammar ourselves when we
e absorbed in historical work; but we have to de-
ne to admit that we cannot guess those cause or
uses.

But guessing is not really necessary. There is
idence attainable — evidence from the batch dis-
edited by the biographer and set out at the back
or in his appendix-basket; and yet a court of law
ould think twice before throwing it out, whereas it
ould be a hardy person who would venture to offer
such a place a good part of the material which is
aced before the readers of this book as '' evi-
nce,'' and so treated by this daring biographer.
nong some letters (in the appendix-basket) from
rs. Godwin, detailing the Godwinian share in the

Shelleyan events of 1814, she tells how Harri
Shelley came to her and her husband, agitated a
weeping, to implore them to forbid Shelley t
house, and prevent his seeing Mary Godwin.

"She related that last November he had fallen in love with M
Turner and paid her such marked attentions Mr. Turner, the husba
had carried off his wife to Devonshire."

The biographer finds a technical fault in thi
"the Shelleys were in *Edinburgh* in November.
What of that? The woman is recalling a convers
tion which is more than two months old; beside
she was probably more intent upon the central an
important fact of it than upon its unimportant dat
Harriet's quoted statement has some sense in it; f
that reason, if for no other, it ought to have bee
put in the body of the book. Still, that would n
have answered; even the biographer's enemy cou
not be cruel enough to ask him to let this re
grievance, this compact and substantial and pictu
esque figure, this rawhead-and-bloody-bones, com
striding in there among those pale shams, thos
rickety spectres labeled WET-NURSE, BONNET-SHO
and so on — no, the father of all malice could n
ask the biographer to expose his pathetic goblins t
a competition like that.

The fabulist finds fault with the statement becaus
it has a technical error in it; and he does this at th
moment that he is furnishing us an error himself
and of a graver sort. He says:

"If Turner carried off his wife to Devonshire he brought her bac

d Shelley was staying with her and her mother on terms of cordial
timacy in March, 1814."

We accept the " cordial intimacy" — it was the
ery thing Harriet was complaining of — but there
 nothing to show that it was Turner who brought
s wife back.   The statement is thrown in as if it
ere not only true, but was proof that Turner was
ot uneasy.   Turner's *movements* are proof of noth-
g.   Nothing but a statement from Turner's mouth
ould have any value here, and he made none.

 Six days after writing his letter Shelley and his
ife were together again for a moment — to get
married according to the rites of the English
hurch.

Within three weeks the new husband and wife
ere apart again, and the former was back in his
dorous paradise.   This time it is the wife who does
e deserting.   She finds Cornelia too strong for
er, probably.   At any rate, she goes away with
er baby and sister, and we have a playful fling at
er from good Mrs. Boinville, the " mysterious
inner Maimuna "; she whose " face was as a
amsel's face, and yet her hair was gray "; she of
hom the biographer has said, " Shelley was indeed
ught in an almost invisible thread spun around
m, but unconsciously, by this subtle and benignant
chantress."   The subtle and benignant enchant-
ss writes to Hogg, April 18: " Shelley is again a
idower; his beauteous half went to town on
hursday."

Then Shelley writes a poem — a chant of gri
over the hard fate which obliges him now to leav
his paradise and take up with his wife again.
seems to intimate that the paradise is cooling towar
him; that he is warned off by acclamation; that h
must not even venture to tempt with one last te
his friend Cornelia's ungentle mood, for her eye
glazed and cold and dares not entreat her lover t
stay:

Exhibit E

. . . .

" Pause not! the time is past! Every voice cries ' Away !'
 Tempt not with one last tear thy friend's ungentle mood;
 Thy lover's eye, so glazed and cold, dares not entreat thy stay:
  Duty and dereliction guide thee back to solitude."

Back to the solitude of his now empty home, tha
is!

 " Away! away! to thy sad and silent home;
  Pour bitter tears on its desolated hearth."

. . . .

But he will have rest in the grave by-and-by
Until that time comes, the charms of Bracknell wi
remain in his memory, along with Mrs. Boinville'
voice and Cornelia Turner's smile:

" Thou in the grave shalt rest — yet, till the phantoms flee
 Which that house and hearth and garden made dear to thee er
  while,
Thy remembrance and repentance and deep musings are not free
 From the music of two voices and the light of one sweet smile."

We *cannot* wonder that Harriet could not stand it
Any of us would have left. We would not even sta

ith a cat that was in this condition. Even the
oinvilles could not endure it; and so, as we have
en, they gave this one notice.

"Early in May, Shelley was in London. He did not yet despair of
conciliation with Harriet, nor had he ceased to love her."

Shelley's poems are a good deal of trouble to his
ographer. They are constantly inserted as " evi-
nce," and they make much confusion. As soon
one of them has proved one thing, another one
llows and proves quite a different thing. The
em just quoted shows that he was in love with
ornelia, but a month later he is in love with Harriet
ain, and there is a poem to prove it.

"In this piteous appeal Shelley declares that he has now no grief but
e — the grief of having known and lost his wife's love."

Exhibit F

" Thy look of love has power to calm
The stormiest passion of my soul."

But without doubt she had been reserving her
oks of love a good part of the time for ten months,
w — ever since he began to lavish his own on
ornelia Turner at the end of the previous July.
e does really seem to have already forgotten Cor-
lia's merits in one brief month, for he eulogizes
arriet in a way which rules all competition out:

" Thou only virtuous, gentle, kind,
Amid a world of hate."

He complains of her hardness, and begs her to
ake the concession of a " slight endurance " — of
s waywardness, perhaps — for the sake of " a
5E

fellow-being's lasting weal.''   But the main force
his appeal is in his closing stanza, and is strong
worded:

> " O trust for once no erring guide!
>   Bid the remorseless feeling flee;
>   'Tis malice, 'tis revenge, 'tis pride,
>   'Tis anything but thee;
>   O deign a nobler pride to prove,
>   And pity if thou canst not love.''

This is in May — apparently towards the end
it.   Harriet and Shelley were corresponding all
time.   Harriet got the poem — a copy exists in
own handwriting; she being the only gentle a
kind person amid a world of hate, according
Shelley's own testimony in the poem, we are p
mitted to think that the daily letters would presen
have melted that kind and gentle heart and brou
about the reconciliation, if there had been time
but there wasn't; for in a very few days — in fa
before the 8th of June — Shelley was in love w
another woman.

And so — perhaps while Harriet was walking
floor nights, trying to get *her* poem by heart —
husband was doing a fresh one — for the other
— Mary Wollstonecraft Godwin — with sentime
like these in it:

Exhibit G

> " To spend years thus and be rewarded,
>   As thou, sweet love, requited me
>   When none were near.
>   . . . thy lips did meet
>   Mine tremblingly; . . .

" Gentle and good and mild thou art,
    Nor can I live if thou appear
  Aught but thyself." . . .

d so on. " Before the close of June it was known
l felt by Mary and Shelley that each was inex-
ssibly dear to the other." Yes, Shelley had
nd this child of sixteen to his liking, and had
)ed and won her in the graveyard. But that is
hing; it was better than wooing her in her
sery, at any rate, where it might have disturbed
other children.

Iowever, she was a child in years only. From
day that she set her masculine grip on Shelley
was to frisk no more. If she had occupied the
y kind and gentle Harriet's place in March it
ild have been a thrilling spectacle to see her in-
e the Boinville rookery and read the riot act.
it holiday of Shelley's would have been of short
ation, and Cornelia's hair would have been as
y as her mother's when the services were over.

Iogg went to the Godwin residence in Skinner
et with Shelley on that 8th of June. They
sed through Godwin's little debt-factory of a
k-shop and went up-stairs hunting for the pro-
tor. Nobody there. Shelley strode about the
m impatiently, making its crazy floor quake under
. Then a door " was partially and softly opened.
hrilling voice called ' Shelley !' A thrilling voice
wered, ' Mary ! ' And he darted out of the room
an arrow from the bow of the far-shooting King.

A very young female, fair and fair-haired, pa
indeed, and with a piercing look, wearing a frock
tartan, an unusual dress in London at that time, h
called him out of the room.''

This is Mary Godwin, as described by Hog
The thrill of the voices shows that the love
Shelley and Mary was already upward of a fortnig
old; therefore it had been born within the mor
of May — born while Harriet was still trying to g
her poem by heart, we think. I must not be ask
how I know so much about that thrill; it is r
secret. The biographer and I have private ways
finding out things when it is necessary to find the
out and the customary methods fail.

Shelley left London that day, and was gone t
days. The biographer conjectures that he spent tl
interval with Harriet in Bath. It would be just li
him. To the end of his days he liked to be in lc
with two women at once. He was more in lo
with Miss Hitchener when he married Harriet th
he was with Harriet, and told the lady so w
simple and unostentatious candor. He was more
love with Cornelia than he was with Harriet in t
end of 1813 and the beginning of 1814, yet he su
plied both of them with love poems of an equ
temperature meantime; he loved Mary and Harr
in June, and while getting ready to run off with t
one, it is conjectured that he put in his odd ti
trying to get reconciled to the other; by-and-b
while still in love with Mary, he will make love

er half-sister by marriage, adoption, and the visita-
on of God, through the medium of clandestine
etters, and she will answer with letters that are for
o eye but his own.

When Shelley encountered Mary Godwin he was
ooking around for another paradise.   He had tastes
f his own, and there were features about the God-
in establishment that strongly recommended it.
odwin was an advanced thinker and an able writer.
ne of his romances is still read, but his philo-
ophical works, once so esteemed, are out of vogue
ow; their authority was already declining when
helley made his acquaintance — that is, it was de-
ining with the public, but not with Shelley.   They
ad been his moral and political Bible, and they
ere that yet.   Shelley the infidel would himself
ave claimed to be less a work of God than a work
Godwin.   Godwin's philosophies had formed his
ind and interwoven themselves into it and become
part of its texture; he regarded himself as God-
in's spiritual son.   Godwin was not without self-
preciation; indeed, it may be conjectured that
om his point of view the last syllable of his name
as surplusage.   He lived serene in his lofty world
philosophy, far above the mean interests that
sorbed smaller men, and only came down to the
ound at intervals to pass the hat for alms to pay
s debts with, and insult the man that relieved him.
everal of his principles were out of the ordinary.
r example, he was opposed to marriage.   He was

5*.*.

not aware that his preachings from this text wer
but theory and wind; he supposed he was in earnes
in imploring people to live together without marry
ing, until Shelley furnished him a working model o
his scheme and a practical example to analyze, b
applying the principle in his own family; the matte
took a different and surprising aspect then. Th
late Matthew Arnold said that the main defect i
Shelley's make-up was that he was destitute of th
sense of humor. This episode must have escape
Mr. Arnold's attention.

But we have said enough about the head of th
new paradise. Mrs. Godwin is described as bein
in several ways a terror; and even when her sou
was in repose she wore green spectacles. But
suspect that her main unattractiveness was born o
the fact that she wrote the letters that are out in th
appendix-basket in the back yard — letters whic
are an outrage and wholly untrustworthy, for the
say some kind things about poor Harriet and te
some disagreeable truths about her husband; an
these things make the fabulist grit his teeth a goo
deal.

Next we have Fanny Godwin — a Godwin b
courtesy only; she was Mrs. Godwin's natur
daughter by a former friend. She was a sweet an
winning girl, but she presently wearied of the Go
win paradise, and poisoned herself.

Last in the list is Jane (or Claire, as she preferre
to call herself) Clairmont, daughter of Mrs. Godw

a former marriage. She was very young and
etty and accommodating, and always ready to do
at she could to make things pleasant. After
elley ran off with her part-sister Mary, she be-
ne the guest of the pair, and contributed a natural
ld to their nursery — Allegra. Lord Byron was
e father.

We have named the several members and advan-
ges of the new paradise in Skinner Street, with its
zy book-shop underneath. Shelley was all right
w, this was a better place than the other; more
iety anyway, and more different kinds of france. One could turn out poetry here without
y trouble at all.

The way the new love-match came about was this:
elley told Mary all his aggravations and sorrows
l griefs, and about the wet-nurse and the bonnet-
op and the surgeon and the carriage, and the
er-in-law that blocked the London game, and
out Cornelia and her mamma, and how they had
ned him out of the house after making so much
him; and how he had deserted Harriet and then
rriet had deserted him, and how the reconciliation
s working along and Harriet getting her poem by
art; and still he was not happy, and Mary pitied
n, for she had had trouble herself. But I am not
isfied with this. It reads too much like statistics.
acks smoothness and grace, and is too earthy and
siness-like. It has the sordid look of a trades-
on procession out on strike. That is not the

E*₊*₊

right form for it. The book does it better; we v
fall back on the book and have a cake-walk:

> " It was easy to divine that some restless grief possessed him; M
> herself was not unlearned in the lore of pain. His generous zeal in
> father's behalf, his spiritual sonship to Godwin, his reverence for
> mother's memory, were guarantees with Mary of his excellence.*   '
> new friends could not lack subjects of discourse, and underneath t
> words about Mary's mother, and ' Political Justice,' and ' Rights
> Woman,' were two young hearts, each feeling towards the other, e
> perhaps unaware, trembling in the direction of the other. The de
> to assuage the suffering of one whose happiness has grown preciou
> us may become a hunger of the spirit as keen as any other, and
> hunger now possessed Mary's heart; when her eyes rested unseen
> Shelley, it was with a look full of the ardor of a ' soothing pity. ' "

Yes, that is better and has more composu
That is just the way it happened. He told h
about the wet-nurse, she told him about politi
justice; he told her about the deadly sister-in-la
she told him about her mother; he told her abc
the bonnet-shop, she murmured back about t
rights of woman; then he assuaged her, then s
assuaged him; then he assuaged her some mo
next she assuaged him some more; then they be
assuaged one another simultaneously; and so th
went on by the hour assuaging and assuaging a
assuaging, until at last what was the result? Th
were in love. It will happen so every time.

> " He had married a woman who, as he now persuaded himself, l
> never truly loved him, who loved only his fortune and his rank, a
> who proved her selfishness by deserting him in his misery."

---

* What she was after was guarantees of his excellence. That
stood ready to desert his wife and child was one of them, apparently.

I think that that is not quite fair to Harriet. We
've no certainty that she knew Cornelia had turned
n out of the house. He went back to Cornelia,
d Harriet may have supposed that he was as
ppy with her as ever. Still, it was judicious to
gin to lay on the whitewash, for Shelley is going
need many a coat of it now, and the sooner the
ader becomes used to the intrusion of the brush
e sooner he will get reconciled to it and stop
etting about it.

After Shelley's (conjectured) visit to Harriet at
th — 8th of June to 18th — '' it seems to have
en arranged that Shelley should henceforth join
e Skinner Street household each day at dinner.''
Nothing could be handier than this; things will
im along now.

'' Although now Shelley was coming to believe that his wedded union
h Harriet was a thing of the past, he had not ceased to regard her
h affectionate consideration ; he wrote to her frequently, and kept
informed of his whereabouts.''

We must not get impatient over these curious
harmoniousnesses and irreconcilabilities in Shel-
y's character. You can see by the biographer's
itude towards them that there is nothing objec-
nable about them. Shelley was doing his best to
ake two adoring young creatures happy: he was
garding the one with affectionate consideration by
il, and he was assuaging the other one at home.

'' Unhappy Harriet, residing at Bath, had perhaps never desired that

the breach between herself and her husband should be irreparable
complete.''

I find no fault with that sentence except that t
'' perhaps '' is not strictly warranted. It shou
have been left out. In support — or shall we s
extenuation? — of this opinion I submit that the
is not sufficient evidence to warrant the uncertain
which it implies. The only '' evidence '' offer
that Harriet was hard and proud and standing o
against a reconciliation is a poem — the poem
which Shelley beseeches her to '' bid the remors
less feeling flee '' and '' pity '' if she '' cannot love
We have just that as '' evidence,'' and out of
meagre materials the biographer builds a cobhou
of conjectures as big as the Coliseum; conjectur
which convince him, the prosecuting attorney, b
ought to fall far short of convincing any fair-mind
jury.

Shelley's love-poems may be very good evidenc
but we know well that they are '' good for this d
and train only.'' We are able to believe that th
spoke the truth for that one day, but we know l
experience that they could not be depended on
speak it the next. The very supplication for a r
warming of Harriet's chilled love was followed
suddenly by the poet's plunge into an adoring pa
sion for Mary Godwin that if it had been a check
would have lost its value before a lazy person cou
have gotten to the bank with it.

Hardness, stubbornness, pride, vindictiveness -

hese may sometimes reside in a young wife and
nother of nineteen, but they are not charged against
Harriet Shelley outside of that poem, and one has
no right to insert them into her character on such
shadowy " evidence " as that. Peacock knew Har-
iet well, and she has a flexible and persuadable
look, as painted by him :

> " Her manners were good, and her whole aspect and demeanor such
> manifest emanations of pure and truthful nature that to be once in her
> company was to know her thoroughly. She was fond of her husband,
> nd accommodated herself in every way to his tastes. If they mixed
> society, she adorned it ; if they lived in retirement, she was satisfied ;
> they travelled, she enjoyed the change of scene."

" Perhaps " she had never desired that the breach
should be irreparable and complete. The truth is,
we do not even know that there was any breach at
all at this time. We know that the husband and
wife went before the altar and took a new oath on
the 24th of March to love and cherish each other
until death — and this may be regarded as a sort of
reconciliation itself, and a wiping out of the old
grudges. Then Harriet went away, and the sister-
n-law removed herself from her society. That was
n April. Shelley wrote his " appeal " in May,
but the corresponding went right along afterwards.
We have a right to doubt that the subject of it was
" reconciliation," or that Harriet had any suspi-
tion that she needed to be reconciled and that her
husband was trying to persuade her to it — as the
biographer has sought to make us believe, with his

Coliseum of conjectures built out of a waste-bask
of poetry. For we have " evidence " now — n
poetry and conjecture. When Shelley had bee
dining daily in the Skinner Street paradise fiftee
days and continuing the love-match which w
already a fortnight old twenty-five days earlier, 1
forgot to write Harriet; forgot it the next day an
the next. During four days Harriet got no lett
from him. Then her fright and anxiety rose
expression-heat, and she wrote a letter to Shelley
publisher which seems to reveal to us that Shelley
letters to her had been the customary affectiona
letters of husband to wife, and had carried no a
peals for reconciliation and had not needed to:

> " BATH (postmark July 7, 1814).
> " MY DEAR SIR,—You will greatly oblige me by giving the enclos
> to Mr. Shelley. I would not trouble you, but it is now four days sin
> I have heard from him, which to me is an age. Will you write by 1
> turn of post and tell me what has become of him ? as I always fan
> something dreadful has happened if I do not hear from him. If y
> tell me that he is well I shall not come to London, but if I do not he
> from you or him I shall certainly come, as I cannot endure this dread
> state of suspense. You are his friend and you can feel for me.
> " I remain yours truly,
> " H. S."

Even without Peacock's testimony that " her who
aspect and demeanor were manifest emanations of
pure and truthful nature," we should hold this 1
be a truthful letter, a sincere letter, a loving lette
it bears those marks; I think it is also the letter
a person accustomed to receiving letters from h

husband frequently, and that they have been of a welcome and satisfactory sort, too, this long time back — ever since the solemn remarriage and reconciliation at the altar most likely.

The biographer follows Harriet's letter with a conjecture. He conjectures that she " would now gladly have retraced her steps." Which means that it is proven that she had steps to retrace — proven by the poem. Well, if the poem is better evidence than the letter, we must let it stand at that.

Then the biographer attacks Harriet Shelley's honor — by authority of random and unverified gossip scavengered from a group of people whose very names make a person shudder: Mary Godwin, mistress to Shelley; her part-sister, discarded mistress of Lord Byron; Godwin, the philosophical tramp, who gathers his share of it from a shadow — that is to say, from a person whom he shirks out of naming. Yet the biographer dignifies this sorry rubbish with the name of " evidence."

Nothing remotely resembling a distinct charge from a named person professing to know is offered among this precious " evidence."

1. " Shelley *believed* " so and so.

2. Byron's discarded mistress says that Shelley told Mary Godwin so and so, and *Mary* told *her.*

3. " Shelley said " so and so — and later " admitted over and over again that he had been in error."

4. The unspeakable Godwin " wrote to Mr. Bax-

ter " that he knew so and so " from unquestionabl
authority " — name not furnished.

How any man in his right mind could bring him
self to defile the grave of a shamefully abused and
defenceless girl with these baseless fabrications, thi
manufactured filth, is inconceivable. How any man
in his right mind or out of it, could sit down and
coldly try to persuade anybody to believe it, o
listen patiently to it, or, indeed, do anything bu
scoff at it and deride it, is astonishing.

The charge insinuated by these odious slanders is
one of the most difficult of all offences to prove; it
is also one which no man has a right to mention
even in a whisper about any woman, living or dead,
unless he knows it to be true, and not even then
unless he can also *prove* it to be true. There is no
justification for the abomination of putting this stuff
in the book.

Against Harriet Shelley's good name there is not
one scrap of tarnishing evidence, and not even a
scrap of evil gossip, that comes from a source that
entitles it to a hearing.

On the credit side of the account we have strong
opinions from the people who knew her best.
Peacock says:

"I feel it due to the memory of Harriet to state my most decided
conviction that her conduct as a wife was as pure, as true, as absolutely faultless, as that of any who for such conduct are held most in
honor."

Thornton Hunt, who had picked and published

slight flaws in Harriet's character, says, as regards
this alleged large one:

"There is not a trace of evidence or a whisper of scandal against
her before her voluntary departure from Shelley."

Trelawney says:

"I was assured by the evidence of the few friends who knew both
Shelley and his wife — Hookham, Hogg, Peacock, and one of the
Godwins — that Harriet was perfectly innocent of all offence."

What excuse was there for raking up a parcel of
foul rumors from malicious and discredited sources
and flinging them at this dead girl's head? Her
very defencelessness should have been her protection. The fact that all letters to her or about her,
with almost every scrap of her own writing, had
been diligently mislaid, leaving her case destitute of
a voice, while every pen-stroke which could help
her husband's side had been as diligently preserved,
should have excused her from being brought to
trial. Her witnesses have all disappeared, yet we
see her summoned in her grave-clothes to plead for
the life of her character, without the help of an ad-
vocate, before a disqualified judge and a packed
jury.

Harriet Shelley wrote her distressed letter on the
7th of July. On the 28th her husband ran away
with Mary Godwin and her part-sister Claire to the
Continent. He deserted his wife when her confine-
ment was approaching. She bore him a child at the
end of November, his mistress bore him another one

something over two months later. The truants were back in London before either of these events occurred.

On one occasion, presently, Shelley was so pressed for money to support his mistress with that he went to his wife and got some money of his that was in her hands — twenty pounds. Yet the mistress was not moved to gratitude; for later, when the wife was troubled to meet her engagements, the mistress makes this entry in her diary:

"Harriet sends her creditors here; nasty woman. Now we shall have to change our lodgings."

The deserted wife bore the bitterness and obloquy of her situation two years and a quarter; then she gave up, and drowned herself. A month afterwards the body was found in the water. Three weeks later Shelley married his mistress.

I must here be allowed to italicize a remark of the biographer's concerning Harriet Shelley:

"*That no act of Shelley's during the two years which immediately preceded her death tended to cause the rash act which brought her life to its close seems certain.*"

Yet her husband had deserted her and her children, and was living with a concubine all that time! Why should a person attempt to write biography when the simplest facts have no meaning to him? This book is littered with as crass stupidities as that one — deductions by the page which bear no discoverable kinship to their premises.

The biographer throws off that extraordinary remark without any perceptible disturbance to his
serenity; for he follows it with a sentimental justification of Shelley's conduct which has not a pang of
conscience in it, but is silky and smooth and undu-
lating and pious — a cake-walk with all the colored
brethren at their best. There may be people who
can read that page and keep their temper, but it is
doubtful.

Shelley's life has the one indelible blot upon it,
but is otherwise worshipfully noble and beautiful.
It even stands out indestructibly gracious and lovely
from the ruck of these disastrous pages, in spite of
the fact that they expose and establish his responsibility for his forsaken wife's pitiful fate — a
responsibility which he himself tacitly admits in a
letter to Eliza Westbrook, wherein he refers to his
taking up with Mary Godwin as an act which Eliza
" might excusably regard as the cause of her sister's
ruin."

6B

FENIMORE COOPER'S LITERARY OFFENCES

The Pathfinder and *The Deerslayer* stand at the head of Cooper's novels as artistic creations. There are others of his works which contain parts as perfect as are to be found in these, and scenes even more thrilling. Not one can be compared with either of them as a finished whole.

The defects in both of these tales are comparatively slight. They were pure works of art. — *Prof. Lounsbury.*

The five tales reveal an extraordinary fulness of invention.

... One of the very greatest characters in fiction, Natty Bumppo. ...

The craft of the woodsman, the tricks of the trapper, all the delicate art of the forest, were familiar to Cooper from his youth up. — *Prof. Brander Matthews.*

Cooper is the greatest artist in the domain of romantic fiction yet produced by America. — *Wilkie Collins.*

IT seems to me that it was far from right for the Professor of English Literature in Yale, the Professor of English Literature in Columbia, and Wilkie Collins to deliver opinions on Cooper's literature without having read some of it. It would have been much more decorous to keep silent and let persons talk who have read Cooper.

Cooper's art has some defects. In one place in *Deerslayer*, and in the restricted space of two-thirds of a page, Cooper has scored 114 offences against

(78)

terary art out of a possible 115. It breaks the
ecord.

There are nineteen rules governing literary art in
the domain of romantic fiction — some say twenty-
vo. In *Deerslayer* Cooper violated eighteen of
them. These eighteen require:

1. That a tale shall accomplish something and
rrive somewhere. But the *Deerslayer* tale accom-
lishes nothing and arrives in the air.

2. They require that the episodes of a tale shall
e necessary parts of the tale, and shall help to de-
elop it. But as the *Deerslayer* tale is not a tale,
nd accomplishes nothing and arrives nowhere, the
pisodes have no rightful place in the work, since
here was nothing for them to develop.

3. They require that the personages in a tale shall
e alive, except in the case of corpses, and that
ways the reader shall be able to tell the corpses
om the others. But this detail has often been
verlooked in the *Deerslayer* tale.

4. They require that the personages in a tale,
oth dead and alive, shall exhibit a sufficient excuse
r being there. But this detail also has been over-
oked in the *Deerslayer* tale.

5. They require that when the personages of a
le deal in conversation, the talk shall sound like
uman talk, and be talk such as human beings would
e likely to talk in the given circumstances, and
ave a discoverable meaning, also a discoverable
urpose. and a show of relevancy, and remain in

the neighborhood of the subject in hand, and be
interesting to the reader, and help out the tale, and
stop when the people cannot think of anything more
to say. But this requirement has been ignored from
the beginning of the *Deerslayer* tale to the end of it.

6. They require that when the author describes
the character of a personage in his tale, the conduct
and conversation of that personage shall justify said
description. But this law gets little or no attention
in the *Deerslayer* tale, as Natty Bumppo's case will
amply prove.

7. They require that when a personage talks like
an illustrated, gilt-edged, tree-calf, hand-tooled,
seven-dollar Friendship's Offering in the beginning
of a paragraph, he shall not talk like a negro min-
strel in the end of it. But this rule is flung down
and danced upon in the *Deerslayer* tale.

8. They require that crass stupidities shall not be
played upon the reader as " the craft of the woods
man, the delicate art of the forest," by either the
author or the people in the tale. But this rule is
persistently violated in the *Deerslayer* tale.

9. They require that the personages of a tale shall
confine themselves to possibilities and let miracle
alone; or, if they venture a miracle, the author
must so plausibly set it forth as to make it look
possible and reasonable. But these rules are not
respected in the *Deerslayer* tale.

10. They require that the author shall make the
reader feel a deep interest in the personages of his

ale and in their fate; and that he shall make the
eader love the good people in the tale and hate the
ad ones.   But the reader of the *Deerslayer* tale dis-
kes the good people in it, is indifferent to the
thers, and wishes they would all get drowned
ogether.

11. They require that the characters in a tale
hall be so clearly defined that the reader can tell
eforehand what each will do in a given emergency.
ut in the *Deerslayer* tale this rule is vacated.

In addition to these large rules there are some
ttle ones.   These require that the author shall

12. *Say* what he is proposing to say, not merely
ome near it.

13. Use the right word, not its second cousin.

14. Eschew surplusage.

15. Not omit necessary details.

16. Avoid slovenliness of form.

17. Use good grammar.

18. Employ a simple and straightforward style.

Even these seven are coldly and persistently vio-
ted in the *Deerslayer* tale.

Cooper's gift in the way of invention was not a
ch endowment; but such as it was he liked to
ork it, he was pleased with the effects, and indeed
 did some quite sweet things with it.   In his little
ox of stage properties he kept six or eight cunning
vices, tricks, artifices for his savages and woods-
en to deceive and circumvent each other with, and
 was never so happy as when he was working

6*.*.*

these innocent things and seeing them go.
favorite one was to make a moccasined pers
tread in the tracks of the moccasined enemy, a
thus hide his own trail. Cooper wore out barr
and barrels of moccasins in working that tric
Another stage-property that he pulled out of l
box pretty frequently was his broken twig. I
prized his broken twig above all the rest of l
effects, and worked it the hardest. It is a restf
chapter in any book of his when somebody does
step on a dry twig and alarm all the reds and whi
for two hundred yards around. Every time
Cooper person is in peril, and absolute silence
worth four dollars a minute, he is sure to step or
dry twig. There may be a hundred handier thin
to step on, but that wouldn't satisfy Coop
Cooper requires him to turn out and find a d
twig; and if he can't do it, go and borrow or
In fact, the Leather Stocking Series ought to ha
been called the Broken Twig Series.

I am sorry there is not room to put in a f
dozen instances of the delicate art of the forest,
practised by Natty Bumppo and some of the otl
Cooperian experts. Perhaps we may venture t
or three samples. Cooper was a sailor — a na
officer; yet he gravely tells us how a vessel, drivi
towards a lee shore in a gale, is steered for a p
ticular spot by her skipper because he knows of
undertow there which will hold her back against
gale and save her. For just pure woodcraft,

dlorcraft, or whatever it is, isn't that neat? For
veral years Cooper was daily in the society of
tillery, and he ought to have noticed that when a
nnon-ball strikes the ground it either buries itself
 skips a hundred feet or so; skips again a hundred
et or so — and so on, till finally it gets tired and
lls.   Now in one place he loses some " females "
 as he always calls women — in the edge of a
od near a plain at night in a fog, on purpose to
ve Bumppo a chance to show off the delicate art
 the forest before the reader.   These mislaid
ople are hunting for a fort.   They hear a cannon-
ist, and a cannon-ball presently comes rolling into
e wood and stops at their feet.   To the females
s suggests nothing.   The case is very different
th the admirable Bumppo.   I wish I may never
ow peace again if he doesn't strike out promptly
d *follow the track* of that cannon-ball across the
in through the dense fog and find the fort.   Isn't
 a daisy?   If Cooper had any real knowledge of
ture's ways of doing things, he had a most deli-
te art in concealing the fact.   For instance: one
 his acute Indian experts, Chingachgook (pro-
unced Chicago, I think), has lost the trail of a
rson he is tracking through the forest.   Appar-
tly that trail is hopelessly lost.   Neither you nor
ould ever have guessed out the way to find it.   It
s very different with Chicago.   Chicago was not
mped for long.   He turned a running stream out
 its course, and there, in the slush in its old

F*₊*₊

bed, were that person's moccasin-tracks. The cur
rent did not wash them away, as it would have don
in all other like cases — no, even the eternal laws o
Nature have to vacate when Cooper wants to put u
a delicate job of woodcraft on the reader.

We must be a little wary when Brander Matthew
tells us that Cooper's books " reveal an extraord
nary fulness of invention.''   As a rule, I am qui
willing to accept Brander Matthews's literary judg
ments and applaud his lucid and graceful phrasin
of them; but that particular statement needs to b
taken with a few tons of salt.   Bless your hear
Cooper hadn't any more invention than a horse
and I don't mean a high-class horse, either; I mea
a clothes-horse.   It would be very difficult to find
really clever " situation " in Cooper's books, an
still more difficult to find one of any kind which h
has failed to render absurd by his handling of i
Look at the episodes of " the caves ''; and at th
celebrated scuffle between Maqua and those othe
on the table-land a few days later; and at Hurr
Harry's queer water-transit from the castle to th
ark; and at Deerslayer's half-hour with his fir
corpse; and at the quarrel between Hurry Har
and Deerslayer later; and at — but choose for you
self; you can't go amiss.

If Cooper had been an observer his inventi
faculty would have worked better; not more interes
ingly, but more rationally, more plausibly.   Cooper
proudest creations in the way of " situations " suff

oticeably from the absence of the observer's pro-
jecting gift. Cooper's eye was splendidly inaccurate.
Cooper seldom saw anything correctly. He saw
nearly all things as through a glass eye, darkly. Of
course a man who cannot see the commonest little
every-day matters accurately is working at a disad-
vantage when he is constructing a " situation." In
the *Deerslayer* tale Cooper has a stream which is
fifty feet wide where it flows out of a lake; it
presently narrows to twenty as it meanders along
for no given reason, and yet when a stream acts like
that it ought to be required to explain itself. Fourteen pages later the width of the brook's outlet from
the lake has suddenly shrunk thirty feet, and become " the narrowest part of the stream." This
shrinkage is not accounted for. The stream has
bends in it, a sure indication that it has alluvial
banks and cuts them; yet these bends are only
thirty and fifty feet long. If Cooper had been a
nice and punctilious observer he would have noticed
that the bends were oftener nine hundred feet long
than short of it.

Cooper made the exit of that stream fifty feet
wide, in the first place, for no particular reason; in
the second place, he narrowed it to less than twenty
to accommodate some Indians. He bends a " sapling " to the form of an arch over this narrow
passage, and conceals six Indians in its foliage.
They are " laying " for a settler's scow or ark
which is coming up the stream on its way to the

lake; it is being hauled against the stiff current by
rope whose stationary end is anchored in the lake
its rate of progress cannot be more than a mile a
hour. Cooper describes the ark, but pretty ob
scurely. In the matter of dimensions " it was littl
more than a modern canal-boat." Let us guess
then, that it was about one hundred and forty fee
long. It was of " greater breadth than common."
Let us guess, then, that it was about sixteen fee
wide. This leviathan had been prowling down bend
which were but a third as long as itself, and scrapin;
between banks where it had only two feet of spac
to spare on each side. We cannot too much admir
this miracle. A low-roofed log dwelling occupie
" two-thirds of the ark's length " — a dwellin;
ninety feet long and sixteen feet wide, let us say —
a kind of vestibule train. The dwelling has tw
rooms — each forty-five feet long and sixteen fee
wide, let us guess. One of them is the bedroom o:
the Hutter girls, Judith and Hetty; the other is th
parlor in the daytime, at night it is papa's bed
chamber. The ark is arriving at the stream's exi
now, whose width has been reduced to less than
twenty feet to accommodate the Indians — say to
eighteen. There is a foot to spare on each side o:
the boat. Did the Indians notice that there was
going to be a tight squeeze there? Did they notice
that they could make money by climbing down out
of that arched sapling and just stepping aboard
when the ark scraped by? No, other Indians

ould have noticed these things, but Cooper's
ndians never notice anything. Cooper thinks they
re marvelous creatures for noticing, but he was
lmost always in error about his Indians. There
as seldom a sane one among them.

The ark is one hundred and forty feet long; the
welling is ninety feet long. The idea of the Indians
 to drop softly and secretly from the arched sap-
ng to the dwelling as the ark creeps along under it
t the rate of a mile an hour, and butcher the
mily. It will take the ark a minute and a half to
ass under. It will take the ninety foot dwelling a
inute to pass under. Now, then, what did the six
ndians do? It would take you thirty years to guess,
nd even then you would have to give it up, I be-
eve. Therefore, I will tell you what the Indians
id. Their chief, a person of quite extraordinary
tellect for a Cooper Indian, warily watched the
anal-boat as it squeezed along under him, and when
e had got his calculations fined down to exactly
he right shade, as he judged, he let go and dropped.
nd *missed the house!* That is actually what he did.
e missed the house, and landed in the stern of the
ow. It was not much of a fall, yet it knocked
im silly. He lay there unconscious. If the house
ad been ninety-seven feet long he would have made
e trip. The fault was Cooper's, not his. The
ror lay in the construction of the house. Cooper
as no architect.

There still remained in the roost five Indians.

The boat has passed under and is now out of their
reach. Let me explain what the five did — you
would not be able to reason it out for yourself.
No. 1 jumped for the boat, but fell in the water
astern of it. Then No. 2 jumped for the boat, but
fell in the water still farther astern of it. Then No.
3 jumped for the boat, and fell a good way astern
of it. Then No. 4 jumped for the boat, and fell in
the water *away* astern. Then even No. 5 made a
jump for the boat — for he was a Cooper Indian.
In the matter of intellect, the difference between a
Cooper Indian and the Indian that stands in front of
the cigar-shop is not spacious. The scow episode
is really a sublime burst of invention; but it does
not thrill, because the inaccuracy of the detail
throws a sort of air of fictitiousness and general
improbability over it. This comes of Cooper's in-
adequacy as an observer.

The reader will find some examples of Cooper's
high talent for inaccurate observation in the account
of the shooting-match in *The Pathfinder*.

"A common wrought nail was driven lightly into the target, its head
having been first touched with paint."

The color of the paint is not stated — an important omission, but Cooper deals freely in important omissions. No, after all, it was not an important
omission; for this nail-head is *a hundred yards from*
the marksmen, and could not be seen by them at
that distance, no matter what its color might be.

How far can the best eyes see a common house-fly?
A hundred yards? It is quite impossible. Very
well; eyes that cannot see a house-fly that is a hundred yards away cannot see an ordinary nail-head at
that distance, for the size of the two objects is the
same. It takes a keen eye to see a fly or a nail-
head at fifty yards — one hundred and fifty feet.
Can the reader do it?

The nail was lightly driven, its head painted, and
game called. Then the Cooper miracles began. The
bullet of the first marksman chipped an edge of the
nail-head; the next man's bullet drove the nail a
little way into the target — and removed all the
paint. Haven't the miracles gone far enough now?
Not to suit Cooper; for the purpose of this whole
scheme is to show off his prodigy, Deerslayer-
Hawkeye - Long - Rifle-Leather-Stocking-Pathfinder-
Bumppo before the ladies.

" ' Be all ready to clench it, boys! ' cried out Pathfinder, stepping
into his friend's tracks the instant they were vacant. ' Never mind a
new nail; I can see that, though the paint is gone, and what I can see
I can hit at a hundred yards, though it were only a mosquito's eye. Be
ready to clench! '
" The rifle cracked, the bullet sped its way, and the head of the nail
was buried in the wood, covered by the piece of flattened lead."

There, you see, is a man who could hunt flies
with a rifle, and command a ducal salary in a Wild
West show to-day if we had him back with us.

The recorded feat is certainly surprising just as it
stands; but it is not surprising enough for Cooper.

Cooper adds a touch. He has made Pathfinder do this miracle with another man's rifle; and not only that, but Pathfinder did not have even the advantage of loading it himself. He had everything against him, and yet he made that impossible shot; and not only made it, but did it with absolute confidence, saying, "Be ready to clench." Now a person like that would have undertaken that same feat with a brickbat, and with Cooper to help he would have achieved it, too.

Pathfinder showed off handsomely that day before the ladies. His very first feat was a thing which no Wild West show can touch. He was standing with the group of marksmen, observing — a hundred yards from the target, mind; one Jasper raised his rifle and drove the centre of the bull's-eye. Then the Quartermaster fired. The target exhibited no result this time. There was a laugh. "It's a dead miss," said Major Lundie. Pathfinder waited an impressive moment or two; then said, in that calm, indifferent, know-it-all way of his, "No, Major, he has covered Jasper's bullet, as will be seen if any one will take the trouble to examine the target."

Wasn't it remarkable! How *could* he see that little pellet fly through the air and enter that distant bullet-hole? Yet that is what he did; for nothing is impossible to a Cooper person. Did any of those people have any deep-seated doubts about this thing? No; for that would imply sanity, and these were all Cooper people.

"The respect for Pathfinder's skill and for his *quickness and accuracy of sight*" (the italics are mine) "was so profound and general, that the instant he made this declaration the spectators began to distrust their own opinions, and a dozen rushed to the target in order to ascertain the fact. There, sure enough, it was found that the Quartermaster's bullet had gone through the hole made by Jasper's, and that, too, so accurately as to require a minute examination to be certain of the circumstance, which, however, was soon clearly established by discovering one bullet over the other in the stump against which the target was placed."

They made a "minute" examination; but never mind, how could they know that there were two bullets in that hole without digging the latest one out? for neither probe nor eyesight could prove the presence of any more than one bullet. Did they dig? No; as we shall see. It is the Pathfinder's turn now; he steps out before the ladies, takes aim, and fires.

But, alas! here is a disappointment; an incredible, an unimaginable disappointment — for the target's aspect is unchanged; there is nothing there but that same old bullet-hole!

"'If one dared to hint at such a thing,' cried Major Duncan, 'I should say that the Pathfinder has also missed the target!'"

As nobody had missed it yet, the "also" was not necessary; but never mind about that, for the Pathfinder is going to speak.

"'No, no, Major,' said he, confidently, 'that *would* be a risky declaration. I didn't load the piece, and can't say what was in it; but if it was lead, you will find the bullet driving down those of the Quartermaster and Jasper, else is not my name Pathfinder.'

"A shout from the target announced the truth of this assertion."

Is the miracle sufficient as it stands? Not f
Cooper. The Pathfinder speaks again, as he " no
slowly advances towards the stage occupied by th
females '':

> " ' That's not all, boys, that's not all; if you find the target touch
> at all, I'll own to a miss. The Quartermaster cut the wood, but you
> find no wood cut by that last messenger."

The miracle is at last complete. He knew —
doubtless *saw* — at the distance of a hundred yard
— that his bullet had passed into the hole *witho*
fraying the edges. There were now three bullets i
that one hole — three bullets embedded procession
ally in the body of the stump back of the targe
Everybody knew this — somehow or other — an
yet nobody had dug any of them out to make sur
Cooper is not a close observer, but he is interesting
He is certainly always that, no matter what happens
And he is more interesting when he is not noticin
what he is about than when he is. This is a con
siderable merit.

The conversations in the Cooper books have
curious sound in our modern ears. To believe th
such talk really ever came out of people's mouth
would be to believe that there was a time when tim
was of no value to a person who thought he ha
something to say; when it was the custom to sprea
a two-minute remark out to ten; when a man'
mouth was a rolling-mill, and busied itself all da
long in turning four-foot pigs of thought into thirty
foot bars of conversational railroad iron by attenua

on; when subjects were seldom faithfully stuck to,
ut the talk wandered all around and arrived no-
here; when conversations consisted mainly of
irrelevancies, with here and there a relevancy, a
relevancy with an embarrassed look, as not being
ble to explain how it got there.

Cooper was certainly not a master in the construc-
on of dialogue. Inaccurate observation defeated
im here as it defeated him in so many other enter-
rises of his. He even failed to notice that the
an who talks corrupt English six days in the week
ust and will talk it on the seventh, and can't help
imself. In the *Deerslayer* story he lets Deerslayer
lk the showiest kind of book-talk sometimes, and
: other times the basest of base dialects. For
stance, when some one asks him if he has a sweet-
eart, and if so, where she abides, this is his
ajestic answer:

" 'She's in the forest — hanging from the boughs of the trees, in a
ft rain — in the dew on the open grass — the clouds that float about
the blue heavens — the birds that sing in the woods — the sweet
rings where I slake my thirst — and in all the other glorious gifts that
me from God's Providence!' "

And he preceded that, a little before, with this:

" 'It consarns me as all things that touches a fri'nd consarns a
'nd.' "

And this is another of his remarks:

" 'If I was Injin born, now, I might tell of this, or carry in the scalp
d boast of the expl'ite afore the whole tribe; or if my inimy had only
en a bear' " — and so on.

7 E

We cannot imagine such a thing as a veteran
Scotch Commander-in-Chief comporting himself in
the field like a windy melodramatic actor, but
Cooper could.   On one occasion Alice and Cora
were being chased by the French through a fog in
the neighborhood of their father's fort:

> " '*Point de quartier aux coquins!*' cried an eager pursuer, who
> seemed to direct the operations of the enemy.
>
> " 'Stand firm and be ready, my gallant 60ths!' suddenly exclaimed
> a voice above them; 'wait to see the enemy; fire low, and sweep the
> glacis.'
>
> " 'Father! father!' exclaimed a piercing cry from out the mist; 'it
> is I! Alice! thy own Elsie! spare, O! save your daughters!'
>
> " 'Hold!' shouted the former speaker, in the awful tones of parental
> agony, the sound reaching even to the woods, and rolling back in solemn
> echo.   ''Tis she! God has restored me my children! Throw open
> the sally-port; to the field, 60ths, to the field! pull not a trigger, lest ye
> kill my lambs!   Drive off these dogs of France with your steel!' "

Cooper's word-sense was singularly dull.   When
a person has a poor ear for music he will flat and
sharp right along without knowing it.   He keeps
near the tune, but it is *not* the tune.   When a person
has a poor ear for words, the result is a literary flatting and sharping; you perceive what he is intending to say, but you also perceive that he doesn'
say it.   This is Cooper.   He was not a word
musician.   His ear was satisfied with the *approxi-
mate* word.   I will furnish some circumstantial
evidence in support of this charge.   My instances
are gathered from half a dozen pages of the tale
called *Deerslayer*.   He uses " verbal," for " oral "
" precision," for " facility "; " phenomena," for

" marvels "; " necessary," for " predetermined ";
" unsophisticated," for " primitive "; " preparation," for " expectancy "; " rebuked," for " subdued "; " dependent on," for " resulting from ";
" fact," for " condition "; " fact," for " conjecture "; " precaution," for " caution "; " explain,"
or " determine "; " mortified," for " disappointed"; "meretricious," for "factitious"; "materially," for " considerably "; " decreasing," for
" deepening "; " increasing," for " disappearing ";
" embedded," for " enclosed "; " treacherous,"
or " hostile "; " stood," for " stooped "; " softened," for " replaced "; " rejoined," for " remarked "; " situation," for " condition "; " different," for " differing "; " insensible," for
" unsentient "; " brevity," for " celerity "; " dis-
trusted," for " suspicious "; " mental imbecility,"
or " imbecility "; " eyes," for " sight "; " coun-
teracting," for " opposing "; " funeral obsequies,"
or " obsequies."

There have been daring people in the world who
claimed that Cooper could write English, but they
re all dead now — all dead but Lounsbury. I don't
remember that Lounsbury makes the claim in so
many words, still he makes it, for he says that *Deerslayer* is a " pure work of art." Pure, in that connection, means faultless — faultless in all details —
and language is a detail. If Mr. Lounsbury had
only compared Cooper's English with the English
which he writes himself — but it is plain that he

didn't; and so it is likely that he imagines until th
day that Cooper's is as clean and compact as h
own.   Now I feel sure, deep down in my heart, tha
Cooper wrote about the poorest English that exis
in our language, and that the English of *Deerslay*
is the very worst that even Cooper ever wrote.

I may be mistaken, but it does seem to me tha
Deerslayer is not a work of art in any sense; it do
seem to me that it is destitute of every detail tha
goes to the making of a work of art; in truth,
seems to me that *Deerslayer* is just simply a literar
delirium tremens.

A work of art? It has no invention; it has n
order, system, sequence, or result; it has no lif
likeness, no thrill, no stir, no seeming of reality;
characters are confusedly drawn, and by their ac
and words they prove that they are not the sort
people the author claims that they are; its humor
pathetic; its pathos is funny; its conversations a
— oh! indescribable; its love-scenes odious;
English a crime against the language.

Counting these out, what is left is Art. I thin
we must all admit that.

AST spring I went out to Chicago to see the
Fair, and although I did not see it my trip was
not wholly lost — there were compensations. In
New York I was introduced to a major in the regular
army who said he was going to the Fair, and we
agreed to go together. I had to go to Boston first,
but that did not interfere; he said he would go
along, and put in the time. He was a handsome
man, and built like a gladiator. But his ways were
gentle, and his speech was soft and persuasive. He
was companionable, but exceedingly reposeful. Yes,
and wholly destitute of the sense of humor. He
was full of interest in everything that went on around
him, but his serenity was indestructible; nothing
disturbed him, nothing excited him.

But before the day was done I found that deep
down in him somewhere he had a passion, quiet as
it was — a passion for reforming petty public
abuses. He stood for citizenship — it was his
hobby. His idea was that every citizen of the re-
public ought to consider himself an unofficial police-
man, and keep unsalaried watch and ward over the
laws and their execution. He thought that the only

7*.*.   (97)

effective way of preserving and protecting pub
rights was for each citizen to do his share in p
venting or punishing such infringements of them
came under his personal notice.

It was a good scheme, but I thought it wo
keep a body in trouble all the time; it seemed
me that one would be always trying to get offe
ing little officials discharged, and perhaps gett
laughed at for all reward. But he said no, I I
the wrong idea; that there was no occasion to
anybody discharged; that in fact you *must n't*
anybody discharged; that that would itself be
failure; no, one must reform the man — reform I
and make him useful where he was.

"Must one report the offender and then beg
superior not to discharge him, but reprimand I
and keep him?"

"No, that is not the idea; you don't report I
at all, for then you risk his bread and butter. Y
can act as if you are *going* to report him — w
nothing else will answer. But that's an extre
case. That is a sort of *force*, and force is b
Diplomacy is the effective thing. Now if a man
tact — if a man will exercise diplomacy — "

For two minutes we had been standing at a t
graph wicket, and during all this time the Major I
been trying to get the attention of one of the yo
operators, but they were all busy skylarking. 1
Major spoke now, and asked one of them to t
his telegram. He got for reply:

" I reckon you can wait a minute, can't you?"
the skylarking went on.

The Major said yes, he was not in a hurry. Then
wrote another telegram:

esident Western Union Tel. Co.:
Come and dine with me this evening. I can tell you how business
onducted in one of your branches."

Presently the young fellow who had spoken so
tly a little before reached out and took the tele-
m, and when he read it he lost color and began
apologize and explain. He said he would lose
place if this deadly telegram was sent, and he
ght never get another. If he could be let off this
e he would give no cause of complaint again.
e compromise was accepted.

As we walked away, the Major said:

" Now, you see, that was diplomacy — and you
how it worked. It wouldn't do any good to
ster, the way people are always doing — that
y can always give you as good as you send, and
u'll come out defeated and ashamed of yourself
etty nearly always. But you see he stands no
ance against diplomacy. Gentle words and diplo-
cy — those are the tools to work with."

" Yes, I see; but everybody wouldn't have had
ur opportunity. It isn't everybody that is on
ose familiar terms with the president of the West-
n Union."

" Oh, you misunderstand. I don't know the
esident — I only use him diplomatically. It is for

G*₊*₂

his good and for the public good. There's no har
in it."

I said, with hesitation and diffidence:

" But is it ever right or noble to tell a lie?"

He took no note of the delicate self-righteousne
of the question, but answered, with undisturb
gravity and simplicity:

" Yes, sometimes. Lies told to injure a perso
and lies told to profit yourself are not justifiable, b
lies told to help another person, and lies told in t
public interest — oh, well, that is quite anoth
matter. Anybody knows that. But never mi
about the methods: you see the result. That you
is going to be useful now, and well-behaved. I
had a good face. He was worth saving. Why,
was worth saving on his mother's account if not I
own. Of course, he has a mother — sisters, to
Damn these people who are always forgetting tha
Do you know, I've never fought a duel in my life
never once — and yet have been challenged, li
other people. I could always see the other mar
unoffending women folks or his little children stan
ing between him and me. *They* hadn't done an
thing — I couldn't break *their* hearts, you know."

He corrected a good many little abuses in t
course of the day, and always without friction
always with a fine and dainty " diplomacy " whi
left no sting behind; and he got such happiness a
such contentment out of these performances tha
was obliged to envy him his trade — and perha

ould have adopted it if I could have managed the
necessary deflections from fact as confidently with
my mouth as I believe I could with a pen, behind
the shelter of print, after a little practice.

Away late that night we were coming up-town in
horse-car when three boisterous roughs got aboard,
and began to fling hilarious obscenities and pro-
fanities right and left among the timid passengers,
some of whom were women and children. Nobody
resisted or retorted; the conductor tried soothing
words and moral suasion, but the roughs only called
him names and laughed at him. Very soon I saw
that the Major realized that this was a matter which
was in his line; evidently he was turning over his
stock of diplomacy in his mind and getting ready.
I felt that the first diplomatic remark he made in
this place would bring down a land-slide of ridicule
upon him and maybe something worse; but before
I could whisper to him and check him he had begun,
and it was too late. He said, in a level and dispassionate tone:

" Conductor, you must put these swine out. I
will help you."

I was not looking for that. In a flash the three
roughs plunged at him. But none of them arrived.
He delivered three such blows as one could not expect to encounter outside the prize-ring, and neither
of the men had life enough left in him to get up from
where he fell. The Major dragged them out and
threw them off the car, and we got under way again.

I was astonished; astonished to see a lamb
so; astonished at the strength displayed, and
clean and comprehensive result; astonished at
brisk and business-like style of the whole thin
The situation had a humorous side to it, consider
how much I had been hearing about mild persuas
and gentle diplomacy all day from this pile-driv
and I would have liked to call his attention to t'
feature and do some sarcasms about it; but whe
looked at him I saw that it would be of no use —
placid and contented face had no ray of humor
it; he would not have understood. When we
the car, I said:

" That was a good stroke of diplomacy — th
good strokes of diplomacy, in fact."

" *That ?* That wasn't diplomacy. You are qu
in the wrong. Diplomacy is a wholly different thin
One cannot apply it to that sort, they would
understand it. No, that was not diplomacy; it v
force."

" Now that you mention it, I — yes, I think p
haps you are right."

" Right? Of course I am right. It was j
force."

" I think, myself, it had the outside aspect of
Do you often have to reform people in that way

" Far from it. It hardly ever happens.
oftener than once in half a year, at the outside."

" Those men will get well?"

" Get well? Why, certainly they will. They

t in any danger.   I know how to hit and where to
t.   You noticed that I did not hit them under the
w.   That would have killed them.''

I believed that.   I remarked — rather wittily, as I
ought — that he had been a lamb all day, but now
d all of a sudden developed into a ram — batter-
g ram; but with dulcet frankness and simplicity
said no, a battering-ram was quite a different
ng and not in use now.   This was maddening,
d I came near bursting out and saying he had no
re appreciation of wit than a jackass — in fact, I
d it right on my tongue, but did not say it, know-
g there was no hurry and I could say it just as
ll some other time over the telephone.

We started to Boston the next afternoon.   The
oking-compartment in the parlor-car was full, and
went into the regular smoker.   Across the aisle
the front seat sat a meek, farmer-looking old man
h a sickly pallor in his face, and he was holding
door open with his foot to get the air.   Presently
big brakeman came rushing through, and when
got to the door he stopped, gave the farmer an
ly scowl, then wrenched the door to with such
ergy as to almost snatch the old man's boot off.
en on he plunged about his business.   Several
ssengers laughed, and the old gentleman looked
thetically shamed and grieved.

After a little the conductor passed along, and the
jor stopped him and asked him a question in his
bitually courteous way:

" Conductor, where does one report the mi
conduct of a brakeman? Does one report to you?

" You can report him at New Haven if you wa
to. What has he been doing?"

The Major told the story. The conductor seeme
amused. He said, with just a touch of sarcasm
his bland tones:

" As I understand you, the brakeman didn't s
anything."

" No, he didn't say anything."

" But he scowled, you say."

" Yes."

" And snatched the door loose in a rough way

" Yes."

" That's the whole business, is it ?"

" Yes, that is the whole of it."

The conductor smiled pleasantly, and said:

" Well, if you want to report him, all right, bu
don't quite make out what it's going to amount
You'll say — as I understand you — that the brak
man insulted this old gentleman. They'll ask y
what he *said*. You'll say he didn't say anything
all. I reckon they'll say, how are you going
make out an insult when you acknowledge yours
that he didn't say a word."

There was a murmur of applause at the c
ductor's compact reasoning, and it gave him ple
ure — you could see it in his face But the Ma
was not disturbed. He said:

" There — now you have touched upon a cry

efect in the complaint-system. The railway offi-
als — as the public think and as you also seem to
think — are not aware that there are any kind of
sults except *spoken* ones. So nobody goes to
eadquarters and reports insults of manner, insults
f gesture, look, and so forth; and yet these are
sometimes harder to bear than any words. They
re bitter hard to bear because there is nothing
ingible to take hold of; and the insulter can always
ay, if called before the railway officials, that he
ever dreamed of intending any offence. It seems
o me that the officials ought to specially and
rgently request the public to report *unworded*
ffronts and incivilities."

The conductor laughed, and said:

" Well, that *would* be trimming it pretty fine,
ure !"

" But not too fine, I think. I will report this
natter at New Haven, and I have an idea that I'll
e thanked for it."

The conductor's face lost something of its com-
placency; in fact, it settled to a quite sober cast as
he owner of it moved away. I said:

" You are not really going to bother with that
rifle, are you?"

" It isn't a trifle. Such things ought always to
be reported. It is a public duty, and no citizen has
a right to shirk it. But I sha'n't have to report this
case."

" Why?"

" It won't be necessary.   Diplomacy will do the
business.   You'll see."

Presently the conductor came on his rounds again,
and when he reached the Major he leaned over and
said:

" That's all right.   You needn't report him.   He's
responsible to me, and if he does it again I'll give
him a talking to."

The Major's response was cordial:

" Now that is what I like!   You mustn't think
that I was moved by any vengeful spirit, for that
wasn't the case.   It was duty — just a sense of
duty, that was all.   My brother-in-law is one of
the directors of the road, and when he learns that
you are going to reason with your brakeman the
very next time he brutally insults an unoffending
old man it will please him, you may be sure of
that."

The conductor did not look as joyous as one might
have thought he would, but on the contrary looked
sickly and uncomfortable.   He stood around a little
then said:

" I think something ought to be done to him
now.   I'll discharge him."

" Discharge him?   What good would that do?
Don't you think it would be better wisdom to teach
him better ways and keep him?"

" Well, there's something in that.   What would
you suggest?"

" He insulted the old gentleman in presence of all

hese people.   How would it do to have him come
nd apologize in their presence?"

"I'll have him here right off.   And I want to say
his: If people would do as you've done, and re-
-ort such things to me instead of keeping mum and
oing off and blackguarding the road, you'd see a
ifferent state of things pretty soon.   I'm much
bliged to you."

The brakeman came and apologized.   After he
vas gone the Major said:

"Now, you see how simple and easy that was.
The ordinary citizen would have accomplished noth-
ng — the brother-in-law of a director can accomplish
nything he wants to."

"But are you really the brother-in-law of a
irector?"

"Always.   Always when the public interests require it.   I have a brother-in-law on all the boards
— everywhere.   It saves me a world of trouble."

"It is a good wide relationship."

"Yes.   I have over three hundred of them."

"Is the relationship never doubted by a con-
luctor?"

"I have never met with a case.   It is the honest
ruth — I never have."

"Why didn't you let him go ahead and discharge
he brakeman, in spite of your favorite policy? You
:now he deserved it."

The Major answered with something which really
iad a sort of distant resemblance to impatience:

" If you would stop and think a moment you
wouldn't ask such a question as that. Is a brake
man a dog, that nothing but dog's methods will d
for him? He is a man, and has a man's fight fo
life. And he always has a sister, or a mother, o
wife and children to support. Always — there ar
no exceptions. When you take his living away fro
him you take theirs away too — and what have the
done to you? Nothing. And where is the profit i
discharging an uncourteous brakeman and hirin
another just like him? It's unwisdom. Don't yo
see that the rational thing to do is to *reform* th
brakeman and keep him? Of course it is."

Then he quoted with admiration the conduct of
certain division superintendent of the Consolidate
road, in a case where a switchman of two year
experience was negligent once and threw a train o
the track and killed several people. Citizens cam
in a passion to urge the man's dismissal, but th
superintendent said:

" No, you are wrong. He has learned his lesso
he will throw no more trains off the track. He
twice as valuable as he was before. I shall ke
him."

We had only one more adventure on the trip. B
tween Hartford and Springfield the train-boy ca
shouting in with an armful of literature and dropp
a sample into a slumbering gentleman's lap, and t
man woke up with a start. He was very angry, a
he and a couple of friends discussed the outra

vith much heat.   They sent for the parlor-car conductor and described the matter, and were deter-
mined to have the boy expelled from his situation.
The three complainants were wealthy Holyoke mer-
hants, and it was evident that the conductor stood
n some awe of them.   He tried to pacify them,
nd explained that the boy was not under his
uthority, but under that of one of the news com-
anies; but he accomplished nothing.

Then the Major volunteered some testimony for
he defence.   He said:

" I saw it all.   You gentlemen have not meant to
xaggerate the circumstances, but still that is what
ou have done.   The boy has done nothing more
han all train-boys do.   If you want to get his ways
oftened down and his manners reformed, I am with
ou and ready to help, but it isn't fair to get him
ischarged without giving him a chance."

But they were angry, and would hear of no com-
romise.   They were well acquainted with the presi-
ent of the Boston & Albany, they said, and would
ut everything aside next day and go up to Boston
nd fix that boy.

The Major said he would be on hand too, and
ould do what he could to save the boy.   One of
he gentlemen looked him over, and said:

" Apparently it is going to be a matter of who
an wield the most influence with the president.   Do
ou know Mr. Bliss personally?"

The Major said, with composure:

8E

" Yes; he is my uncle."

The effect was satisfactory. There was an awk
ward silence for a minute or more; then th
hedging and the half-confessions of over-haste an
exaggerated resentment began, and soon everythin
was smooth and friendly and sociable, and it wa
resolved to drop the matter and leave the boy'
bread-and-butter unmolested.

It turned out as I had expected: the president o
the road was not the Major's uncle at all — excep
by adoption, and for this day and train only.

We got into no episodes on the return journey
Probably it was because we took a night train an
slept all the way.

We left New York Saturday night by the Pennsyl
vania road. After breakfast the next morning w
went into the parlor-car, but found it a dull plac
and dreary. There were but few people in it an
nothing going on. Then we went into the littl
smoking-compartment of the same car and foun
three gentlemen in there. Two of them were grum
bling over one of the rules of the road — a rul
which forbade card-playing on the trains on Sunday
They had started an innocent game of high-low-jacl
and been stopped. The Major was interested. H
said to the third gentleman:

" Did you object to the game?"

" Not at all. I am a Yale professor and a relig
ious man, but my prejudices are not extensive."

Then the Major said to the others:

" You are at perfect liberty to resume your game,
gentlemen; no one here objects."

One of them declined the risk, but the other one
said he would like to begin again if the Major would
join him. So they spread an overcoat over their
knees and the game proceeded. Pretty soon the
parlor-car conductor arrived, and said brusquely:

" There, there, gentlemen, that won't do. Put
up the cards— it's not allowed."

The Major was shuffling. He continued to shuffle,
and said :

" By whose order is it forbidden?"

" It's my order. I forbid it."

The dealing began. The Major asked:

" Did you invent the idea?"

" What idea?"

" The idea of forbidding card-playing on Sunday."

" No — of course not."

" Who did?"

" The company."

" Then it isn't your order, after all, but the company's. Is that it?"

" Yes. But you don't stop playing; I have to
require you to stop playing immediately."

" Nothing is gained by hurry, and often much is
lost. Who authorized the company to issue such an
order?"

" My dear sir, that is a matter of no consequence
to me, and — "

" But you forget that you are not the only pers○
concerned. It may be a matter of consequence
me. It is indeed a matter of very great importan○
to me. I cannot violate a legal requirement of n○
country without dishonoring myself; I cannot allo○
any man or corporation to hamper my liberties wi○
illegal rules — a thing which railway companies a○
always trying to do — without dishonoring n○
citizenship. So I come back to that question: F
whose authority has the company issued this order ?○

" I don't *know*. That's *their* affair."

" Mine, too. I doubt if the company has an○
right to issue such a rule. This road runs throug○
several States. Do you know what State we are○
now, and what its laws are in matters of th○
kind?"

" Its laws do not concern me, but the company○
orders do. It is my duty to stop this game, gentl○
men, and it *must* be stopped."

" Possibly; but still there is no hurry. In hote○
they post certain rules in the rooms, but they alway○
quote passages from the State laws as authority f○
these requirements. I see nothing posted here ○
this sort. Please produce your authority and let ○
arrive at a decision, for you see yourself that y○
are marring the game."

" I have nothing of the kind, but I have m○
orders, and that is sufficient. They must ○
obeyed."

" Let us not jump to conclusions. It will ○

tter all around to examine into the matter without
at or haste, and see just where we stand before
her of us makes a mistake — for the curtailing of
e liberties of a citizen of the United States is a
uch more serious matter than you and the railroads
em to think, and it cannot be done in my person
til the curtailer proves his right to do so.
ow — ''

" My dear sir, *will* you put down those cards?"

" All in good time, perhaps. It depends. You
y this order must be obeyed. *Must.* It is a
ong word. You see yourself how strong it is.
wise company would not arm you with so drastic
order as this, of *course*, without appointing a
nalty for its infringement. Otherwise it runs the
k of being a dead letter and a thing to laugh at.
hat is the appointed penalty for an infringement
this law?"

" Penalty? I never heard of any."

" Unquestionably you must be mistaken. Your
mpany orders you to come here and rudely break
an innocent amusement, and furnishes you no
ay to enforce the order? Don't you see that that
nonsense? What do you *do* when people refuse
obey this order? Do you take the cards away
om them?"

" No."

" Do you put the offender off at the next station?"

" Well, no — of course we couldn't if he had a
cket."

8***

" Do you have him up before a court?"

The conductor was silent and apparently trouble

The Major started a new deal, and said:

" You see that you are helpless, and that t
company has placed you in a foolish position. Y
are furnished with an arrogant order, and you c
liver it in a blustering way, and when you come
look into the matter you find you haven't any w
of enforcing obedience."

The conductor said, with chill dignity:

" Gentlemen, you have heard the order, and r
duty is ended. As to obeying it or not, you will
as you think fit."   And he turned to leave.

" But wait. The matter is not yet finished.
think you are mistaken about your duty bei
ended; but if it really is, I myself have a duty
perform yet."

" How do you mean?"

" Are you going to report my disobedience
headquarters in Pittsburg?"

" No. What good would that do?"

" You must report me, or I will report you."

" Report me for what?"

" For disobeying the company's orders in n
stopping this game. As a citizen it is my duty
help the railway companies keep their servants
their work."

" Are you in earnest?"

" Yes, I am in earnest. I have nothing agai
you as a man, but I have this against you as

cer — that you have not carried out that order,
d if you do not report me I must report you.
d I will."

The conductor looked puzzled, and was thought-
a moment; then he burst out with:

" I seem to be getting *myself* into a scrape! It's
a muddle; I can't make head or tail of it; it's
ver happened before; they always knocked under
d never said a word, and so *I* never saw how
iculous that stupid order with no penalty is. *I*
n't want to report anybody, and I don't want to
reported — why, it might do me no end of harm!
w *do* go on with the game — play the whole day
you want to — and don't let's have any more
uble about it!"

" No, I only sat down here to establish this
ntleman's rights — he can have his place now.
t before you go won't you tell me what you think
e company made this rule for? Can you imagine
excuse for it? I mean a rational one — an ex-
se that is not on its face silly, and the invention
an idiot?"

" Why, surely I can. The reason it was made is
in enough. It is to save the feelings of the other
ssengers — the religious ones among them, I
an. They would not like it, to have the Sabbath
secrated by card-playing on the train."

" I just thought as much. They are willing to
secrate it themselves by traveling on Sunday, but
y are not willing that other people — "

H*⁎*⁎

" By gracious, you've hit it! I never thought
that before. The fact is, it *is* a silly rule when y
come to look into it."

At this point the train-conductor arrived, and v
going to shut down the game in a very high-hand
fashion, but the parlor-car conductor stopped h
and took him aside to explain. Nothing more v
heard of the matter.

I was ill in bed eleven days in Chicago and got
glimpse of the Fair, for I was obliged to return e
as soon as I was able to travel. The Major secu
and paid for a state-room in a sleeper the day bef
we left, so that I could have plenty of room and
comfortable; but when we arrived at the station
mistake had been made and our car had not be
put on. The conductor had reserved a section
us — it was the best he could do, he said. But
Major said we were not in a hurry, and would w
for the car to be put on. The conductor respond
with pleasant irony:

" It may be that *you* are not in a hurry, just
you say, but we *are*. Come, get aboard, gent
men, get aboard — don't keep us waiting."

But the Major would not get aboard himself
allow me to do it. He wanted his car, and said
must have it. This made the hurried and perspir
conductor impatient, and he said:

" It's the best we can *do* — we can't do impos
bilities. You will take the section or go witho
A mistake has been made and can't be rectified

s late hour. It's a thing that happens now and
:n, and there is nothing for it but to put up with
and make the best of it.   Other people do.''

" Ah, that is just it, you see. If they had stuck
 their rights and enforced them you wouldn't be
ing to trample mine under foot in this bland way
w.   I haven't any disposition to give you un-
:essary trouble, but it is my duty to protect the
xt man from this kind of imposition.   So I must
ve my car.   Otherwise I will wait in Chicago and
: the company for violating its contract.''

" Sue the company? — for a thing like that!''

" Certainly.''

" Do you really mean that?''

" Indeed, I do.''

The conductor looked the Major over wonder-
;ly, and then said:

" It beats me — it's bran-new — I've never struck
: mate to it before. But I swear I think you'd
 it.   Look here, I'll send for the station-master.''

When the station-master came he was a good deal
noyed — at the Major, not at the person who had
de the mistake.   He was rather brusque, and
>k the same position which the conductor had
:en in the beginning; but he failed to move the
t-spoken artilleryman, who still insisted that he
ist have his car.   However, it was plain that there
s only one strong side in this case, and that that
le was the Major's.   The station-master banished
s annoyed manner, and became pleasant and even

half-apologetic. This made a good opening for
compromise, and the Major made a concession. I
said he would give up the engaged state-room, b
he must have *a* state-room. After a deal
ransacking, one was found whose owner was p
suadable; he exchanged it for our section, and
got away at last. The conductor called on us in t
evening, and was kind and courteous and obligi
and we had a long talk and got to be good frien
He said he wished the public would make trou
oftener — it would have a good effect. He s
that the railroads could not be expected to do th
whole duty by the traveler unless the traveler wo
take some interest in the matter himself.

I hoped that we were done reforming for the t
now, but it was not so. In the hotel-car, in t
morning, the Major called for broiled chicken. T
waiter said:

" It's not in the bill of fare, sir; we do not se
anything but what is in the bill."

" That gentleman yonder is eating a broi
chicken."

" Yes, but that is different. He is one of
superintendents of the road."

" Then all the more must I have broiled chick
I do not like these discriminations. Please hurry
bring me a broiled chicken."

The waiter brought the steward, who explai
in a low and polite voice that the thing was imp
sible — it was against the rule, and the rule was rig

" Very well, then, you must either apply it im-
rtially or break it impartially. You must take
at gentleman's chicken away from him or bring
e one."

The steward was puzzled, and did not quite know
at to do. He began an incoherent argument,
t the conductor came along just then, and asked
at the difficulty was. The steward explained that
re was a gentleman who was insisting on having a
icken when it was dead against the rule and not in
e bill. The conductor said:

" Stick by your rules — you haven't any option.
ait a moment — is this the gentleman?" Then he
ghed and said: " Never mind your rules — it's
advice, and sound; give him anything he wants
don't get him started on his rights. Give him
atever he asks for; and if you haven't got it,
p the train and get it."

The Major ate the chicken, but said he did it from
ense of duty and to establish a principle, for he
not like chicken.

I missed the Fair, it is true, but I picked up
ne diplomatic tricks which I and the reader may
d handy and useful as we go along.

PRIVATE HISTORY OF THE "JUMPING FROG" STORY

FIVE or six years ago a lady from Finland asked me to tell her a story in our negro dialect, so that she could get an idea of what that variety of speech was like. I told her one of Hopkinson Smith's negro stories, and gave her a copy of *Harper's Monthly* containing it. She translated it for a Swedish newspaper, but by an oversight named me as the author of it instead of Smith. I was very sorry for that, because I got a good lashing in the Swedish press, which would have fallen to his share but for that mistake; for it was shown that Boccaccio had told that very story, in his curt and meagre fashion, five hundred years before Smith took hold of it and made a good and tellable thing out of it.

I have always been sorry for Smith. But my own turn has come now. A few weeks ago Professor Van Dyke, of Princeton, asked this question:

" Do you know how old your Jumping Frog story is?"

And I answered:

" Yes — forty-five years. The thing happened in ▮laveras County in the spring of 1849."

" No; it happened earlier — a couple of thousand ▮ars earlier; it is a Greek story."

I was astonished — and hurt. I said:

" I am willing to be a literary thief if it has been ordained; I am even willing to be caught robbing ▮e ancient dead alongside of Hopkinson Smith, for ▮ is my friend and a good fellow, and I think would ▮ as honest as any one if he could do it without ▮casioning remark; but I am not willing to ante-▮te his crimes by fifteen hundred years. I must ▮k you to knock off part of that."

But the professor was not chaffing; he was in ▮rnest, and could not abate a century. He named ▮e Greek author, and offered to get the book and ▮nd it to me and the college text-book containing ▮e English translation also. I thought I would like ▮e translation best, because Greek makes me tired. ▮nuary 30th he sent me the English version, and I ▮ll presently insert it in this article. It is my ▮mping Frog tale in every essential. It is not ▮rung out as I have strung it out, but it is all ▮ere.

To me this is very curious and interesting. ▮urious for several reasons. For instance:

I heard the story told by a man who was not tell-▮g it to his hearers as a thing new to them, but as ▮ thing which *they had witnessed and would re-▮ember*. He was a dull person, and ignorant; he

had no gift as a story-teller, and no invention; i
his mouth this episode was merely history — histor
and statistics; and the gravest sort of history, too
he was entirely serious, for he was dealing with wh:
to him were austere facts, and they interested hi
solely because they *were* facts; he was drawing c
his memory, not his mind; he saw no humor in h
tale, neither did his listeners; neither he nor the
ever smiled or laughed; in my time I have n
attended a more solemn conference. To him an
to his fellow gold-miners there were just two thing
in the story that were worth considering. One w:
the smartness of the stranger in taking in its her
Jim Smiley, with a loaded frog; and the other was tl
stranger's deep knowledge of a frog's nature — f
he knew (as the narrator asserted and the listene
conceded) that a frog *likes shot* and is always reac
to eat it. Those men discussed those two point
and those only. They were hearty in their admir
tion of them, and none of the party was aware th
a first-rate story had been told in a first-rate wa
and that it was brimful of a quality whose presen
they never suspected — humor.

Now, then, the interesting question is, *did* tl
frog episode happen in Angel's Camp in the sprir
of '49, as told in my hearing that day in the fall
1865? I am perfectly sure that it did. I am al
sure that its duplicate happened in Bœotia a coup
of thousand years ago. I think it must be a case
history actually repeating itself, and not a case of

ood story floating down the ages and surviving be-
ause too good to be allowed to perish.

I would now like to have the reader examine the
Greek story and the story told by the dull and
solemn Californian, and observe how exactly alike
they are in essentials.

[*Translation.*]

THE ATHENIAN AND THE FROG.*

An Athenian once fell in with a Bœotian who was sitting by the road-
side looking at a frog.   Seeing the other approach, the Bœotian said his
was a remarkable frog, and asked if he would agree to start a contest of
ogs, on condition that he whose frog jumped farthest should receive a
rge sum of money.   The Athenian replied that he would if the other
ould fetch him a frog, for the lake was near.   To this he agreed, and
hen he was gone the Athenian took the frog, and, opening its mouth,
oured some stones into its stomach, so that it did not indeed seem
rger than before, but could not jump.   The Bœotian soon returned
th the other frog, and the contest began.   The second frog first was
nched, and jumped moderately; then they pinched the Bœotian frog.
nd he gathered himself for a leap, and used the utmost effort, but
could not move his body the least.   So the Athenian departed with
e money.   When he was gone the Bœotian, wondering what was the
atter with the frog, lifted him up and examined him.   And being
rned upside down, he opened his mouth and vomited out the stones.

And here is the way it happened in California:

FROM "THE CELEBRATED JUMPING FROG OF CALAVERAS COUNTY."

Well, thish-yer Smiley had rat-tarriers, and chicken cocks, and tom-
ts, and all them kind of things, till you couldn't rest, and you couldn't
ch nothing for him to bet on but he'd match you.   He ketched a
g one day, and took him home, and said he cal'lated to educate him;
d so he never done nothing for three months but set in his back yard

---

* Sidgwick, *Greek Prose Composition*, page 116.

and learn that frog to jump. And you bet you he *did* learn him, to
He'd give him a little punch behind, and the next minute you'd s
that frog whirling in the air like a doughnut — see him turn one summe
set, or maybe a couple if he got a good start, and come down flat-foot
and all right, like a cat. He got him up so in the matter of ketchi
flies, and kep' him in practice so constant, that he'd nail a fly every ti
as fur as he could see him. Smiley said all a frog wanted was educ
tion, and he could do 'most anything — and I believe him. Why, I'
seen him set Dan'l Webster down here on this floor — Dan'l Webs
was the name of the frog — and sing out "Flies, Dan'l, flies!" a
quicker'n you could wink he'd spring straight up and snake a fly off
the counter there, and flop down on the floor ag'in as solid as a gob
mud, and fall to scratching the side of his head with his hind foot
indifferent as if he hadn't no idea he'd been doin' any more'n any fr
might do. You never see a frog so modest and straightfor'ard as
was, for all he was so gifted. And when it come to fair and squa
jumping on a dead level, he could get over more ground at one strade
than any animal of his breed you ever see. Jumping on a dead le
was his strong suit, you understand; and when it came to that, Smi
would ante up money on him as long as he had a red. Smiley w
monstrous proud of his frog, and well he might be, for fellers that h
traveled and been everywheres all said he laid over any frog that e
they see.

Well, Smiley kep' the beast in a little lattice box, and he used
fetch him down-town sometimes and lay for a bet. One day a fell
— a stranger in the camp, he was — come acrost him with his bo
and says:

"What might it be that you've got in the box?"

And Smiley says, sorter indifferent-like, "It might be a parrot, or
might be a canary, maybe, but it ain't — it's only just a frog."

And the feller took it, and looked at it careful, and turned it round th
way and that, and says, "H'm — so 'tis. Well, what's *he* good for?

"Well," Smiley says, easy and careless, "he's good enough for o
thing, I should judge — he can outjump any frog in Calaveras County.

The feller took the box again and took another long, particular loo
and gave it back to Smiley, and says, very deliberate, "Well," he say
"I don't see no p'ints about that frog that's any better'n any oth
frog."

"Maybe you don't," Smiley says. "Maybe you understand fro

nd maybe you don't understand 'em; maybe you've had experience, nd maybe you ain't only a amature, as it were. Anyways, I've got *y* opinion, and I'll resk forty dollars that he can outjump any frog in alaveras County.''

And the feller studies a minute, and then says, kinder sad-like, Well, I'm only a stranger here, and I ain't got no frog, but if I had frog I'd bet you.''

And then Smiley says: "That's all right — that's all right — if you'll old my box a minute, I'll go and get you a frog.'' And so the feller ok the box and put up his forty dollars along with Smiley's and set wn to wait.

So he set there a good while thinking and thinking to hisself, and en he got the frog out and prized his mouth open and took a teaspoon d filled him full of quail shot — filled him pretty near up to his chin - and set him on the floor. Smiley he went to the swamp and slopped ound in the mud for a long time, and finally he ketched a frog and tched him in and give him to this feller, and says:

"Now, if you're ready, set him alongside of Dan'l, with his fore-paws st even with Dan'l's, and I'll give the word.'' Then he says, "One two — three — *git!*'' and him and the feller touched up the frogs m behind, and the new frog hopped off lively; but Dan'l give a ave, and hysted up his shoulders — so — like a Frenchman, but it rn't no use — he couldn't budge; he was planted as solid as a church, d he couldn't no more stir than if he was anchored out. Smiley was good deal surprised, and he was disgusted, too, but he didn't have no a what the matter was, of course.

The feller took the money and started away; and when he was going t at the door he sorter jerked his thumb over his shoulder — so — at n'l, and says again, very deliberate: "Well,'' he says, "*I* don't see p'ints about that frog that's any better'n any other frog.''

Smiley he stood scratching his head and looking down at Dan'l a g time, and at last he says, "I do wonder what in the nation that g throw'd off for — I wonder if there ain't something the matter with n — he 'pears to look mighty baggy, somehow.'' And he ketched n'l by the nap of the neck, and hefted him, and says, "Why, blame cats if he don't weigh five pound!'' and turned him upside down, d he belched out a double handful of shot. And then he see how it s, and he was the maddest man — he set the frog down and took ou er that feller, but he never ketched him.

9B

The resemblances are deliciously exact. The
you have the wily Bœotian and the wily Jim Smile
waiting — two thousand years apart — and waitin
each equipped with his frog and " laying " for tl
stranger. A contest is proposed — for money. T
Athenian would take a chance " if the other wou
fetch him a frog "; the Yankee says: " I'm only
stranger here, and I ain't got no frog; but if I ha
a frog I'd bet you." The wily Bœotian and tl
wily Californian, with that vast gulf of two thousar
years between, retire eagerly and go frogging in tl
marsh; the Athenian and the Yankee remain behir
and work a base advantage, the one with pebble
the other with shot. Presently the contest bega
In the one case " they pinched the Bœotian frog '
in the other, " him and the feller touched up tl
frogs from behind." The Bœotian frog " gather
himself for a leap " (you can just *see* him!), " b
could not move his body in the least ": the Ca
fornian frog " give a heave, but it warn't no use -
he couldn't budge." In both the ancient and tl
modern cases the strangers departed with the mone
The Bœotian and the Californian wonder what is tl
matter with their frogs; they lift them and examin
they turn them upside down and out spills the i
forming ballast.

Yes, the resemblances are curiously exact.
used to tell the story of the Jumping Frog in Sa
Francisco, and presently Artemus Ward came alor
and wanted it to help fill out a little book which l

as about to publish; so I wrote it out and sent it
his publisher, Carleton; but Carleton thought the
ok had enough matter in it, so he gave the story
Henry Clapp as a present, and Clapp put it in
s *Saturday Press*, and it killed that paper with a
ddenness that was beyond praise. At least the
per died with that issue, and none but envious
ople have ever tried to rob me of the honor and
edit of killing it. The " Jumping Frog " was the
st piece of writing of mine that spread itself
rough the newspapers and brought me into public
tice. Consequently, the *Saturday Press* was a
coon and I the worm in it; also, I was the gay-
lored literary moth which its death set free. This
nile has been used before.

Early in '66 the " Jumping Frog " was issued in
ok form, with other sketches of mine. A year or
ɔ later Madame Blanc translated it into French
d published it in the *Revue des Deux Mondes*,
t the result was not what should have been ex-
cted, for the *Revue* struggled along and pulled
ough, and is alive yet. I think the fault must
ve been in the translation. I ought to have trans-
ed it myself. I think so because I examined into
: matter and finally retranslated the sketch from
French back into English, to see what the
uble was; that is, to see just what sort of a focus
French people got upon it. Then the mystery
s explained. In French the story is too confused,
l chaotic, and unreposeful, and ungrammatical,

and insane; consequently it could only cause gri
and sickness — it could not kill. A glance at n
re-translation will show the reader that this must
true.

[*My Re-translation.*]

THE FROG JUMPING OF THE COUNTY OF CALAVERAS.

Eh bien! this Smiley nourished some terriers à rats, and some co
of combat, and some cats, and all sort of things; and with his rage
betting one no had more of repose. He trapped one day a frog
him imported with him (et l'emporta chez lui) saying that he preten
to make his education. You me believe if you will, but during th
months he not has nothing done but to him apprehend to ju
(apprendre à sauter) in a court retired of her mansion (de sa maiso
And I you respond that he have succeeded. He him gives a sr
blow by behind, and the instant after you shall see the frog turn in
air like a grease-biscuit, make one summersault, sometimes two, w
she was well started, and re-fall upon his feet like a cat. He him
accomplished in the art of to gobble the flies (gober des mouches),
him there exercised continually — so well that a fly at the most far that
appeared was a fly lost. Smiley had custom to say that all which lac
to a frog it was the education, but with the education she could do ne
all — and I him believe. Tenez, I him have seen pose Daniel Web
there upon this plank — Daniel Webster was the name of the frog —
to him sing, "Some flies, Daniel, some flies!" — in a flash of the
Daniel had bounded and seized a fly here upon the counter, then jun
anew at the earth, where he rested truly to himself scratch the head
his behind-foot, as if he no had not the least idea of his superic
Never you not have seen frog as modest, as natural, sweet as she
And when he himself agitated to jump purely and simply upon
earth, she does more ground in one jump than any beast of his sp
than you can know.

To jump plain — this was his strong. When he himself agitate
that Smiley multiplied the bets upon her as long as there to him rema
a red. It must to know, Smiley was monstrously proud of his frog
he of it was right, for some men who were traveled, who had all
said that they to him would be injurious to him compare to another
Smiley guarded Daniel in a little box latticed which he carried by
to the village for some bet.

One day an individual stranger at the camp him arrested with his box nd him said:

"What is this that you have then shut up there within?"

Smiley said, with an air indifferent:

"That could be a paroquet, or a syringe (*ou un serin*), but this no is othing of such, it not is but a frog."

The individual it took, it regarded with care, it turned from one side nd from the other, then he said:

"*Tiens !* in effect! — At what is she good?"

"My God!" respond Smiley, always with an air disengaged, "she is ood for one thing, to my notice (*à mon avis*), she can batter in jump- ng (*elle peut batter en sautant*) all frogs of the county of Calaveras."

The individual re-took the box, it examined of new longly, and it endered to Smiley in saying with an air deliberate:

"*Eh bien !* I no saw not that that frog had nothing of better than each rog." (*Je ne vois pas que cette grenouille ait rien de mieux qu'aucune grenouille.*) [If that isn't grammar gone to seed, then I count myself o judge. — M. T.]

"Possible that you not it saw not," said Smiley, "possible that you — you comprehend frogs; possible that you not you there comprehend othing; possible that you had of the experience, and possible that you ot be but an amateur. Of all manner (*De toute manière*) I bet forty ollars that she batter in jumping no matter which frog of the county of Calaveras."

The individual reflected a second, and said like sad:

"I not am but a stranger here, I no have not a frog; but if I of it ad one, I would embrace the bet."

"Strong, well!" respond Smiley; "nothing of more facility. If ou will hold my box a minute, I go you to search a frog (*j'irai vous hercher*)."

Behold, then, the individual, who guards the box, who puts his forty ollars upon those of Smiley, and who attends (*et qui attend*). He ttended enough longtimes, reflecting all solely. And figure you that e takes Daniel, him opens the mouth by force and with a teaspoon im fills with shot of the hunt, even him fills just to the chin, then he im puts by the earth. Smiley during these times was at slopping in a wamp. Finally he trapped (*attrape*) a frog, him carried to that indi- vidual, and said:

"Now if you be ready, put him all against Daniel, with their before-

9*₊*₊

feet upon the same line, and I give the signal"—then he added "One, two, three—advance!"

Him and the individual touched their frogs by behind, and the fro new put to jump smartly, but Daniel himself lifted ponderously, exalte the shoulders thus, like a Frenchman—to what good? he could n budge, he is planted solid like a church, he not advance no more than one him had put at the anchor.

Smiley was surprised and disgusted, but he not himself doubted n of the turn being intended (*mais il ne se doutait pas du tour bie entendu*). The individual empocketed the silver, himself with it wen and of it himself in going is that he no gives not a jerk of thumb ov the shoulder—like that—at the poor Daniel, in saying with his a deliberate—(*L'individu empoche l'argent s'en va et en s'en allant e ce qu'il ne donne pas un coup de pouce par-dessus l'épaule, comme, ça au pauvre Daniel, en disant de son air délibéré.*)

"Eh bien! *I no see not that that frog has nothing of better tha another.*"

Smiley himself scratched longtimes the head, the eyes fixed up Daniel, until that which at last he said:

"I me demand how the devil it makes itself that this beast has refuse Is it that she had something? One would believe that she is stuffed." He grasped Daniel by the skin of the neck, him lifted and said: "The wolf me bite if he no weigh not five pounds."

He him reversed and the unhappy belched two handfuls of sh (*et le malheureux*, etc.).—When Smiley recognized how it was, l was like mad. He deposited his frog by the earth and ran after th individual, but he not him caught never.

It may be that there are people who can translat better than I can, but I am not acquainted with them

So ends the private and public history of th Jumping Frog of Calaveras County, an incider which has this unique feature about it — that it both old and new, a " chestnut " and not a " ches nut "; for it was original when it happened tw thousand years ago, and was again original when happened in California in our own time.

MENTAL TELEGRAPHY AGAIN

HAVE three or four curious incidents to tell about. They seem to come under the head of hat I named "Mental Telegraphy" in a paper ritten seventeen years ago, and published long fterwards.*

Several years ago I made a campaign on the plat- orm with Mr. George W. Cable. In Montreal we ere honored with a reception. It began at two in ie afternoon in a long drawing-room in the Wind- or Hotel. Mr. Cable and I stood at one end of this oom, and the ladies and gentlemen entered it at the ther end, crossed it at that end, then came up the ong left-hand side, shook hands with us, said a ord or two, and passed on, in the usual way. My ght is of the telescopic sort, and I presently recog- ized a familiar face among the throng of strangers rifting in at the distant door, and I said to myself, ith surprise and high gratification, "That is Mrs. ..; I had forgotten that she was a Canadian." She ad been a great friend of mine in Carson City, evada, in the early days. I had not seen her or

---

* The paper entitled "Mental Telegraphy," which originally appeared
Harper's Magazine for December, 1893, is included in the volume
ntitled *The American Claimant and Other Stories and Sketches.*

I*₊*₊   (131)

heard of her for twenty years; I had not bee
thinking about her; there was nothing to sugge:
her to me, nothing to bring her to my mind; i
fact, to me she had long ago ceased to exist, an
had disappeared from my consciousness. But
knew her instantly; and I saw her so clearly that
was able to note some of the particulars of her dres:
and did note them, and they remained in my mind
I was impatient for her to come. In the midst c
the hand-shakings I snatched glimpses of her an
noted her progress with the slow-moving file acros
the end of the room; then I saw her start up th
side, and this gave me a full front view of her fac
I saw her last when she was within twenty-five fee
of me. For an hour I kept thinking she must sti
be in the room somewhere and would come at last
but I was disappointed.

When I arrived in the lecture-hall that evenin
some one said: " Come into the waiting-room
there's a friend of yours there who wants to se
you. You'll not be introduced — you are to do th
recognizing without help if you can."

I said to myself: " It is Mrs. R.; I shan't hav
any trouble."

There were perhaps ten ladies present, all seated
In the midst of them was Mrs. R., as I had ex
pected. She was dressed exactly as she was when
had seen her in the afternoon. I went forward an
shook hands with her and called her by name, an
said:

" I knew you the moment you appeared at the
reception this afternoon."

She looked surprised, and said: " But I was not
at the reception.   I have just arrived from Quebec,
and have not been in town an hour."

It was my turn to be surprised now.   I said: " I
can't help it.   I give you my word of honor that it
is as I say.   I saw you at the reception, and you
were dressed precisely as you are now.   When they
told me a moment ago that I should find a friend in
this room, your image rose before me, dress and
all, just as I had seen you at the reception."

Those are the facts.   She was not at the reception
at all, or anywhere near it; but I saw her there nevertheless, and most clearly and unmistakably.   To that
could make oath.   How is one to explain this?   I
was not thinking of her at the time; had not thought
of her for years.   But she had been thinking of me,
no doubt; did her thoughts flit through leagues of
air to me, and bring with it that clear and pleasant
vision of herself?   I think so.   That was and remains
my sole experience in the matter of apparitions — 1
mean apparitions that come when one is (ostensibly)
awake.   I could have been asleep for a moment;
the apparition could have been the creature of a
dream.   Still, that is nothing to the point; the
feature of interest is the happening of the thing just
at that time, instead of at an earlier or later time,
which is argument that its origin lay in thought-
transference.

My next incident will be set aside by most person
as being merely a " coincidence," I suppose. Year
ago I used to think sometimes of making a lecturin
trip through the antipodes and the borders of th
Orient, but always gave up the idea, partly becaus
of the great length of the journey and partly becaus
my wife could not well manage to go with me
Towards the end of last January that idea, after a
interval of years, came suddenly into my head agai
— forcefully, too, and without any apparent reason
Whence came it? What suggested it? I will touc'
upon that presently.

I was at that time where I am now — in Paris.
wrote at once to Henry M. Stanley (London), an
asked him some questions about his Australian lec
ture tour, and inquired who had conducted him an
what were the terms. After a day or two his answe
came. It began:

" The lecture agent for Australia and New Zealand is *par excellen*
Mr. R. S. Smythe, of Melbourne."

He added his itinerary, terms, sea expenses, an
some other matters, and advised me to write Mr
Smythe, which I did — February 3d. I began m
letter by saying in substance that while he did no
know me personally we had a mutual friend i
Stanley, and that would answer for an introduction
Then I proposed my trip, and asked if he would giv
me the same terms which he had given Stanley.

I mailed my letter to Mr. Smythe February 6th
and three days later I got a letter from the selfsam

Smythe, dated Melbourne, December 17th. I would as soon have expected to get a letter from the late George Washington. The letter began somewhat as mine to him had begun — with a self-introduction :

"DEAR MR. CLEMENS, — It is so long since Archibald Forbes and spent that pleasant afternoon in your comfortable house at Hartford that you have probably quite forgotten the occasion."

In the course of his letter this occurs :

"I am willing to give you" [here he named the terms which he had given Stanley] "for an antipodean tour to last, say, three months."

Here was the single essential detail of my letter answered three days after I had mailed my inquiry. I might have saved myself the trouble and the postage — and a few years ago I would have done that very thing, for I would have argued that my sudden and strong impulse to write and ask some questions of a stranger on the under side of the globe meant that the impulse came from that stranger, and that he would answer my questions of his own motion if I would let him alone.

Mr. Smythe's letter probably passed under my nose on its way to lose three weeks traveling to America and back, and gave me a whiff of its contents as it went along. Letters often act like that. Instead of the *thought* coming to you in an instant from Australia, the (apparently) unsentient letter imparts it to you as it glides invisibly past your elbow in the mail-bag.

Next incident. In the following month — March — I was in America. I spent a Sunday at Irvingtonon-the-Hudson with Mr. John Brisben Walker, of the *Cosmopolitan* magazine. We came into New York next morning, and went to the Century Club for luncheon. He said some praiseful things about the character of the club and the orderly serenity and pleasantness of its quarters, and asked if I had never tried to acquire membership in it. I said I had not, and that New York clubs were a continuous expense to the country members without being of frequent use or benefit to them.

"And now I've got an idea!" said I. "There's the Lotos — the first New York club I was ever a member of — my very earliest love in that line. I have been a member of it for considerably more than twenty years, yet have seldom had a chance to look in and see the boys. They turn gray and grow old while I am not watching. And *my dues go on!* I am going to Hartford this afternoon for a day or two, but as soon as I get back I will go to John Elderkin very privately and say: 'Remember the veteran and confer distinction upon him, for the sake of old times. Make me an honorary member and abolish the tax. If you haven't any such thing as honorary membership, all the better — create it for my honor and glory.' That would be a great thing; I will go to John Elderkin as soon as I get back from Hartford."

I took the last express that afternoon, first telegraphing Mr. F. G. Whitmore to come and see me next day. When he came he asked:

" Did you get a letter from Mr. John Elderkin, :cretary of the Lotos Club, before you left New ork?"

" No."

" Then it just missed you. If I had known you ere coming I would have kept it. It is beautiful, id will make you proud. The Board of Directors, y unanimous vote, have made you a life member, id *squelched those dues ;* and, you are to be on and and receive your distinction on the night of ιe 30th, which is the twenty-fifth anniversary of ιe founding of the club, and it will not surprise me they have some great times there."

What put the honorary membership in my head ιat day in the Century Club? for I had never ιought of it before. I don't know what brought ιe thought to me at *that* particular time instead of arlier, but I am well satisfied that it originated with ιe Board of Directors, and had been on its way to ιy brain through the air ever since the moment that ιw their vote recorded.

Another incident. I was in Hartford two or three ays as a guest of the Rev. Joseph H. Twichell. I ave held the rank of Honorary Uncle to his chil- ren for a quarter of a century, and I went out with im in the trolley-car to visit one of my nieces, who ι at Miss Porter's famous school in Farmington. ʹhe distance is eight or nine miles. On the way, ιlking, I illustrated something with an anecdote. ʹhis is the anecdote:

Two years and a half ago I and the family arrive
at Milan on our way to Rome, and stopped at th
Continental.   After dinner I went below and took
seat in the stone-paved court, where the customar
lemon-trees stand in the customary tubs, and said t
myself, " Now *this* is comfort, comfort and repos
and nobody to disturb it; I do not know anybod
in Milan."

Then a young gentleman stepped up and shoo
hands, which damaged my theory. He said, i
substance :

" You won't remember me, Mr. Clemens, but
remember you very well. I was a cadet at We
Point when you and Rev. Joseph H. Twichell cam
there some years ago and talked to us on a Hu
dredth Night. I am a lieutenant in the regular arm
now, and my name is H. I am in Europe, a
alone, for a modest little tour; my regiment is i
Arizona."

We became friendly and sociable, and in th
course of the talk he told me of an adventure whic
had befallen him — about to this effect :

" I was at Bellagio, stopping at the big hot
there, and ten days ago I lost my letter of credit.
did not know what in the world to do. I was
stranger; I knew no one in Europe; I hadn't
penny in my pocket; I couldn't even send a tel
gram to London to get my lost letter replaced; m
hotel bill was a week old, and the presentation of i
imminent — so imminent that it could happen a

any moment now. I was so frightened that my wits seemed to leave me. I tramped and tramped, back and forth, like a crazy person. If anybody approached me I hurried away, for no matter what a person looked like, I took him for the head waiter with the bill.

" I was at last in such a desperate state that I was ready to do any wild thing that promised even the shadow of help, and so this is the insane thing that I did. I saw a family lunching at a small table on the veranda, and recognized their nationality — Americans — father, mother, and several young daughters — young, tastefully dressed, and pretty — the rule with our people. I went straight there in my civilian costume, named my name, said I was a lieutenant in the army, and told my story and asked for help.

" What do you suppose the gentleman did? But you would not guess in twenty years. He took out a handful of gold coin and told me to help myself — freely. That is what he did."

The next morning the lieutenant told me his new letter of credit had arrived in the night, so we strolled to Cook's to draw money to pay back the benefactor with. We got it, and then went strolling through the great arcade. Presently he said, " Yonder they are; come and be introduced." I was introduced to the parents and the young ladies; then we separated, and I never saw him or them any
1 —

" Here we are at Farmington," said Twichell
interrupting.

We left the trolley-car and tramped through the
mud a hundred yards or so to the school, talking
about the time we and Warner walked out there
years ago, and the pleasant time we had.

We had a visit with my niece in the parlor, then
started for the trolley again. Outside the house we
encountered a double rank of twenty or thirty of
Miss Porter's young ladies arriving from a walk, and
we stood aside, ostensibly to let them have room to
file past, but really to look at them. Presently one
of them stepped out of the rank and said:

" You don't know me, Mr. Twichell, but I know
your daughter, and that gives me the privilege of
shaking hands with you."

Then she put out her hand to me, and said:

" And I wish to shake hands with you too, Mr
Clemens. You don't remember me, but you were
introduced to me in the arcade in Milan two years
and a half ago by Lieutenant H."

What had put that story into my head after all
that stretch of time? Was it just the proximity of
that young girl, or was it merely an odd accident?

WHAT PAUL BOURGET THINKS OF US

HE reports the American joke correctly. In Boston they ask, How much does he know? In New York, How much is he worth? in Philadelphia, Who were his parents? And when an alien observer turns his telescope upon us — advertisedly in our own special interest — a natural apprehension moves us to ask, What is the diameter of his reflector?

I take a great interest in M. Bourget's chapters, for I know by the newspapers that there are several Americans who are expecting to get a whole education out of them; several who foresaw, and also foretold, that our long night was over, and a light almost divine about to break upon the land.

"His utterances concerning us are bound to be weighty and well *med."*

"He gives us an object-lesson which should be thoughtfully and *profitably studied."*

These well-considered and important verdicts were of a nature to restore public confidence, which had been disquieted by questionings as to whether so young a teacher would be qualified to take so large a class as 70,000,000, distributed over so extensive

a schoolhouse as America, and pull it through with
out assistance.

I was even disquieted myself, although I am of
cold, calm temperament, and not easily disturbed
I feared for my country. And I was not wholl
tranquilized by the verdicts rendered as above. .
seemed to me that there was still room for doub
In fact, in looking the ground over I became mor
disturbed than I was before. Many worrying que:
tions came up in my mind. Two were prominen
Where had the teacher gotten his equipment? Wh:
was his method?

He had gotten his equipment in France.

Then as to his method! I saw by his own intim:
tions that he was an Observer, and had a System –
that used by naturalists and other scientists. Th
naturalist collects many bugs and reptiles and butte:
flies and studies their ways a long time patientl
By this means he is presently able to group the:
creatures into families and subdivisions of famili
by nice shadings of differences observable in the
characters. Then he labels all those shaded bug
and things with nicely descriptive group names, an
is now happy, for his great work is completed, an
as a result he intimately knows every bug and shac
of a bug there, inside and out. It may be true, b
a person who was not a naturalist would feel saf
about it if he had the opinion of the bug. I thin
it is a pleasant System, but subject to error.

The Observer of Peoples has to be a Classifier,

Grouper, a Deducer, a Generalizer, a Psychologizer; and, first and last, a Thinker. He has to be all these, and when he is at home, observing his own folk, he is often able to prove competency. But history has shown that when he is abroad observing unfamiliar peoples the chances are heavily against him. He is then a naturalist observing a bug, with no more than a naturalist's chance of being able to tell the bug anything new about itself, and no more than a naturalist's chance of being able to teach it any new ways which it will prefer to its own.

To return to that first question. M. Bourget, as teacher, would simply be France teaching America. It seemed to me that the outlook was dark — almost Egyptian, in fact. What would the new teacher, representing France, teach us? Railroading? No. France knows nothing valuable about railroading. Steamshipping? No. France has no superiorities over us in that matter. Steamboating? No. French steamboating is still of Fulton's date — 1809. Postal service? No. France is a back number there. Telegraphy? No, we taught her that ourselves. Journalism? No. Magazining? No, that is our own specialty. Government? No; Liberty, Equality, Fraternity, Nobility, Democracy, Adultery — the system is too variegated for our climate. Religion? No, not variegated enough for our climate. Morals? No, we cannot rob the poor to enrich ourselves. Novel-writing? No. M. Bour-

get and the others know only one plan, and whe
that is expurgated there is nothing left of the bool

I wish I could think what he is going to teach u
Can it be Deportment? But he experimented in th.
at Newport and failed to give satisfaction, except
a few. Those few are pleased. They are enjoyi
their joy as well as they can. They confess the
happiness to the interviewer. They feel pret
striped, but they remember with reverent reco
nition that they had sugar between the cuts. Tru
sugar with sand in it, but sugar. And true, th
had some trouble to tell which was sugar and whi
was sand, because the sugar itself looked just like t
sand, and also had a gravelly taste; still, they kn
that the sugar was there, and would have been ve
good sugar indeed if it had been screened. Y
they are pleased; not noisily so, but pleased;
vaded, or streaked, as one may say, with little
current shivers of joy — subdued joy, so to spe
not the overdone kind. And they commune
gether, these, and massage each other with comf
ing sayings, in a sweet spirit of resignation a
thankfulness, mixing these elements in the sa
proportions as the sugar and the sand, as a mer
rial, and saying, the one to the other, and to
interviewer: " It was severe — yes, it was bitt
severe; but oh, how true it was; and it will do
so much good !"

If it isn't Deportment, what is left? It was
this point that I seemed to get on the right track

ιst. M. Bourget would teach us to know ourselves;
hat was it: he would reveal us to ourselves. That
γould be an education. He would explain us to
urselves. Then we should understand ourselves;
nd after that be able to go on more intelligently.

It seemed a doubtful scheme. He could explain
s to *him*self — that would be easy. That would
e the same as the naturalist explaining the bug to
imself. But to explain the bug to the bug — that
ι quite a different matter. The bug may not know
imself perfectly, but he knows himself better than
ιe naturalist can know him, at any rate.

A foreigner can photograph the exteriors of a
ιtion, but I think that that is as far as he can get.
think that no foreigner can report its interior — its
ɔul, its life, its speech, its thought. I think that a
nowledge of these things is acquirable in only one
ιy; not two or four or six—*absorption;* years and
ears of unconscious absorption; years and years
f intercourse with the life concerned; of living it,
ιdeed; sharing personally in its shames and prides,
s joys and griefs, its loves and hates, its pros-
erities and reverses, its shows and shabbinesses,
s deep patriotisms, its whirlwinds of political pas-
on, its adorations — of flag, and heroic dead, and
ιe glory of the national name. Observation? Of
hat real value is it? One learns peoples through
ιe heart, not the eyes or the intellect.

There is only one expert who is qualified to ex-
mine the souls and the life of a people and make a
10*₊*₊

valuable report — the native novelist. This expert is
so rare that the most populous country can never
have fifteen conspicuously and confessedly competent
ones in stock at one time. This native specialist is
not qualified to begin work until he has been absorb-
ing during twenty-five years. How much of his
competency is derived from conscious " observation"? The amount is so slight that it counts for
next to nothing in the equipment. Almost the
whole capital of the novelist is the slow accumula-
tion of *un*conscious observation — absorption. The
native expert's intentional observation of manners,
speech, character, and ways of life can have value,
for the native knows what they mean without having
to cipher out the meaning. But I should be astonished to see a foreigner get at the right meanings,
catch the elusive shades of these subtle things.
Even the native novelist becomes a foreigner, with a
foreigner's limitations, when he steps from the State
whose life is familiar to him into a State whose life
he has not lived. Bret Harte got his California and
his Californians by unconscious absorption, and put
both of them into his tales alive. But when he
came from the Pacific to the Atlantic and tried to
do Newport life from study — conscious observation — his failure was absolutely monumental.
Newport is a disastrous place for the unacclimated
observer, evidently.

To return to novel-building. Does the native
novelist try to generalize the nation? No, he lays

plainly before you the ways and speech and life of a
few people grouped in a certain place — his own
place — and that is one book.   In time he and his
brethren will report to you the life and the people
of the whole nation — the life of a group in a New
England village; in a New York village; in a Texan
village; in an Oregon village; in villages in fifty
States and Territories; then the farm-life in fifty
States and Territories; a hundred patches of life
and groups of people in a dozen widely separated
cities.   And the Indians will be attended to; and
the cowboys; and the gold and silver miners; and
the negroes; and the Idiots and Congressmen; and
the Irish, the Germans, the Italians, the Swedes,
the French, the Chinamen, the Greasers; and the
Catholics, the Methodists, the Presbyterians, the
Congregationalists, the Baptists, the Spiritualists,
the Mormons, the Shakers, the Quakers, the Jews,
the Campbellites, the infidels, the Christian Scientists, the Mind-Curists, the Faith-Curists, the train-
robbers, the White Caps, the Moonshiners.   And
when a thousand able novels have been written,
there you have the soul of the people, the life of
the people, the speech of the people; and not anywhere else can these be had.   And the shadings of
character, manners, feelings, ambitions, will be
infinite.

  " *The nature of a people* is always of a similar shade in its vices and
its virtues, in its frivolities and in its labor. *It is this physiognomy
which it is necessary to discover*, and every document is good, from the

J*₊*₊

hall of a casino to the church, from the foibles of a fashionable woman
to the suggestions of a revolutionary leader. I am therefore quite sure
that this *American soul*, the principal interest and the great object of
my voyage, appears behind the records of Newport for those who choose
to see it." — *M. Paul Bourget.*

[The italics are mine.] It is a large contract
which he has undertaken. "Records" is a pretty
poor word there, but I think the use of it is due to
hasty translation. In the original the word is *fastes.*
I think M. Bourget meant to suggest that he expected to find the great "American soul" secreted
behind the *ostentations* of Newport; and that he
was going to get it out and examine it, and generalize it, and psychologize it, and make it reveal to
him its hidden vast mystery: "the nature of the
people" of the United States of America. We
have been accused of being a nation addicted to
inventing wild schemes. I trust that we shall be
allowed to retire to second place now.

There isn't a single human characteristic that can
be safely labeled "American." There isn't a single
human ambition, or religious trend, or drift of
thought, or peculiarity of education, or code of
principles, or breed of folly, or style of conversation, or preference for a particular subject for discussion, or form of legs or trunk or head or face or
expression or complexion, or gait, or dress, or
manners, or disposition, or any other human detail
inside or outside, that can rationally be generalized
as "American."

Whenever you have found what seems to be a

" American " peculiarity, you have only to cross a
frontier or two, or go down or up in the social scale,
and you perceive that it has disappeared. And you
can cross the Atlantic and find it again. There
may be a Newport religious drift, or sporting drift,
or conversational style or complexion, or cut of
face, but there are entire empires in America, north,
south, east, and west, where you could not find
your duplicates. It is the same with everything
else which one might propose to call " American."
M. Bourget thinks he has found the American
Coquette. If he had really found her he would also
have found, I am sure, that she was not new, that
she exists in other lands in the same forms, and
with the same frivolous heart and the same ways
and impulses. I think this because I have seen our
coquette; I have seen her in life; better still, I have
seen her in our novels, and seen her twin in foreign
novels. I wish M. Bourget had seen ours. He
thought he saw her. And so he applied his System
to her. She was a Species. So he gathered a
number of samples of what seemed to be her, and
put them under his glass, and divided them into
groups which he calls " types," and labeled them in
his usual scientific way with " formulas " — brief
sharp descriptive flashes that make a person blink,
sometimes, they are so sudden and vivid. As a
rule they are pretty far-fetched, but that is not an
important matter; they surprise, they compel admiration, and I notice by some of the comments

which his efforts have called forth that they deceive
the unwary.   Here are a few of the coquette variants
which he has grouped and labeled:

THE COLLECTOR.

THE EQUILIBREE.

THE PROFESSIONAL BEAUTY.

THE BLUFFER.

THE GIRL-BOY.

If he had stopped with describing these characters
we should have been obliged to believe that they
exist; that they exist, and that he has seen them and
spoken with them.   But he did not stop there; he
went further and furnished to us light-throwing
samples of their behavior, and also light-throwing
samples of their speeches.   He entered those things
in his note-book without suspicion, he takes them
out and delivers them to the world with a candor
and simplicity which show that he believed them
genuine.   They throw altogether too much light.
They reveal to the native the origin of his find.   I
suppose he knows how he came to make that novel
and captivating discovery, by this time.   If he
does not, any American can tell him — any American to whom he will show his anecdotes.   It was
" put up " on him, as we say.   It was a jest — to
be plain, it was a series of frauds.   To my mind it
was a poor sort of jest, witless and contemptible.
The players of it have their reward, such as it is;
they have exhibited the fact that whatever they may
be they are not ladies.   M. Bourget did not discover

a type of coquette; he merely discovered a type of
practical joker.   One may say *the* type of practical
joker, for these people are exactly alike all over the
world.   Their equipment is always the same: a
vulgar mind, a puerile wit, a cruel disposition as a
rule, and always the spirit of treachery.

In his Chapter IV. M. Bourget has two or three
columns gravely devoted to the collating and examining and psychologizing of these sorry little
frauds.   One is not moved to laugh.   There is
nothing funny in the situation; it is only pathetic.
The stranger gave those people his confidence, and
they dishonorably treated him in return.

But one must be allowed to suspect that M.
Bourget was a little to blame himself.   Even a
practical joker has some little judgment.   He has
to exercise some degree of sagacity in selecting his
prey if he would save himself from getting into
trouble.   In my time I have seldom seen such daring
things marketed at any price as these conscienceless
folk have worked off at par on this confiding observer.   It compels the conviction that there was
something about him that bred in those speculators
a quite unusual sense of safety, and encouraged
them to strain their powers in his behalf.   They
seem to have satisfied themselves that all he wanted
was "significant" facts, and that he was not accustomed to examine the source whence they proceeded.   It is plain that there was a sort of conspiracy against him almost from the start — a

conspiracy to freight him up with all the strang
extravagances those people's decayed brains coul
invent.

The lengths to which they went are next t
incredible. They told him things which surel
would have excited any one else's suspicion, bu
they did not excite his. Consider this:

" There is not in all the United States an entirely nude statue."

If an angel should come down and say such
thing about heaven, a reasonably cautious observe
would take that angel's number and inquire a littl
further before he added it to his catch. What doe
the present observer do? Adds it. Adds it at once
Adds it, and labels it with this innocent comment:

" This small fact is strangely significant."

It does seem to me that this kind of observing i
defective.

Here is another curiosity which some libera
person made him a present of. I should think i
ought to have disturbed the deep slumber of hi
suspicion a little, but it didn't. It was a note fron
a fog-horn for strenuousness, it seems to me, bu
the doomed voyager did not catch it. If he had bu
caught it, it would have saved him from severa
disasters:

" If the American knows that you are traveling to take notes, he i
interested in it, and at the same time rejoices in it, as in a tribute."

Again, this is defective observation. It is humar
to like to be praised; one can even notice it in the

French. But it is not human to like to be ridiculed, even when it comes in the form of a " tribute." I think a little psychologizing ought to have come in there. Something like this: A dog does not like to be ridiculed, a redskin does not like to be ridiculed, a negro does not like to be ridiculed, a Chinaman does not like to be ridiculed; let us deduce from these significant facts this formula: the American's grade being higher than these, and the chain of argument stretching unbroken all the way up to him, there is room for suspicion that the person who said the American likes to be ridiculed, and regards it as a tribute, is not a capable observer.

I feel persuaded that in the matter of psychologizing, a professional is too apt to yield to the fascinations of the loftier regions of that great art, to the neglect of its lowlier walks. Every now and then, at half-hour intervals, M. Bourget collects a hatful of airy inaccuracies and dissolves them in a panful of assorted abstractions, and runs the charge into a mould and turns you out a compact principle which will explain an American girl, or an American woman, or why new people yearn for old things, or any other impossible riddle which a person wants answered.

It seems to be conceded that there are a few human peculiarities that can be generalized and located here and there in the world and named by the name of the nation where they are found. I wonder what they are. Perhaps one of them is

temperament. One speaks of French vivacity an
German gravity and English stubbornness. Then
is no American temperament. The nearest that on
can come at it is to say there are two — the com
posed Northern and the impetuous Southern; an
both are found in other countries. Morals? Purit
of women may fairly be called universal with u
but that is the case in some other countries. W
have no monopoly of it; it cannot be named Amer
can. I think that there is but a single specialty wit
us, only one thing that can be called by the wic
name " American." That is the national devotic
to ice-water. All Germans drink beer, but th
British nation drinks beer, too; so neither of tho
peoples is *the* beer-drinking nation. I suppose v
do stand alone in having a drink that nobody lik
but ourselves. When we have been a month
Europe we lose our craving for it, and we final
tell the hotel folk that they needn't provide it an
more. Yet we hardly touch our native shore agai
winter or summer, before we are eager for it. Th
reasons for this state of things have not be
psychologized yet. I drop the hint and say
more.

It is my belief that there are some " national
traits and things scattered about the world that a
mere superstitions, frauds that have lived so loi
that they have the solid look of facts. One of the
is the dogma that the French are the only chas
people in the world. Ever since I arrived in Fran

his last time I have been accumulating doubts about
that; and before I leave this sunny land again I will
gather in a few random statistics and psychologize
the plausibilities out of it.   If people are to come
over to America and find fault with our girls and
our women, and psychologize every little thing they
do, and try to teach them how to behave, and how
to cultivate themselves up to where one cannot tell
them from the French model, I intend to find out
whether those missionaries are qualified or not.   A
nation ought always to examine into this detail
before engaging the teacher for good.   This last one
has let fall a remark which renewed those doubts of
mine when I read it:

" In our high Parisian existence, for instance, we find applied to arts
and luxury, and to debauchery, all the powers and all the weaknesses of
the French soul."

You see, it amounts to a trade with the French
soul; a profession; a science; the serious business
of life, so to speak, in our high Parisian existence.
I do not quite like the look of it.   I question if
it can be taught with profit in our country, except, of course, to those pathetic, neglected minds
that are waiting there so yearningly for the education which M. Bourget is going to furnish them
from the serene summits of our high Parisian life.

I spoke a moment ago of the existence of some
superstitions that have been parading the world as
facts this long time.   For instance, consider the
dollar.   The world seems to think that the love of

money is " American "; and that the mad desire t
get suddenly rich is " American." I believe th
both of these things are merely and broadly humar
not American monopolies at all. The love of mone
is natural to all nations, for money is a good an
strong friend. I think that this love has existe
everywhere, ever since the Bible called it the root c
all evil.

I think that the reason why we Americans seer
to be so addicted to trying to get rich suddenly i
merely because the *opportunity* to make promisin
efforts in that direction has offered itself to us wit
a frequency out of all proportion to the Europea
experience. For eighty years this opportunity ha
been offering itself in one new town or region afte
another straight westward, step by step, all the wa
from the Atlantic coast to the Pacific. When
mechanic could buy ten town lots on tolerably lon
credit for ten months' savings out of his wages, an
reasonably expect to sell them in a couple of year
for ten times what he gave for them, it was huma
for him to try the venture, and he did it no matte
what his nationality was. He would have done it i
Europe or China if he had had the same chance.

In the flush times in the silver regions a cook o
any other humble worker stood a very good chanc
to get rich out of a trifle of money risked in a stoc
deal; and that person promptly took that risk, n
matter what his or her nationality might be. I wa
there, and saw it.

But these opportunities have not been plenty in
ur Southern States; so there you have a prodigious
egion where the rush for sudden wealth is almost an
nknown thing — and has been, from the beginning.

Europe has offered few opportunities for poor
'om, Dick, and Harry; but when she has offered
ne, there has been no noticeable difference between
,uropean eagerness and American. England saw
uis in the wild days of the Railroad King; France
aw it in 1720 — time of Law and the Mississippi
ubble. I am sure I have never seen in the gold
nd silver mines any madness, fury, frenzy to get
ıddenly rich which was even remotely comparable
» that which raged in France in the Bubble day.
' I had a cyclopædia here I could turn to that
lemorable case, and satisfy nearly anybody that the
unger for the sudden dollar is no more " Ameri-
ın " than it is French. And if I could furnish an
merican opportunity to staid Germany, I think I
ould wake her up like a house afire.

But I must return to the Generalizations, Psychol-
zizings, Deductions. When M. Bourget is ex-
.oiting these arts, it is then that he is peculiarly and
articularly himself. His ways are wholly original
hen he encounters a trait or a custom which is new
 him. Another person would merely examine the
ıd, verify it, estimate its value, and let it go; but
.at is not sufficient for M. Bourget: he always
ants to know *why* that thing exists, he wants to
low how it came to happen; and he will not let go

IIE

of it until he has found out.   And in every instance
he will find that reason where no one but himself
would have thought of looking for it.   He does n
seem to care for a reason that is not picturesque
located; one might almost say picturesquely and
impossibly located.

He found out that in America men do not try
hunt down young married women.   At once,
usual, he wanted to know *why*.   Any one cou
have told him.   He could have divined it by th
lights thrown by the novels of the country.   B
no, he preferred to find out for himself.   He has
trustfulness as regards men and facts which is fin
and unusual; he is not particular about the sour
of a fact, he is not particular about the charact
and standing of the fact itself; but when it comes
pounding out the reason for the existence of th
fact, he will trust no one but himself.

In the present instance here was his fact: Amer
can young married women are not pursued by th
corruptor; and here was the question: What is
that protects her?

It seems quite unlikely that that problem cou
have offered difficulties to any but a trained philos
pher.   Nearly any person would have said to M
Bourget: " Oh, that is very simple.   It is ve
seldom in America that a marriage is made on
commercial basis; our marriages, from the begi
ning, have been made for love; and where love
there is no room for the corruptor."

Now, it is interesting to see the formidable way
which M. Bourget went at that poor, humble
ttle thing.   He moved upon it in column — three
lumns — and with artillery.

" Two reasons of a very different kind explain "
- that fact.

And now that I have got so far, I am almost afraid
say what his two reasons are, lest I be charged
th inventing them.   But I will not retreat now; I
ll condense them and print them, giving my word
at I am honest and not trying to deceive any one.

1.   Young married women are protected from the
proaches of the seducer in New England and
cinity by the diluted remains of a prudence created
 a Puritan law of two hundred years ago, which
r a while punished adultery with death.

2.   And young married women of the other forty
fifty States are protected by laws which afford
traordinary facilities for divorce.

If I have not lost my mind I have accurately con-
yed those two Vesuvian irruptions of philosophy.
t the reader can consult Chapter IV. of *Outre-
er*, and decide for himself.   Let us examine this
ralyzing Deduction or Explanation by the light
 a few sane facts.

1. This universality of " protection " has existed
 our country *from the beginning;* before the
ath penalty existed in New England, and during
 the generations that have dragged by since it
 s annulled.

2. Extraordinary facilities for divorce are of such recent creation that any middle-aged American can remember a time when such things had not yet been thought of.

Let us suppose that the first easy divorce law went into effect forty years ago, and got noised around and fairly started in business thirty-five years ago, when we had, say, 25,000,000 of white population. Let us suppose that among 5,000,000 of them the young married women were " protected " by the surviving shudder of that ancient Puritan scare — what is M. Bourget going to do about those who lived among the 20,000,000? They were clean in their morals, they were pure, yet there was no easy divorce law to protect them.

Awhile ago I said that M. Bourget's method of truth-seeking — hunting for it in out-of-the-way places — was new; but that was an error. I remember that when Leverrier discovered the Milky Way, he and the other astronomers began to theorize about it in substantially the same fashion which M. Bourget employs in his reasonings about American social facts and their origin. Leverrier advanced the hypothesis that the Milky Way was caused by gaseous protoplasmic emanations from the field of Waterloo, which, ascending to an altitude determinable by their own specific gravity, became luminous through the development and exposure — by the natural processes of animal decay — of the phosphorus contained in them.

This theory was warmly complimented by Ptolemy, ho, however, after much thought and research, cided that he could not accept it as final. His wn theory was that the Milky Way was an emigra- on of lightning bugs; and he supported and rein- rced this theorem by the well-known fact that the custs do like that in Egypt.

Giordano Bruno also was outspoken in his praises Leverrier's important contribution to astronomical ience, and was at first inclined to regard it as con- usive; but later, conceiving it to be erroneous, he onounced against it, and advanced the hypothesis at the Milky Way was a detachment or corps of ars which became arrested and held in *suspenso spensorum* by refraction of gravitation while on e march to join their several constellations; a oposition for which he was afterwards burned at e stake in Jacksonville, Illinois.

These were all brilliant and picturesque theories, d each was received with enthusiasm by the scien- ic world; but when a New England farmer, who s not a thinker, but only a plain sort of person o tried to account for large facts in simple ways, me out with the opinion that the Milky Way was st common, ordinary stars, and was put where it s because God "wanted to hev it so," the ad- rable idea fell perfectly flat.

As a literary artist, M. Bourget is as fresh and iking as he is as a scientific one. He says, Above all, I do not believe much in anecdotes.''

11*₊*₊

Why? " In history they are all false " — a sufficiently broad statement — " in literature all libelous " — also a sufficiently sweeping statement,
coming from a critic who notes that we are a
people who are peculiarly extravagant in our language — " and when it is a matter of social life
almost all biased." It seems to amount to stultifi-
cation, almost. He has built two or three breeds
of American coquettes out of anecdotes — mainly
" biased " ones, I suppose; and, as they occur
" in literature," furnished by his pen, they must be
" all libelous." Or did he mean not *in* literature
or anecdotes *about* literature or literary people?
am not able to answer that. Perhaps the original
would be clearer, but I have only the translation of
this installment by me. I think the remark had an
intention; also that this intention was booked for
the trip; but that either in the hurry of the remark's
departure it got left, or in the confusion of changing
cars at the translator's frontier it got side-tracked.

" But on the other hand I believe in statistics;
and those on divorces appear to me to be most con-
clusive." And he sets himself the task of explaining — in a couple of columns — the process by
which Easy-Divorce conceived, invented, originated,
developed, and perfected an empire-embracing condition of sexual purity in the States. *In 40 years?*
No, he doesn't state the interval. With all his
passion for statistics he forgot to ask how long it
took to produce this gigantic miracle.

I have followed his pleasant but devious trail through those columns, but I was not able to get hold of his argument and find out what it was. I was not even able to find out where it left off. It seemed to gradually dissolve and flow off into other matters. I followed it with interest, for I was anxious to learn how easy-divorce eradicated adultery in America, but I was disappointed; I have no idea yet how it did it. I only know it didn't. But that is not valuable; I knew it before.

Well, humor is the great thing, the saving thing, after all. The minute it crops up, all our hardnesses yield, all our irritations and resentments flit away, and a sunny spirit takes their place. And so, when M. Bourget said that bright thing about our grandfathers, I broke all up. I remember exploding its American countermine once, under that grand hero, Napoleon. He was only First Consul then, and I was Consul-General — for the United States, of course; but we were very intimate, notwithstanding the difference in rank, for I waived that. One day something offered the opening, and he said:

"Well, General, I suppose life can never get entirely dull to an American, because whenever he can't strike up any other way to put in his time he can always get away with a few years trying to find out who his grandfather was!"

I fairly shouted, for I had never heard it sound better; and then I was back at him as quick as a flash:

K *₊*₊

" Right, your Excellency! But I reckon a
Frenchman's got *his* little stand-by for a dull time
too; because when all other interests fail he can
turn in and see if he can't find out who his father
was !"

Well, you should have heard him just whoop, and
cackle, and carry on ! He reached up and hit me
one on the shoulder, and says:

" Land, but it's good! It's im-mensely good !
I'George, I never heard it said so good in my life
before ! Say it again."

So I said it again, and he said his again, and I
said mine again, and then he did, and then I did,
and then he did, and we kept on doing it, and doing
it, and I *never* had such a good time, and he said
the same. In my opinion there isn't anything that
is as killing as one of those dear old ripe pensioners
if you know how to snatch it out in a kind of a
fresh sort of original way.

But I wish M. Bourget had read more of our
novels before he came. It is the only way to
thoroughly understand a people. When I found he
was coming to Paris, I read *La Terre*.

LITTLE NOTE TO M. PAUL BOURGET

[The preceding squib was assailed in the *North American Review* in a article entitled " Mark Twain and Paul Bourget," by Max O'Rell. ne following little note is a Rejoinder to that article. It is possible at the position assumed here — that M. Bourget dictated the O'Rell ticle himself — is untenable.]

YOU have every right, my dear M. Bourget, to retort upon me by dictation, if you prefer that ethod to writing at me with your pen; but if I ay say it without hurt — and certainly I mean no fence — I believe you would have acquitted your-lf better with the pen. With the pen you are at ome; it is your natural weapon; you use it with ace, eloquence, charm, persuasiveness, when men e to be convinced, and with formidable effect when ey have earned a castigation. But I am sure I see gns in the above article that you are either unac-stomed to dictating or are out of practice. If you ll re-read it you will notice, yourself, that it lacks efiniteness; that it lacks purpose; that it lacks herence; that it lacks a subject to talk about; at it is loose and wabbly; that it wanders around; at it loses itself early and does not find itself any ore. There are some other defects, as you will

notice, but I think I have named the main ones. I
feel sure that they are all due to your lack of practice in dictating.

Inasmuch as you had not signed it I had the impression at first that you had not dictated it. But
only for a moment. Certain quite simple and
definite facts reminded me that the article *had* to
come from you, for the reason that it could not
come from any one else without a specific invitation
from you or from me. I mean, it could not except
as an intrusion, a transgression of the law which
forbids strangers to mix into a private dispute between friends, unasked.

Those simple and definite facts were these: I had
published an article in this magazine, with you for
my subject; just you yourself; I stuck strictly to
that one subject, and did not interlard any other.
No one, of course, could call me to account but you
alone, or your authorized representative. I asked
some questions — asked them of myself. I answered them myself. My article was thirteen pages
long, and all devoted to you; devoted to you, and
divided up in this way: one page of guesses as to
what subjects you would instruct us in, as teacher;
one page of doubts as to the effectiveness of your
method of examining us and our ways; two or three
pages of criticism of your method, and of certain
results which it furnished you; two or three pages
of attempts to show the justness of these same
criticisms; half a dozen pages made up of slight

ault-findings with certain minor details of your
iterary workmanship, of extracts from your *Outre-
Mer* and comments upon them; then I closed with
an anecdote. I repeat — for certain reasons — that
I closed with an anecdote.

When I was asked by this magazine if I wished to
" answer " a " reply " to that article of mine, I
said " yes," and waited in Paris for the proof-sheets
of the " reply " to come. I already knew, by the
cablegram, that the " reply " would not be signed
by you, but upon reflection I knew it would be dictated by you, because no volunteer would feel himself at liberty to assume your championship in a
private dispute, unasked, in view of the fact that
you are quite well able to take care of your matters
of that sort yourself and are not in need of any
one's help. No, a volunteer could not make such a
venture. It would be too immodest. Also too
gratuitously generous. And a shade too self-
sufficient. No, he could not venture it. It would
look too much like anxiety to get in at a feast
where no plate had been provided for him. In fact
he could not get in at all, except by the back way,
and with a false key; that is to say, a pretext — a
pretext invented for the occasion by putting into
my mouth words which I did not use, and by
wresting sayings of mine from their plain and true
meaning. Would he resort to methods like those to
get in? No; there are no people of that kind. So
then I knew for a certainty that you dictated the

Reply yourself. I knew you did it to save yourse
manual labor.

And you had the right, as I have already said
and I am content — perfectly content. Yet it woul
have been little trouble to you, and a great kindnes
to me, if you had written your Reply all out wit
your own capable hand.

Because then it would have replied — and that
really what a Reply is for. Broadly speaking, i
function is to refute — as you will easily conced
That leaves something for the other person to tal
hold of: he has a chance to reply to the Reply, l
has a chance to refute the refutation. This wou
have happened if you had written it out instead
dictating. Dictating is nearly sure to unconcentra
the dictator's mind, when he is out of practice, co
fuse him, and betray him into using one set
literary rules when he ought to use a quite differe
set. Often it betrays him into employing the RULI
FOR CONVERSATION BETWEEN A SHOUTER AND
DEAF PERSON — as in the present case — when I
ought to employ the RULES FOR CONDUCTING DI
CUSSION WITH A FAULT-FINDER. The great found
tion-rule and basic principle of discussion with
fault-finder is relevancy and concentration upon tl
subject; whereas the great foundation-rule and bas
principle governing conversation between a shout
and a deaf person is irrelevancy and persiste
desertion of the topic in hand. If I may be allow
to illustrate by quoting example IV., section

om chapter ix. of " Revised Rules for Conducting
onversation between a Shouter and a Deaf Per-
n," it will assist us in getting a clear idea of the
fference between the two sets of rules:

Shouter. Did you say his name is WETHERBY?

Deaf Person. Change? Yes, I think it will.
hough if it should clear off I —

Shouter. It's his NAME I want — his NAME.

Deaf Person. Maybe so, maybe so; but it will
ily be a shower, I think.

Shouter. No, no, *no!* — you have quite mis-
aderSTOOD me. If —

Deaf Person. Ah! GOOD morning; I am sorry
ou must go. But call again, and let me continue
be of assistance to you in every way I can.

You see it is a perfect kodak of the article you
ave dictated. It is really curious and interesting
hen you come to compare it with yours; in detail,
ith my former article to which it is a Reply in
our hand. I talk twelve pages about your Ameri-
an instruction projects, and your doubtful scientific
ystem, and your painstaking classification of non-
xistent things, and your diligence and zeal and
ncerity, and your disloyal attitude towards anec-
otes, and your undue reverence for unsafe statistics
nd for facts that lack a pedigree; and you turn
round and come back at me with eight pages of
eather.

I do not see how a person can act so. It is good
f you to repeat, with change of language, in the

bulk of your rejoinder, so much of my own articl
and adopt my sentiments, and make them ove
and put new buttons on; and I like the complimen
and am frank to say so; but *agreeing* with a perso
cripples controversy and ought not to be allowe
It is weather; and of almost the worst sort.
pleases me greatly to hear you discourse with su
approval and expansiveness upon my text:

"A foreigner can photograph the exteriors of
nation, but I think that is as far as he can get.
think that no foreigner can report its interior;'
which is a quite clear way of saying that a foreigner
report is only valuable when it restricts itself
impressions. It pleases me to have you follow n
lead in that glowing way, but it leaves me nothin
to combat. You should give me something to der
and refute; I would do as much for you.

It pleases me to have you playfully warn tl
public against taking one of your books seriously
Because I used to do that cunning thing myself
earlier days. I did it in a prefatory note to a boc
of mine called *Tom Sawyer*.

---

* And you say: "A man of average intelligence, who has passed
months among a people, cannot express opinions that are worth jotti
down, but he can form impressions that are worth repeating. For »
part, I think that foreigners' impressions are more interesting than nati
opinions. After all, such impressions merely mean 'how the coun'
struck the foreigner.'"

† When I published *Jonathan and his Continent*, I wrote in a prefa
addressed to Jonathan: "If ever you should insist in seeing in this lit
volume a serious study of your country and of your countrymen, I wa
you that your world-wide fame for humor will be exploded."

NOTICE.

Persons attempting to find a motive in this narrative will be prosecuted; persons attempting to find a moral in it will be banished; persons attempting to find a plot in it will be shot.

BY ORDER OF THE AUTHOR
PER G. G., CHIEF OF ORDNANCE.

The kernel is the same in both prefaces, you see — the public must not take us too seriously. If we remove that kernel we remove the life-principle, and the preface is a corpse. Yes, it pleases me to have you use that idea, for it is a high compliment. But is leaves me nothing to combat; and that is damage to me.

Am I seeming to say that your Reply is not a reply at all, M. Bourget? If so, I must modify that; it is too sweeping. For you have furnished a general answer to my inquiry as to what France — through you — can teach us.*   It is a good answer.

---

* "What could France teach America?" exclaims Mark Twain. France can teach America all the higher pursuits of life, and there is more artistic feeling and refinement in a street of French workingmen than in many avenues inhabited by American millionaires. She can teach her, not perhaps how to work, but how to rest, how to live, how to be happy. She can teach her that the aim of life is not money-making, but that money-making is only a means to obtain an end. She can teach her that wives are not expensive toys, but useful partners, friends, and confidants, who should always keep men under their wholesome influence by their diplomacy, their tact, their common-sense, without umptiousness. These qualities, added to the highest standard of morality (not angular and morose, but cheerful morality), are conceded to Frenchwomen by whoever knows something of French life outside of the Paris boulevards, and Mark Twain's ill-natured sneer cannot even so much as stain them.

I might tell Mark Twain that in France a man who was seen tipsy in

It relates to manners, customs, and morals — thre
things concerning which we can never have ex
haustive and determinate statistics, and so th
verdicts delivered upon them must always lack cor
clusiveness and be subject to revision; but you hav
stated the truth, possibly, as nearly as any on
could do it, in the circumstances. But why did yo
choose a detail of my question which could b
answered only with vague hearsay evidence, an
go right by one which could have been answere
with deadly facts? — facts in everybody's reach
facts which none can dispute. I asked what Franc
could teach us about government. I laid mysel
pretty wide open, there; and I thought I was hand
somely generous, too, when I did it. France ca
teach us how to levy village and city taxes whicl
distribute the burden with a nearer approach to per
fect fairness than is the case in any other land; an
she can teach us the wisest and surest system of col
lecting them that exists. She can teach us how to
elect a President in a sane way; and also how to do
it without throwing the country into earthquake
and convulsions that cripple and embarrass business
stir up party hatred in the hearts of men, and make

---

his club would immediately see his name canceled from membership. A
man who had settled his fortune on his wife to avoid meeting his cred
itors would be refused admission into any decent society. Many a
Frenchman has blown his brains out rather than declare himself a bankrupt. Now would Mark Twain remark to this: "An American is not
such a fool: when a creditor stands in his way he closes his doors, and
reopens them the following day. When he has been a bankrupt three
times he can retire from business?"

aceful people wish the term extended to thirty
ars. France can teach us — but enough of that
rt of the question. And what else can France
ch us? She can teach us all the fine arts — and
es. She throws open her hospitable art acade-
es, and says to us, "Come" — and we come,
ops and troops of our young and gifted; and she
s over us the ablest masters in the world and
aring the greatest names; and she teaches us all
t we are capable of learning, and persuades us
d encourages us with prizes and honors, much
if we were somehow children of her own; and
en this noble education is finished and we are
dy to carry it home and spread its gracious
nistries abroad over our nation, and we come
h homage and gratitude and ask France for the
— *there is nothing to pay*. And in return for this
perial generosity, what does America do? She
urges a duty on French works of art!

I wish I had your end of this dispute; I should
ve something worth talking about. If you would
y furnish me something to argue, something to
ute — but you persistently won't. You leave
od chances unutilized and spend your strength
proving and establishing unimportant things.
r instance, you have proven and established these
ht facts here following — a good score as to
mber, but not worth while:

Mark Twain is —
1. " Insulting."
12B

2. (Sarcastically speaking) " This refined hum
ist."

3. Prefers the manure-pile to the violets.

4. Has uttered " an ill-natured sneer."

5. Is " nasty."

6. Needs a " lesson in politeness and good m
ners."

7. Has published a " nasty article."

8. Has made remarks " unworthy of a gent
man."* These are all true, but really they are
valuable; no one cares much for such finds.
our American magazines we recognize this and s
press them. We avoid naming them. Americ
writers never allow themselves to name them.
would look as if they were in a temper, and we h
that exhibitions of temper in public are not g
form — except in the very young and inexperienc
And even if we had the disposition to name the

* " It is more funny than his " (Mark Twain's) " anecdote,
would have been less insulting."

A quoted remark of mine " is a gross insult to a nation friend
America."

" He has read *La Terre*, this refined humorist."

" When Mark Twain visits a garden . . . he goes in the far-a
corner where the soil is prepared."

" Mark Twain's ill-natured sneer cannot so much as stain the
(the Frenchwomen).

" When he " (Mark Twain) " takes his revenge he is unkind,
fair, bitter, nasty."

" But not even your nasty article on my country, Mark," etc.

" Mark might certainly have derived from it " (M. Bourget's be
" a lesson in politeness and good manners."

A quoted remark of mine is " unworthy of a gentleman."

order to fill up a gap when we were short of ideas
d arguments, our magazines would not allow us to
it, because they think that such words sully their
ges.   This present magazine is particularly stren-
us about it.   Its note to me announcing the
rwarding of your proof-sheets to France closed
us — for your protection:

*" It is needless to ask you to avoid anything that
    might consider as personal."*

It was well enough, as a measure of precaution,
t really it was not needed.   You can trust me im-
icitly, M. Bourget; I shall never call you any
mes in print which I should be ashamed to call
u with your unoffending and dearest ones present.
Indeed, we are reserved, and particular in America
a degree which you would consider exaggerated.
r instance, we should not write notes like that one
yours to a lady for a small fault — or a large
e.*   We should not think it kind.   No matter

---

* When M. Paul Bourget indulges in a little chaffing at the expense
the Americans, " who can always get away with a few years' trying
ind out who their grandfathers were," he merely makes an allusion
an American foible; but, forsooth, what a kind man, what a humor-
Mark Twain is when he retorts by calling France a nation of
tards!   How the Americans of culture and refinement will admire
1 for thus speaking in their name!

Snobbery. . . . I could give Mark Twain an example of the Ameri-
specimen.   It is a piquant story.   I never published it because I
red my readers might think that I was giving them a typical illustra-
1 of American character instead of a rare exception.

I was once booked by my manager to give a *causerie* in the drawing-
m of a New York millionaire.   I accepted with reluctance.   I do

how much we might have associated with kings an
nobilities, we should not think it right to crush h
with it and make her ashamed of her lowlier walk
life; for we have a saying, "Who humiliates m
mother includes his own."

Do I seriously imagine you to be the author
that strange letter, M. Bourget? Indeed I do no
I believe it to have been surreptitiously inserted b
your amanuensis when your back was turned.
think he did it with a good motive, expecting it

---

not like private engagements. At five o'clock on the day the *cause*
was to be given, the lady sent to my manager to say that she wou
expect me to arrive at nine o'clock and to speak for about an hou
Then she wrote a postscript. Many women are unfortunate the
Their minds are full of after-thoughts, and the most important part
their letters is generally to be found after their signature. This lad
P. S. ran thus: "I suppose he will not expect to be entertained af
the lecture."

I fairly shouted, as Mark Twain would say, and then, indulgi
myself in a bit of snobbishness, I was back at her as quick as a flash

"Dear Madam: As a literary man of some reputation, I have ma
times had the pleasure of being entertained by the members of the
aristocracy of France. I have also many times had the pleasure
being entertained by the members of the old aristocracy of Englar
If it may interest you, I can even tell you that I have several times h
the honor of being entertained by royalty; but my ambition has ne
been so wild as to expect that one day I might be entertained by t
aristocracy of New York. No, I do not expect to be entertained
you, nor do I want you to expect me to entertain you and your frier
to-night, for I decline to keep the engagement."

Now, I could fill a book on America with reminiscences of this so
adding a few chapters on bosses and boodlers, on New York *chroniq
scandaleuse*, on the tenement houses of the large cities, on the gamblir
hells of Denver, and the dens of San Francisco, and what not! I
not even your nasty article on my country, Mark, will make me do it.

d force and piquancy to your article, but it does
t reflect your nature, and I know it will grieve
u when you see it. I also think he interlarded
any other things which you will disapprove of
en you see them. I am certain that all the harsh
mes discharged at me come from him, not you.
doubt you could have proved me entitled to
em with as little trouble as it has cost him to do it,
t it would have been your disposition to hunt
me of a higher quality.

Why, I even doubt if it is you who furnish me all
at excellent information about Balzac and those
ers.* All this in simple justice to you — and to
; for, to gravely accept those interlardings as
urs would be to wrong your head and heart, and
the same time convict myself of being equipped

"Now the style of M. Bourget and many other French writers is
arently a closed letter to Mark Twain; but let us leave that alone.
s he read Erckmann-Chatrian, Victor Hugo, Lamartine, Edmond
ut, Cherbuliez, Renan? Has he read Gustave Droz's *Monsieur*,
dame, et Bébé, and those books which leave for a long time a per-
e about you? Has he read the novels of Alexandre Dumas, Eugène
, George Sand, and Balzac? Has he read Victor Hugo's *Les Misé-
les* and *Notre Dame de Paris?* Has he read or heard the plays of
deau, Augier, Dumas, and Sardou, the works of those Titans of
dern literature, whose names will be household words all over the
ld for hundreds of years to come? He has read *La Terre* — this
d-hearted, refined humorist! When Mark Twain visits a garden
s he smell the violets, the roses, the jasmine, or the honeysuckle?
, he goes in the far-away corner where the soil is prepared. Hear
at he says: "I wish M. Paul Bourget had read more of our novels
ore he came. It is the only way to thoroughly understand a people.
en I found I was coming to Paris I read *La Terre*."

12***

with a vacancy where my penetration ought to
lodged.

And now finally I must uncover the secret pai
the wee sore from which the Reply grew —*t.
anecdote which closed my recent article*—and co
sider how it is that this pimple has spread to the
cancerous dimensions. If any but you had dictat
the Reply, M. Bourget, I would know that th
anecdote was twisted around and its intention ma
nified some hundreds of times, in order that it mig
be used as a pretext to creep in the back way.   B
I accuse you of nothing — nothing but error. Wh
you say that I " retort by calling France a nation
bastards," it is an error. And not a small one, b
a large one. I made no such remark, nor anythir
resembling it. Moreover, the magazine would n
have allowed me to use so gross a word as that.

You told an anecdote. A funny one—I adm
that. It hit a foible of our American aristo
racy, and it stung me — I admit that; it stung n
sharply. It was like this: You found some ancie
portraits of French kings in the gallery of one of o
aristocracy, and you said:

" He has the Grand Monarch, but *where is t.
portrait of his grandfather?*" That is, the Amer
can aristocrat's grandfather.

Now that hits only a few of us, I grant — just tl
upper crust only — but it hits exceedingly hard.

I wondered if there was any way of getting bac
at you. In one of your chapters I found this chance

" In our high Parisian existence, for instance, we
⸺d applied to arts and luxury, and to debauchery,
⸺ the powers and all the weaknesses of the French
⸺ul."

You see? Your " higher Parisian " class — not
⸺erybody, not the nation, but only the *top crust* of
⸺e nation — *applies to debauchery all the powers of*
⸺ *soul.*

I argued to myself that that energy must produce
⸺sults. So I built an anecdote out of your remark.
⸺ it I make Napoleon Bonaparte say to me — but
⸺e for yourself the anecdote (ingeniously clipped
⸺d curtailed) in paragraph eleven of your Reply.*

---

* So, I repeat, Mark Twain does not like M. Paul Bourget's book.
⸺ long as he makes light fun of the great French writer he is at home,
⸺ is pleasant, he is the American humorist we know.   When he takes
⸺ revenge (and where is the reason for taking a revenge?) he is unkind,
⸺fair, bitter, nasty.
⸺For example:
⸺See his answer to a Frenchman who jokingly remarks to him:
" I suppose life can never get entirely dull to an American, because
⸺enever he can't strike up any other way to put in his time, he can
⸺ways get away with a few years trying to find out who his grandfather
⸺s."
⸺Hear the answer:
" I reckon a Frenchman's got *his* little standby for a dull time, too;
⸺cause when all other interests fail, he can turn in and see if he can't
⸺d out who his father was."
⸺The first remark is a good-humored bit of chaffing on American snob-
⸺ry.   I may be utterly destitute of humor, but I call the second remark
⸺ gratuitous charge of immorality hurled at the French women — a
⸺mark unworthy of a man who has the ear of the public, unworthy of
⸺gentleman, a gross insult to a nation friendly to America, a nation that
⸺lped Mark Twain's ancestors in their struggle for liberty, a nation

L*₊*₊

Now, then, your anecdote about the grandfathe
hurt me. Why? Because it had a *point*. It wouldn
have hurt me if it hadn't had point. You wouldn
have wasted space on it if it hadn't had point.

My anecdote has hurt you. Why? Because it h.
point, I suppose. It wouldn't have hurt you if
hadn't had point. I judged from your remark abo
the diligence and industry of the high Parisian upp
crust that it would have *some* point, but really I h
no idea what a gold-mine I had struck. I nev
suspected that the point was going to stick into t
entire nation; but of course you know your nati
better than I do, and if you think it punctures the
all, I have to yield to your judgment. But you a
to blame, your own self. Your remark misled n
I supposed the industry was confined to that lit
unnumerous upper layer.

Well, now that the unfortunate thing has be
done, let us do what we can to undo it. The
must be a way, M. Bourget, and I am willing to
anything that will help; for I am as sorry as y
can be yourself.

I will tell you what I think will be the very thir

---

where to-day it is enough to say that you are American to see e
door open wide to you.

If Mark Twain was hard up in search of a French " chestnut,
might have told him the following little anecdote. It is more fu
than his, and would have been less insulting: Two little street boys
abusing each other. "Ah, hold your tongue," says one, "you a
got no father."

"Ain't got no father!" replies the other; "I've got more fat
than you."

will *swap anecdotes*. I will take your anecdote
I you take mine. I will say to the dukes and
ints and princes of the ancient nobility of France:
Ha, ha! You must have a pretty hard time trying
find out who your grandfathers were?"

They will merely smile indifferently and not feel
rt, because they can trace their lineage back
ough centuries.

And you will hurl mine at every individual in the
nerican nation, saying:

" And *you* must have a pretty hard time trying to
d out who your *fathers* were." They will merely
ile indifferently, and not feel hurt, because they
ven't any difficulty in finding their fathers.

Do you get the idea? The whole harm in the
ecdotes is in the *point*, you see; and when we
ap them around that way, they *haven't* any.

That settles it perfectly and beautifully, and I am
d I thought of it. I am very glad indeed, M.
urget; for it was just that little wee thing that
used the whole difficulty and made you dictate the
ply, and your amanuensis call me all those hard
mes which the magazines dislike so. And I did it
in fun, too, trying to cap your funny anecdote
th another one — on the give-and-take principle,
u know — which is American. *I* didn't know
at with the French it was all give and no take, and
u didn't tell me. But now that I have made
erything comfortable again, and fixed both anec-
tes so they can never have any point any more, I
ow you will forgive me.

THE INVALID'S STORY

I SEEM sixty and married, but these effects are d
to my condition and sufferings, for I am
bachelor, and only forty-one. It will be hard f
you to believe that I, who am now but a shado
was a hale, hearty man two short years ago,-
a man of iron, a very athlete! — yet such is t
simple truth. But stranger still than this fa
is the way in which I lost my health. I lost
through helping to take care of a box of gu
on a two-hundred-mile railway journey one winter
night. It is the actual truth, and I will tell y
about it.

I belong in Cleveland, Ohio. One winter's nigh
two years ago, I reached home just after dark, in
driving snow-storm, and the first thing I heard when
entered the house was that my dearest boyhood frie
and schoolmate, John B. Hackett, had died the d
before, and that his last utterance had been a desi
that I would take his remains home to his poor o
father and mother in Wisconsin. I was great
shocked and grieved, but there was no time to was
in emotions; I must start at once. I took t

card, marked " Deacon Levi Hackett, Bethlehem, Wisconsin," and hurried off through the whistling storm to the railway station. Arrived there I found the long white-pine box which had been described to me; I fastened the card to it with some tacks, saw it put safely aboard the express car, and then ran into the eating-room to provide myself with a sandwich and some cigars. When I returned, presently, there was my coffin-box *back again*, apparently, and a young fellow examining around it, with a card in his hands, and some tacks and a hammer! I was astonished and puzzled. He began to nail on his card, and I rushed out to the express car, in a good deal of a state of mind, to ask for an explanation. But no — there was my box, all right, in the express car; it hadn't been disturbed. The fact is that without my suspecting it a prodigious mistake had been made. I was carrying off a box of *guns* which that young fellow had come to the station to ship to a rifle company in Peoria, Illinois, and *he* had got my corpse!] Just then the conductor sung out " All aboard," and I jumped into the express car and got a comfortable seat on a bale of buckets. The expressman was there, hard at work,— a plain man of fifty, with a simple, honest, good-natured face, and a breezy, practical heartiness in his general style. As the train moved off a stranger skipped into the car and set a package of peculiarly mature and capable Limburger cheese on one end of my coffin-box — I mean my box of guns. That is

to say. I know _now_ that it was Limburger chees
but at that time I never had heard of the article
my life, and of course was wholly ignorant of i
character. Well, we sped through the wild nigh
the bitter storm raged on, a cheerless misery stc
over me, my heart went down, down, down! T.
old expressman made a brisk remark or two abo
the tempest and the arctic weather, slammed l
sliding doors to, and bolted them, closed his windo
down tight, and then went bustling around, here a
there and yonder, setting things to rights, and all t
time contentedly humming "Sweet By and By,"
a low tone, and flatting a good deal. Presently
began to detect a most evil and searching odor stea
ing about on the frozen air. This depressed n
spirits still more, because of course I attributed it
my poor departed friend. There was something i
finitely saddening about his calling himself to my r
membrance in this dumb pathetic way, so it w
hard to keep the tears back. Moreover, it distress
me on account of the old expressman, who, I w
afraid, might notice it. However, he went hummi
tranquilly on, and gave no sign; and for this I w
grateful. Grateful, yes, but still uneasy; and so
I began to feel more and more uneasy every minut
for every minute that went by that odor thicken
up the more, and got to be more and more gam
and hard to stand. Presently, having got thin
arranged to his satisfaction, the expressman got so
wood and made up a tremendous fire in his stov

This distressed me more than I can tell, for I could not but feel that it was a mistake. I was sure that the effect would be deleterious upon my poor departed friend. Thompson — the expressman's name was Thompson, as I found out in the course of the night — now went poking around his car, stopping up whatever stray cracks he could find, remarking that it didn't make any difference what kind of a night it was outside, he calculated to make *us* comfortable, anyway. I said nothing, but I believed he was not choosing the right way. Meantime he was humming to himself just as before; and meantime, too, the stove was getting hotter and hotter, and the place closer and closer. I felt myself growing pale and qualmish, but grieved in silence and said nothing. Soon I noticed that the " Sweet By and By " was gradually fading out; next it ceased altogether, and there was an ominous stillness. After a few moments Thompson said,—

" Pfew! I reckon it ain't no cinnamon 't I've loaded up thish-yer stove with !"

He gasped once or twice, then moved toward the cof—gun-box, stood over that Limburger cheese part of a moment, then came back and sat down near me, looking a good deal impressed. After a contemplative pause, he said, indicating the box with a gesture,—

" Friend of yourn ?"

" Yes," I said with a sigh.

" He's pretty ripe, *ain't* he !"

Nothing further was said for perhaps a couple of minutes, each being busy with his own thoughts; then Thompson said, in a low, awed voice,—

" Sometimes it's uncertain whether they're really gone or not,— *seem* gone, you know — body warm, joints limber — and so, although you *think* they're gone, you don't really know. I've had cases in my car. It's perfectly awful, becuz *you* don't know what minute they'll rise up and look at you! " Then, after a pause, and slightly lifting his elbow toward the box,—" But *he* ain't in no trance! No, sir, I go bail for *him!* "

We sat some time, in meditative silence, listening to the wind and the roar of the train; then Thompson said, with a good deal of feeling,—

" Well-a-well, we've all got to go, they ain't no getting around it. Man that is born of woman is of few days and far between, as Scriptur' says. Yes, you look at it any way you want to, it's awful solemn and cur'us: they ain't *nobody* can get around it; *all's* got to go — just *everybody*, as you may say. One day you're hearty and strong " — here he scrambled to his feet and broke a pane and stretched his nose out at it a moment or two, then sat down again while I struggled up and thrust my nose out at the same place, and this we kept on doing every now and then —" and next day he's cut down like the grass, and the places which knowed him then knows him no more forever, as Scriptur' says. Yes'ndeedy, it's awful solemn and cur'us; but we've all got to

go, one time or another; they ain't no getting
around it."

There was another long pause; then,—

" What did he die of?"

I said I didn't know.

" How long has he ben dead?"

It seemed judicious to enlarge the facts to fit the
probabilities; so I said,—

" Two or three days."

But it did no good; for Thompson received it
with an injured look which plainly said, " Two or
three *years*, you mean." Then he went right along,
placidly ignoring my statement, and gave his views
at considerable length upon the unwisdom of putting
off burials too long. Then he lounged off toward
the box, stood a moment, then came back on a sharp
trot and visited the broken pane, observing,—

" 'Twould 'a' ben a dum sight better, all around,
if they'd started him along last summer."

Thompson sat down and buried his face in his red
silk handkerchief, and began to slowly sway and
rock his body like one who is doing his best to
endure the almost unendurable. By this time the
fragrance — if you may call it fragrance — was just
about suffocating, as near as you can come at it.
Thompson's face was turning gray; I knew mine
hadn't any color left in it. By and by Thompson
rested his forehead in his left hand, with his elbow
on his knee, and sort of waved his red handkerchief
towards the box with his other hand, and said,—

" I've carried a many a one of 'em,— some o' 'em considerable overdue, too,— but, lordy, he jus' lays over 'em all! — and does it *easy*. Cap., they was heliotrope to *him!* "

This recognition of my poor friend gratified me in spite of the sad circumstances, because it had so much the sound of a compliment.

Pretty soon it was plain that something had go' to be done. I suggested cigars. Thompson though' it was a good idea. He said,—

" Likely it'll modify him some."

We puffed gingerly along for a while, and tried hard to imagine that things were improved. Bu' it wasn't any use. Before very long, and withou' any consultation, both cigars were quietly dropped from our nerveless fingers at the same moment. Thompson said, with a sigh,—

" No, Cap., it don't modify him worth a cent. Fact is, it makes him worse, becuz it appears to stir up his ambition. What do you reckon we better do, now?"

I was not able to suggest anything; indeed, I had to be swallowing and swallowing, all the time, and did not like to trust myself to speak. Thompson fell to maundering, in a desultory and low-spirited way, about the miserable experiences of this night; and he got to referring to my poor friend by various titles,— sometimes military ones, sometimes civil ones; and I noticed that as fast as my poor friend's effectiveness grew, Thompson promoted him ac-

:ordingly,— gave him a bigger title.   Finally he
;aid,—

" I've got an idea.   Suppos'n we buckle down to
t and give the Colonel a bit of a shove towards
'other end of the car? — about ten foot, say.   He
vouldn't have so much influence, then, don't you
·eckon?"

I said it was a good scheme.   So we took in
a good fresh breath at the broken pane, calculat-
ng to hold it till we got through;   then we went
here and bent over that deadly cheese and took a
grip on the box.   Thompson nodded "All ready,"
and then we threw ourselves forward with all our
night;   but Thompson slipped, and slumped down
vith his nose on the cheese, and his breath got
oose.   He gagged and gasped, and floundered up
and made a break for the door, pawing the air
and saying hoarsely, "Don't hender me! — gimme
he road!   I'm a-dying;   gimme the road!"   Out
on the cold platform I sat down and held his head
a while, and he revived.   Presently he said,—

" Do you reckon we started the Gen'rul any?"
I said no; we hadn't budged him.

" Well, then, *that* idea's up the flume.   We got
o think up something else.   He's suited wher' he
s, I reckon;   and if that's the way he feels about it,
and has made up his mind that he don't wish to be
disturbed, you bet he's a-going to have his own way
n the business.   Yes, better leave him right wher'
he is, long as he wants it so;   becuz he holds all the

13B

trumps, don't you know, and so it stands to reason
that the man that lays out to alter his plans for him
is going to get left.''

But we couldn't stay out there in that mad storm
we should have frozen to death. So we went in
again and shut the door, and began to suffer once
more and take turns at the break in the window. By
and by, as we were starting away from a station where
we had stopped a moment Thompson pranced in
cheerily, and exclaimed,—

''We're all right, now! I reckon we've got the
Commodore this time. I judge I've got the stuff
here that'll take the tuck out of him.''

It was carbolic acid. He had a carboy of it. He
sprinkled it all around everywhere; in fact he
drenched everything with it, rifle-box, cheese and all.
Then we sat down, feeling pretty hopeful. But it
wasn't for long. You see the two perfumes began
to mix, and then — well, pretty soon we made a
break for the door; and out there Thompson swabbed
his face with his bandanna and said in a kind of dis-
heartened way,—

'' It ain't no use. We can't buck agin *him*. He
just utilizes everything we put up to modify him with,
and gives it his own flavor and plays it back on us.
Why, Cap., don't you know, it's as much as a
hundred times worse in there now than it was when
he first got a-going. I never *did* see one of 'em
warm up to his work so, and take such a dumnation
interest in it. No, sir, I never did, as long as I'

THESE GAVE IT A BETTER HOLD

n on the road; and I've carried a many a one of
m, as I was telling you.''

We went in again after we were frozen pretty
iff; but my, we couldn't *stay* in, now. So
: just waltzed back and forth, freezing, and
awing, and stifling, by turns. In about an hour
: stopped at another station; and as we left it
lompson came in with a bag, and said,—

"Cap., I'm a-going to chance him once more,—
st this once; and if we don't fetch him this time,
e thing for us to do, is to just throw up the sponge
d withdraw from the canvass. That's the way *I*
t it up.''

He had brought a lot of chicken feathers, and
led apples, and leaf tobacco, and rags, and old
oes, and sulphur, and asafœtida, and one thing or
other; and he piled them on a breadth of sheet
n in the middle of the floor, and set fire to them.
When they got well started, I couldn't see, myself,
w even the corpse could stand it. All that went
fore was just simply poetry to that smell,—but
nd you, the original smell stood up out of it just
sublime as ever,—fact is, these other smells just
:med to give it a better hold; and my, how rich it
s! I didn't make these reflections there — there
sn't time — made them on the platform. And
:aking for the platform, Thompson got suffocated
d fell; and before I got him dragged out, which I
. by the collar, I was mighty near gone myself.
1en we revived, Thompson said dejectedly,—

" We got to stay out here, Cap.   We got to do i
They ain't no other way.   The Governor want t
travel alone, and he's fixed so he can outvote us."

And presently he added,—

" And don't you know, we're *pisoned*. It's ou
last trip, you can make up your mind to it.   Typhoi
fever is what's going to come of this.   I feel it a
coming right now.   Yes, sir, we're elected, just as
sure as you're born."

We were taken from the platform an hour late
frozen and insensible, at the next station, and I wer
straight off into a virulent fever, and never knew any
thing again for three weeks.   I found out, then, tha
I had spent that awful night with a harmless box o
rifles and a lot of innocent cheese; but the news wa
too late to save *me;* imagination had done its worl
and my health was permanently shattered; neithe
Bermuda nor any other land can ever bring it bac
to me.   This is my last trip; I am on my way hom
to die.

THE CAPTAIN'S STORY

THERE was a good deal of pleasant gossip about old Captain " Hurricane " Jones, of the Pacific Ocean,— peace to his ashes! Two or three of us present had known him; I, particularly well, for I had made four sea-voyages with him. He was a very remarkable man. He was born on a ship; he picked up what little education he had among his shipmates; he began life in the forecastle, and climbed grade by grade to the captaincy. More than fifty years of his sixty-five were spent at sea. He had sailed all oceans, seen all lands, and borrowed a tint from all climates. When a man has been fifty years at sea, he necessarily knows nothing of men, nothing of the world but its surface, nothing of the world's thought, nothing of the world's learning but its A B C, and that blurred and distorted by the unfocused lenses of an untrained mind. Such a man is only a gray and bearded child. That is what old Hurricane Jones was,— simply an innocent, lovable old infant. When his spirit was in repose he was as sweet and gentle as a girl; when his wrath was up he was a hurricane that made his nickname seem tamely descriptive. He was formidable in a fight, for he was of powerful build and dauntless courage. He was frescoed from head to heel with pictures and mottoes tattooed in red and blue India ink. I was with him one voyage when he got his last vacant space tattooed; this vacant space was around his left ankle. During three days he stumped about the ship with his ankle bare and swollen, and this legend gleaming red and angry out from a clouding of India ink: "Virtue is its own R'd." (There was a lack of room.) He was deeply and sincerely pious, and swore like a fish-woman. He considered swearing blameless, because sailors would not understand an order unilluminated by it. He was a profound Biblical scholar, — that is, he thought he was. He believed everything in the Bible, but he had his own methods of arriving at his beliefs. He was of the "advanced" school of thinkers, and applied natural laws to the interpretation of all miracles, somewhat on the plan of the people who make the six days of creation six geological epochs, and so forth. Without being aware of it, he was a rather severe satire on modern scientific religionists. Such a man as I have been describing is rabidly fond of disquisition and argument; one knows that without being told it.

One trip the captain had a clergyman on board, but did not know he was a clergyman, since the passenger list did not betray the fact. He took a great liking to this Rev. Mr. Peters, and talked

with him a great deal: told him yarns, gave him
toothsome scraps of personal history, and wove a
glittering streak of profanity through his garru-
ous fabric that was refreshing to a spirit weary
of the dull neutralities of undecorated speech. One
day the captain said, " Peters, do you ever read
the Bible?"

" Well — yes."

" I judge it ain't often, by the way you say it.
Now, you tackle it in dead earnest once, and you'll
find it'll pay. Don't you get discouraged, but hang
right on. First, you won't understand it; but by
and by things will begin to clear up, and then you
wouldn't lay it down to eat."

" Yes, I have heard that said."

" And it's so, too. There ain't a book that begins
with it. It lays over 'em all, Peters. There's some
pretty tough things in it,— there ain't any getting
round that,— but you stick to them and think them
out, and when once you get on the inside everything's plain as day."

" The miracles, too, captain?"

" Yes, sir! the miracles, too. Every one of them.
Now, there's that business with the prophets of
Baal; like enough that stumped you?"

" Well, I don't know but —"

" Own up, now; it stumped you. Well, I don't
wonder. You hadn't had any experience in raveling
such things out, and naturally it was too many for
you. Would you like to have me explain that thing
M*ₐ*ₑ

to you, and show you how to get at the meat of
these matters?"

"Indeed, I would, captain, if you don't mind."

Then the captain proceeded as follows: "I'll do
it with pleasure. First, you see, I read and read,
and thought and thought, till I got to understand
what sort of people they were in the old Bible times,
and then after that it was clear and easy. Now, this
was the way I put it up, concerning Isaac* and the
prophets of Baal. There was some mighty sharp
men amongst the public characters of that old
ancient day, and Isaac was one of them. Isaac had
his failings,— plenty of them, too; it ain't for me to
apologize for Isaac; he played on the prophets of
Baal, and like enough he was justifiable, considering
the odds that was against him. No, all I say is,
't wa'n't any miracle, and that I'll show you so's't
you can see it yourself.

"Well, times had been getting rougher and
rougher for prophets,— that is, prophets of Isaac's
denomination. There were four hundred and fifty
prophets of Baal in the community, and only one
Presbyterian; that is, if Isaac *was* a Presbyterian,
which I reckon he was, but it don't say. Naturally,
the prophets of Baal took all the trade. Isaac was
pretty low-spirited, I reckon, but he was a good deal
of a man, and no doubt he went a-prophesying
around, letting on to be doing a land-office busi-

---

* This is the captain's own mistake.

ness, but 't wa'n't any use; he couldn't run any
opposition to amount to anything. By and by
things got desperate with him; he sets his head
to work and thinks it all out, and then what does
he do? Why, he begins to throw out hints that
the other parties are this and that and t'other,—
nothing very definite, may be, but just kind of
undermining their reputation in a quiet way. This
made talk, of course, and finally got to the king.
The king asked Isaac what he meant by his talk.
Says Isaac, ' Oh, nothing particular; only, can
they pray down fire from heaven on an altar? It
ain't much, maybe, your majesty, only can they
do it? That's the idea.' So the king was a good
deal disturbed, and he went to the prophets of
Baal, and they said, pretty airy, that if he had
an altar ready, *they* were ready; and they intimated he better get it insured, too.

" So next morning all the children of Israel and
their parents and the other people gathered themselves together. Well, here was that great crowd of
prophets of Baal packed together on one side, and
Isaac walking up and down all alone on the other,
putting up his job. When time was called, Isaac let
on to be comfortable and indifferent; told the other
team to take the first innings. So they went at it,
the whole four hundred and fifty, praying around the
altar, very hopeful, and doing their level best. They
prayed an hour,— two hours,— three hours,— and
so on, plumb till noon. It wa'n't any use; they

hadn't took a trick. Of course they felt kind
of ashamed before all those people, and well they
might. Now, what would a magnanimous man
do? Keep still, wouldn't he? Of course. What
did Isaac do? He graveled the prophets of Baal
every way he could think of. Says he, ' You
don't speak up loud enough; your god's asleep,
like enough, or maybe he's taking a walk; you
want to holler, you know,' — or words to that effect; I don't recollect the exact language. Mind
I don't apologize for Isaac; he had his faults.

" Well, the prophets of Baal prayed along the best
they knew how all the afternoon, and never raised a
spark. At last, about sundown, they were all
tuckered out, and they owned up and quit.

" What does Isaac do, now? He steps up and
says to some friends of his, there, ' Pour four barrels
of water on the altar ! ' Everybody was astonished
for the other side had prayed at it dry, you know,
and got whitewashed. They poured it on. Says he
' Heave on four more barrels.' Then he says,
' Heave on four more.' Twelve barrels, you see,
altogether. The water ran all over the altar, and all
down the sides, and filled up a trench around it that
would hold a couple of hogsheads,— ' measures,' it
says; I reckon it means about a hogshead. Some
of the people were going to put on their things and
go, for they allowed he was crazy. They didn't
know Isaac. Isaac knelt down and began to pray:
he strung along, and strung along, about the heathen

in distant lands, and about the sister churches, and
about the state and the country at large, and about
those that's in authority in the government, and all
the usual programme, you know, till everybody had
got tired and gone to thinking about something
else, and then, all of a sudden, when nobody was
noticing, he outs with a match and rakes it on
the under side of his leg, and pff! up the whole
thing blazes like a house afire! Twelve barrels of
water? *Petroleum*, sir, PETROLEUM! that's what
it was!"

"Petroleum, captain?"

"Yes, sir; the country was full of it. Isaac
knew all about that. You read the Bible. Don't
you worry about the tough places. They ain't tough
when you come to think them out and throw light
on them. There ain't a thing in the Bible but what
is true; all you want is to go prayerfully to work and
cipher out how 't was done."

STIRRING TIMES IN AUSTRIA

I. THE GOVERNMENT IN THE FRYING-PAN

HERE in Vienna in these closing days of 1897 one's blood gets no chance to stagnate. The atmosphere is brimful of political electricity. All conversation is political; every man is a battery, with brushes overworn, and gives out blue sparks when you set him going on the common topic. Everybody has an opinion, and lets you have it frank and hot, and out of this multitude of counsel you get merely confusion and despair. For no one really understands this political situation, or can tell you what is going to be the outcome of it.

Things have happened here recently which would set any country but Austria on fire from end to end, and upset the government to a certainty; but no one feels confident that such results will follow here. Here, apparently, one must wait and see what will happen, then he will know, and not before; guessing is idle; guessing cannot help the matter. This is

hat the wise tell you; they all say it; they say it
very day, and it is the sole detail upon which they
ll agree.

There is some approach to agreement upon an-
ther point: that there will be no revolution. Men
ay: "Look at our history — revolutions have not
een in our line; and look at our political map
— its construction is unfavorable to an organized
prising, and without unity what could a revolt
ccomplish? It is *dis*union which has held our
mpire together for centuries, and what it has
one in the past it may continue to do now and
n the future."

The most intelligible sketch I have encountered
f this unintelligible arrangement of things was con-
ibuted to the *Travelers Record* by Mr. Forrest
Iorgan, of Hartford, three years ago. He says:

The Austro-Hungarian Monarchy is the patchwork quilt, the Mid-
ay Plaisance, the national chain-gang of Europe; a state that is not a
ation but a collection of nations, some with national memories and
pirations and others without, some occupying distinct provinces almost
urely their own, and others mixed with alien races, but each with a
fferent language, and each mostly holding the others foreigners as
uch as if the link of a common government did not exist. Only one of
 races even now comprises so much as *one-fourth* of the whole, and
t another so much as *one-sixth;* and each has remained for ages as
achanged in isolation, however mingled together in locality, as glob-
es of oil in water. There is nothing else in the modern world that is
early like it, though there have been plenty in past ages; it seems un-
al and impossible even though we know it is true; it violates all our
eling as to what a country should be in order to have a right to exist;
nd it seems as though it was too ramshackle to go on holding together
ny length of time. Yet it has survived, much in its present shape, two

centuries of storms that have swept perfectly unified countries fro
existence and others that have brought it to the verge of ruin, has su
vived formidable European coalitions to dismember it, and has steadi
gained force after each; forever changing in its exact make-up, losir
in the West but gaining in the East, the changes leave the structure as fi
as ever, like the dropping off and adding on of logs in a raft, its mecha
ical union of pieces showing all the vitality of genuine national life.

That seems to confirm and justify the prevaler
Austrian faith that in this confusion of unrelated an
irreconcilable elements, this condition of incurabl
disunion, there is strength — for the governmen
Nearly every day some one explains to me that
revolution would not succeed here. " It couldn'
you know. Broadly speaking, all the nations in th
empire hate the government — but they all hate eac
other, too, and with devoted and enthusiastic bitte
ness; no two of them can combine; the nation th;
rises must rise alone; then the others would joyfull
join the government against her, and she would hav
just a fly's chance against a combination of spider
This government is entirely independent. It can g
its own road, and do as it pleases; it has nothing t
fear. In countries like England and America, whei
there is one tongue and the public interests ai
common, the government must take account of publ
opinion; but in Austria-Hungary there are ninetee
public opinions — one for each state. No — two (
three for each state, since there are two or thre
nationalities in each. A government cannot satisf
all these public opinions; it can only go through th
motions of trying. This government does that.

goes through the motions, and they do not succeed;
but that does not worry the government much.''

The next man will give you some further information. '' The government has a policy — a wise one
— and sticks steadily to it. This policy is — *tranquillity:* keep this hive of excitable nations as quiet
as possible; encourage them to amuse themselves
with things less inflammatory than politics. To this
end it furnishes them an abundance of Catholic priests
to teach them to be docile and obedient, and to be
diligent in acquiring ignorance about things here
below, and knowledge about the kingdom of heaven,
to whose historic delights they are going to add the
charm of their society by-and-by; and further — to
this same end — it cools off the newspapers every
morning at five o'clock, whenever warm events are
happening.'' There is a censor of the press, and
apparently he is always on duty and hard at work.
A copy of each morning paper is brought to him at
five o'clock. His official wagons wait at the doors
of the newspaper offices and scud to him with the
first copies that come from the press. His company
of assistants read every line in these papers, and mark
everything which seems to have a dangerous look;
then he passes final judgment upon these markings.
Two things conspire to give to the results a capricious
and unbalanced look: his assistants have diversified
notions as to what is dangerous and what isn't; he
can't get time to examine their criticisms in much
detail; and so sometimes the very same matter which

is suppressed in one paper fails to be damned in another one, and gets published in full feather and unmodified. Then the paper in which it was suppressed blandly copies the forbidden matter into its evening edition — provokingly giving credit and detailing all the circumstances in courteous and inoffensive language — and of course the censor cannot say a word.

Sometimes the censor sucks all the blood out of a newspaper and leaves it colorless and inane; sometimes he leaves it undisturbed, and lets it talk out its opinions with a frankness and vigor hardly to be surpassed, I think, in the journals of any country. Apparently the censor sometimes revises his verdicts upon second thought, for several times lately he has suppressed journals after their issue and partial distribution. The distributed copies are then sent for by the censor and destroyed. I have two of these, but at the time they were sent for I could not remember what I had done with them.

If the censor did his work before the morning edition was printed, he would be less of an inconvenience than he is; but of course the papers cannot wait many minutes after five o'clock to get his verdict; they might as well go out of business as do that; so they print, and take the chances. Then, if they get caught by a suppression, they must strike out the condemned matter and print the edition over again. That delays the issue several hours, and is expensive besides. The government gets the sup-

pressed edition for nothing. If it bought it, that
would be joyful, and would give great satisfaction.
Also, the edition would be larger. Some of the
papers do not replace the condemned paragraphs
with other matter; they merely snatch them out and
leave blanks behind — mourning blanks, marked
' *Confiscated*.''

The government discourages the dissemination of
newspaper information in other ways. For instance,
it does not allow newspapers to be sold on the streets;
therefore the newsboy is unknown in Vienna. And
there is a stamp duty of nearly a cent upon each
copy of a newspaper's issue. Every American paper
that reaches me has a stamp upon it, which has been
pasted there in the post-office or downstairs in the
hotel office; but no matter who put it there, I have
to pay for it, and that is the main thing. Sometimes
friends send me so many papers that it takes all I
can earn that week to keep this government going.

I must take passing notice of another point in the
government's measures for maintaining tranquillity.
Everybody says it does not like to see any individual
attain to commanding influence in the country, since
such a man can become a disturber and an inconvenience.   '' We have as much talent as the other
nations,'' says the citizen, resignedly, and without
bitterness, '' but for the sake of the general good of
the country we are discouraged from making it over-
conspicuous; and not only discouraged, but tactfully
and skillfully prevented from doing it, if we show

14E

too much persistence. Consequently we have no
renowned men; in centuries we have seldom produced one — that is, seldom allowed one to produce
himself. We can say to-day what no other nation
of first importance in the family of Christian civil-
izations can say: that there exists no Austrian who
has made an enduring name for himself which is familiar all around the globe."

Another helper toward tranquillity is the army. I
is as pervasive as the atmosphere. It is everywhere.
All the mentioned creators, promoters, and pre-
servers of the public tranquillity do their severa
shares in the quieting work. They make a restfu
and comfortable serenity and reposefulness. This i
disturbed sometimes for a little while: a mob as
sembles to protest against something; it gets noisy
— noisier — still noisier — finally *too* noisy; the
the persuasive soldiery come charging down upon it
and in a few minutes all is quiet again, and there i
no mob.

There is a Constitution and there is a Parliament
The House draws its membership of 425 deputie
from the nineteen or twenty states heretofore men
tioned. These men represent peoples who speal
eleven languages. That means eleven distinct varie
ties of jealousies, hostilities, and warring interests
This could be expected to furnish forth a parlia
ment of a pretty inharmonious sort, and make legis
lation difficult at times — and it does that. Th
parliament is split up into many parties — the Cler

als, the Progressists, the German Nationalists, the
oung Czechs, the Social Democrats, the Christian
ocialists, and some others — and it is difficult to
t up working combinations among them. They
efer to fight apart sometimes.

The recent troubles have grown out of Count
deni's necessities. He could not carry on his
vernment without a majority vote in the House
his back, and in order to secure it he had to make
trade of some sort. He made it with the Czechs
the Bohemians. The terms were not easy for
n: he must pass a bill making the Czech tongue
official language in Bohemia in place of the
rman. This created a storm. All the Germans
Austria were incensed. In numbers they form
: a fourth part of the empire's population, but
y urge that the country's public business should
conducted in one common tongue, and that
gue a world language — which German is.

Iowever, Badeni secured his majority. The
rman element in parliament was apparently
ome helpless. The Czech deputies were ex-
nt.

Then the music began. Badeni's voyage, instead
being smooth, was disappointingly rough from
start. The government must get the *Ausgleich*
ugh. It must not fail. Badeni's majority was
ly to carry it through; but the minority was
rmined to obstruct it and delay it until the ob-
ious Czech-language measure should be shelved.

The *Ausgleich* is an Adjustment, Arrangement, Settlement, which holds Austria and Hungary together. It dates from 1867, and has to be renewed every ten years. It establishes the share which Hungary must pay toward the expenses of the imperial government. Hungary is a kingdom (the Emperor of Austria is its King), and has its own parliament and governmental machinery. But it has no foreign office, and it has no army — at least its army is a part of the imperial army, is paid out of the imperial treasury, and is under the control of the imperial war office.

The ten-year rearrangement was due a year ago, but failed to connect. At least completely. A year's compromise was arranged. A new arrangement must be effected before the last day of this year. Otherwise the two countries become separate entities. The Emperor would still be King of Hungary — that is, King of an independent foreign country. There would be Hungarian custom-houses on the Austrian frontier, and there would be a Hungarian army and a Hungarian foreign office. Both countries would be weakened by this, both would suffer damage.

The Opposition in the House, although in the minority, had a good weapon to fight with in the pending *Ausgleich*. If it could delay the *Ausgleich* a few weeks, the government would doubtless have to withdraw the hated language bill or lose Hungary.

The Opposition began its fight. Its arms were the Rules of the House. It was soon manifest that by applying these Rules ingeniously it could make the majority helpless, and keep it so as long as it pleased. It could shut off business every now and then with a motion to adjourn. It could require the ayes and noes on the motion, and use up thirty minutes on that detail. It could call for the reading and verification of the minutes of the preceding meeting, and use up half a day in that way. It could require that several of its members be entered upon the list of permitted speakers previously to the opening of a sitting; and as there is no time limit, further delays could thus be accomplished.

These were all lawful weapons, and the men of the Opposition (technically called the Left) were within their rights in using them. They used them to such dire purpose that all parliamentary business was paralyzed. The Right (the government side) could accomplish nothing. Then it had a saving idea. This idea was a curious one. It was to have the President and the Vice-Presidents of the Parliament trample the Rules under foot upon occasion!

This, for a profoundly embittered minority constructed out of fire and gun-cotton! It was time for idle strangers to go and ask leave to look down out of a gallery and see what would be the result of it.

14*.*.

II. A MEMORABLE SITTING

And now took place that memorable sitting of the House which broke two records. It lasted the best part of two days and a night, surpassing by half an hour the longest sitting known to the world's previous parliamentary history, and breaking the long-speech record with Dr. Lecher's twelve-hour effort, the longest flow of unbroken talk that ever came out of one mouth since the world began.

At 8:45, on the evening of the 28th of October, when the House had been sitting a few minutes short of ten hours, Dr. Lecher was granted the floor. It was a good place for theatrical effects. I think that no other Senate House is so shapely as this one, or so richly and showily decorated. Its plan is that of an opera-house. Up toward the straight side of it — the stage side — rise a couple of terraces of desks for the ministry, and the official clerks or secretaries — terraces thirty feet long, and each supporting about half a dozen desks with spaces between them. Above these is the President's terrace, against the wall. Along it are distributed the proper accommodations for the presiding officer and his assistants. The wall is of richly colored marble highly polished, its paneled sweep relieved by fluted columns and pilasters of distinguished grace and dignity, which glow softly and frostily in the electric light. Around the spacious half-circle of the floor bends the great two-storied curve of the boxes, its frontage elaborately ornamented and sumptuously gilded. On the floor

of the House the 425 desks radiate fanwise from the
President's tribune.

The galleries are crowded on this particular evening,
for word has gone about that the *Ausgleich* is before
the House; that the President, Ritter von Abrahamowicz, has been throttling the Rules; that the
Opposition are in an inflammable state in consequence, and that the night session is likely to be
of an exciting sort.

The gallery guests are fashionably dressed, and
the finery of the women makes a bright and pretty
show under the strong electric light.   But down on
the floor there is no costumery.

The deputies are dressed in day clothes; some of
the clothes neat and trim, others not; there may be
three members in evening dress, but not more.
There are several Catholic priests in their long black
gowns, and with crucifixes hanging from their necks.
No member wears his hat.   One may see by these
details that the aspects are not those of an evening
sitting of an English House of Commons, but rather
those of a sitting of our House of Representatives.

In his high place sits the President, Abrahamowicz,
object of the Opposition's limitless hatred.   He is
sunk back in the depths of his arm-chair, and has his
chin down.   He brings the ends of his spread fingers
together in front of his breast, and reflectively taps
them together, with the air of one who would like to
begin business, but must wait, and be as patient as
he can.   It makes you think of Richelieu.   Now

N*₊*₊

and then he swings his head up to the left or to the right and answers something which some one has bent down to say to him. Then he taps his fingers again. He looks tired, and maybe a trifle harassed. He is a gray-haired, long, slender man, with a colorless long face, which, in repose, suggests a deathmask; but when not in repose is tossed and rippled by a turbulent smile which washes this way and that, and is not easy to keep up with — a pious smile, a holy smile, a saintly smile, a deprecating smile, a beseeching and supplicating smile; and when it is at work the large mouth opens and the flexible lips crumple, and unfold, and crumple again, and move around in a genial and persuasive and angelic way, and expose large glimpses of the teeth; and that interrupts the sacredness of the smile and gives it momentarily a mixed worldly and political and satanic cast. It is a most interesting face to watch. And then the long hands and the body — they furnish great and frequent help to the face in the business of adding to the force of the statesman's words.

To change the tense. At the time of which I have just been speaking the crowds in the galleries were gazing at the stage and the pit with rapt interest and expectancy. One half of the great fan of desks was in effect empty, vacant; in the other half several hundred members were bunched and jammed together as solidly as the bristles in a brush; and they also were waiting and expecting. Presently the Chair delivered this utterance:

" Dr. Lecher has the floor."

Then burst out such another wild and frantic and deafening clamor as has not been heard on this planet since the last time the Comanches surprised a white settlement at midnight.   Yells from the Left, counter-yells from the Right, explosions of yells from all sides at once, and all the air sawed and pawed and clawed and cloven by a writhing confusion of gesturing arms and hands.   Out of the midst of this thunder and turmoil and tempest rose Dr. Lecher, serene and collected, and the providential length of him enabled his head to show out above it.   He began his twelve-hour speech.   At any rate, his lips could be seen to move, and that was evidence.   On high sat the President imploring order, with his long hands put together as in prayer, and his lips visibly but not hearably speaking.   At intervals he grasped his bell and swung it up and down with vigor, adding its keen clamor to the storm weltering there below.

Dr. Lecher went on with his pantomime speech, contented, untroubled.   Here and there and now and then powerful voices burst above the din, and de-livered an ejaculation that was heard.   Then the din ceased for a moment or two, and gave opportunity to hear what the Chair might answer ; then the noise broke out again.   Apparently the President was being charged with all sorts of illegal exercises of power in the interest of the Right (the government side) : among these, with arbitrarily closing an Order of Business before it was finished ; with an unfair dis-

tribution of the right to the floor; with refusal of
the floor, upon quibble and protest, to members entitled to it; with stopping a speaker's speech upon
quibble and protest; and with other transgressions
of the Rules of the House. One of the interrupters
who made himself heard was a young fellow of slight
build and neat dress, who stood a little apart from
the solid crowd and leaned negligently, with folded
arms and feet crossed, against a desk. Trim and
handsome; strong face and thin features; black hair
roughed up; parsimonious mustache; resonant great
voice, of good tone and pitch. It is Wolf, capable
and hospitable with sword and pistol; fighter of the
recent duel with Count Badeni, the head of the
government. He shot Badeni through the arm, and
then walked over in the politest way and inspected
his game, shook hands, expressed regret, and all
that. Out of him came early this thundering peal,
audible above the storm:

"I demand the floor. I wish to offer a motion."

In the sudden lull which followed, the President
answered, " Dr. Lecher has the floor."

Wolf. " I move the close of the sitting!"

P. " Representative Lecher has the floor."
[Stormy outburst from the Left — that is, the
Opposition.]

Wolf. " I demand the floor for the introduction
of a formal motion. [Pause.] Mr. President, are
you going to grant it, or not? [Crash of approval

from the Left.]   I will keep on demanding the floor
till I get it."

P.   " I call Representative Wolf to order.   **Dr.**
Lecher has the floor."

Wolf.   " Mr. President, are you going to observe
the Rules of this House?"   [Tempest of applause
and confused ejaculations from the Left — a boom
and roar which long endured, and stopped all business for the time being.]

Dr. von Pessler.   " By the Rules motions are in
order, and the Chair *must* put them to vote."

For answer the President (who is a Pole — I make
this remark in passing) began to jangle his bell with
energy at the moment that that wild pandemonium
of voices burst out again.

Wolf (hearable above the storm).   " Mr. President, I demand the floor.   We intend to find out,
here and now, which is the hardest, *a Pole's skull or
a German's !*"

This brought out a perfect cyclone of satisfaction
from the Left.   In the midst of it some one again
moved an adjournment.   The President blandly
answered that Dr. Lecher had the floor.   Which was
true; and he was speaking, too, calmly, earnestly,
and argumentatively; and the official stenographers
had left their places and were at his elbows taking
down his words, he leaning and orating into their ears
— a most curious and interesting scene.

Dr. von Pessler (to the Chair).   " Do not drive
us to extremities !"

The tempest burst out again; yells of approval
from the Left, catcalls, an ironical laughter from
the Right.   At this point a new and most effective
noisemaker was pressed into service. Each desk has
an extension, consisting of a removable board
eighteen inches long, six wide, and a half-inch thick.
A member pulled one of these out and began to
belabor the top of his desk with it.   Instantly other
members followed suit, and perhaps you can imagine
the result.   Of all conceivable rackets it is the most
ear-splitting, intolerable, and altogether fiendish.

The persecuted President leaned back in his chair,
closed his eyes, clasped his hands in his lap, and a
look of pathetic resignation crept over his long face.
It is the way a country schoolmaster used to look in
days long past when he had refused his school a
holiday and it had risen against him in ill-mannered
riot and violence and insurrection.   Twice a motion
to adjourn had been offered — a motion always in
order in other Houses, and doubtless so in this one
also.   The President had refused to put these motions.
By consequence, he was not in a pleasant place now,
and was having a right hard time.   Votes upon
motions, whether carried or defeated, could make
endless delay, and postpone the *Ausgleich* to next
century.

In the midst of these sorrowful circumstances and
this hurricane of yells and screams and satanic clatter
of desk-boards, Representative Dr. Kronawetter un-
feelingly reminds the Chair that a motion has been

offered, and adds: " Say yes, or no! What do
you sit there for, and give no answer?"

P. " After I have given a speaker the floor, I
cannot give it to another. After Dr. Lecher is
through, I will put your motion." [Storm of in-
dignation from the Left.]

Wolf (to the Chair). " Thunder and lightning!
look at the Rule governing the case! "

Kronawetter. " I move the close of the sitting!
And I demand the ayes and noes! "

Dr. Lecher. " Mr. President, have I the floor? "

P. " You have the floor."

Wolf (to the Chair, in a stentorian voice which
cleaves its way through the storm). " It is by such
brutalities as these that you drive us to extremities!
Are you waiting till some one shall throw into your
face the word that shall describe what you are bringing
about?*   [Tempest of insulted fury from the Right.]
Is that what you are waiting for, old Grayhead?"
[Long-continued clatter of desk-boards from the Left,
with shouts of " The vote! the vote! " An ironical
shout from the Right, " Wolf is boss! "]

Wolf keeps on demanding the floor for his motion.
At length —

P. " I call Representative Wolf to order! Your
conduct is unheard-of, sir! You forget that you are
in a parliament; you must remember where you are,
sir." [Applause from the Right. Dr. Lecher is still

---

* That is, *revolution.*

peacefully speaking, the stenographers listening
his lips.]

Wolf (banging on his desk with his desk-board)
" I demand the floor for my motion! I won't stan
this trampling of the Rules under foot — no, not
I die for it! I will never yield! You have got to sto
me by force. Have I the floor?"

P. " Representative Wolf, what kind of behavic
is this? I call you to order again. You should hav
some regard for your dignity."

Dr. Lecher speaks on. Wolf turns upon him wit
an offensive innuendo.

Dr. Lecher. " Mr. Wolf, I beg you to refrai
from that sort of suggestions." [Storm of hand
clapping from the Right.]

This was applause from the enemy, for Leche
himself, like Wolf, was an Obstructionist.

Wolf growls to Lecher: " You can scribble tha
applause in your album!"

P. " Once more I call Representative Wolf t
order! Do not forget that you are a Representativ
sir!"

Wolf (slam-banging with his desk-board). "
will force this matter! Are you going to grant m
the floor, or not?"

And still the sergeant-at-arms did not appear.
was because there wasn't any. It is a curious thing
but the Chair has no effectual means of compellin
order.

After some more interruptions:

Wolf (banging with his board).   " I demand the
or.   I will not yield!"

P. " I have no recourse against Representative
olf.   In the presence of behavior like this it is to
regretted that such is the case."   [A shout from
Right, " Throw him out!"]

It is true, he had no effective recourse.   He had
official called an " Ordner," whose help he could
oke in desperate cases, but apparently the Ordner
only a persuader, not a compeller.   Apparently
is a sergeant-at-arms who is not loaded; a good
ough gun to look at, but not valuable for business.
For another twenty or thirty minutes Wolf went
banging with his board and demanding his rights;
n at last the weary President threatened to sum-
n the dread order-maker.   But both his manner
his words were reluctant.   Evidently it grieved
to have to resort to this dire extremity.   He
d to Wolf, " If this goes on, I shall feel obliged
summon the Ordner, and beg him to restore
er in the House."

Wolf. " I'd like to see you do it!   Suppose you
ch in a few policemen, too!   [Great tumult.]
you going to put my motion to adjourn, or
?"

)r. Lecher continues his speech.   Wolf accom-
ies him with his board-clatter.

The President despatches the Ordner, Dr. Lang
mself a deputy), on his order-restoring mission.
lf, with his board uplifted for defence, confronts

the Ordner with a remark which Boss Tweed migh
have translated into " Now let's see what you ar
going to do about it!" [Noise and tumult all ove
the House.]

Wolf stands upon his rights, and says he will main
tain them till he is killed in his tracks. Then he re
sumes his banging, the President jangles his bel
and begs for order, and the rest of the House aug
ments the racket the best it can.

Wolf. " I require an adjournment, because I find
myself personally threatened. [Laughter from th
Right.] Not that I fear for myself; I am only
anxious about what will happen to the man wh
touches me."

The Ordner. " I am not going to fight with you."

Nothing came of the efforts of the angel of peace
and he presently melted out of the scene and dis
appeared. Wolf went on with his noise and with hi
demands that he be granted the floor, resting hi
board at intervals to discharge criticisms and epithet
at the Chair. Once he reminded the Chairman o
his violated promise to grant him (Wolf) the floor
and said, " Whence I came, we call promise-breaker
rascals!" And he advised the Chairman to take hi
conscience to bed with him and use it as a pillow
Another time he said that the Chair was making itsel
ridiculous before all Europe. In fact, some of Wolf'
language was almost unparliamentary. By-and-by h
struck the idea of beating out a *tune* with his board
Later he decided to stop asking for the floor, an

o confer it upon himself.   And so he and Dr.
Lecher now spoke at the same time, and mingled
their speeches with the other noises, and nobody
heard either of them.   Wolf rested himself now and
then from speech-making by reading, in his clarion
voice, from a pamphlet.

I will explain that Dr. Lecher was not making
twelve-hour speech for pastime, but for an important purpose.   It was the government's intention
to push the *Ausgleich* through its preliminary stages
in this one sitting (for which it was the Order of the
Day), and then by vote refer it to a select committee.
It was the Majority's scheme — as charged by the
Opposition — to drown debate upon the bill by pure
noise — drown it out and stop it.   The debate being
thus ended, the vote upon the reference would follow
— with victory for the government.   But into the
government's calculations had not entered the
possibility of a single-barreled speech which should
occupy the entire time-limit of the sitting, and also
get itself delivered in spite of all the noise.   Goliah
was not expecting David.   But David was there;
and during twelve hours he tranquilly pulled statis-
tical, historical, and argumentative pebbles out of his
scrip and slung them at the giant; and when he was
done he was victor, and the day was saved.

In the English House an obstructionist has held
the floor with Bible-readings and other outside
matters; but Dr. Lecher could not have that restful
and recuperative privilege — he must confine himself

15E

strictly to the subject before the House. More th
once, when the President could not hear him becau
of the general tumult, he sent persons to listen a
report as to whether the orator was speaking to t
subject or not.

The subject was a peculiarly difficult one, and
would have troubled any other deputy to stick tc
three hours without exhausting his ammunitic
because it required a vast and intimate knowledge
detailed and particularized knowledge — of the co
mercial, railroading, financial, and international ba
ing relations existing between two great sovereignti
Hungary and the Empire. But Dr. Lecher is Pre
dent of the Board of Trade of his city of Brünn, a
was master of the situation. His speech was
formally prepared. He had a few notes jotted do
for his guidance; he had his facts in his head;
heart was in his work; and for twelve hours he stc
there, undisturbed by the clamor around him,
with grace and ease and confidence poured out
riches of his mind, in closely reasoned argume
clothed in eloquent and faultless phrasing.

He is a young man of thirty-seven. He is
and well-proportioned, and has cultivated and fo
fied his muscle by mountain-climbing. If he wei
little handsomer he would sufficiently reproduce
me the Chauncey Depew of the great New Engl
dinner nights of some years ago; he has Depe
charm of manner and graces of language
delivery.

There was but one way for Dr. Lecher to hold the
·or — he must stay on his legs. If he should sit
·wn to rest a moment, the floor would be taken
·m him by the enemy in the Chair. When he had
·en talking three or four hours he himself proposed
 adjournment, in order that he might get some rest
·m his wearing labors; but he limited his motion
·th the condition that if it was lost he should be
·owed to continue his speech, and if it carried he
·ould have the floor at the next sitting. Wolf was
·w appeased, and withdrew his own thousand-times
·ered motion, and Dr. Lecher's was voted upon —
·d lost. So he went on speaking.

By one o'clock in the morning, excitement and
·ise-making had tired out nearly everybody but the
·ator. Gradually the seats of the Right underwent
·population; the occupants had slipped out to the
·reshment-rooms to eat and drink, or to the cor-
·ors to chat. Some one remarked that there was
 longer a quorum present, and moved a call of the
·use. The Chair (Vice-President Dr. Kramarz)
·used to put it to vote. There was a small dispute
·er the legality of this ruling, but the Chair held its
·ound.

The Left remained on the battle-field to support
·ir champion. He went steadily on with his speech;
·d always it was strong, virile, felicitous, and to
· point. He was earning applause, and this enabled
· party to turn that fact to account. Now and then
·y applauded him a couple of minutes on a stretch,

and during that time he could stop speaking and res
his voice without having the floor taken from him.

At a quarter to two a member of the Left de
manded that Dr. Lecher be allowed a recess for rest
and said that the Chairman was " heartless." Dr
Lecher himself asked for ten minutes. The Chai
allowed him five. Before the time had run out Dr
Lecher was on his feet again.

Wolf burst out again with a motion to adjourn
Refused by the Chair. Wolf said the whole par
liament wasn't worth a pinch of powder. Th
Chair retorted that that was true in a case wher
a single member was able to make all parliamentary
business impossible. Dr. Lecher continued hi
speech.

The members of the Majority went out by detach
ments from time to time and took naps upon sofa
in the reception-rooms; and also refreshed them
selves with food and drink — in quantities nearly
unbelievable — but the Minority staid loyally by
their champion. Some distinguished deputies of th
Majority staid by him, too, compelled thereto b
admiration of his great performance. When a ma
has been speaking eight hours, is it conceivable tha
he can still be interesting, still fascinating? Whe
Dr. Lecher had been speaking eight hours he wa
still compactly surrounded by friends who would no
leave him and by foes (of all parties) who *could* not
and all hung enchanted and wondering upon hi
words, and all testified their admiration with constan

nd cordial outbursts of applause. Surely this was
triumph without precedent in history.

During the twelve-hour effort friends brought to
he orator three glasses of wine, four cups of coffee,
nd one glass of beer — a most stingy re-enforce-
nent of his wasting tissues, but the hostile Chair
vould permit no addition to it. But no matter, the
Chair could not beat that man. He was a garrison
olding a fort, and was not to be starved out.

When he had been speaking eight hours his pulse
vas 72; when he had spoken twelve, it was 100.

He finished his long speech in these terms, as
early as a permissibly free translation can convey
hem:

"I will now hasten to close my examination of
he subject. I conceive that we of the Left have
nade it clear to the honorable gentlemen of the other
ide of the House that we are stirred by no in-
emperate enthusiasm for this measure in its present
hape. . . .

"What we require, and shall fight for with all
awful weapons, is a formal, comprehensive, and
efinitive solution and settlement of these vexed
natters. We desire the restoration of the earlier
ondition of things; the cancellation of all this in-
apable government's pernicious trades with Hun-
ary; and then — release from the sorry burden of
he Badeni ministry!

"I voice the hope — I know not if it will be ful-
lled — I voice the deep and sincere and patriotic
    15*͙*͙*͙

hope that the committee into whose hands this bill
will eventually be committed will take its stand upon
high ground, and will return the *Ausgleich-Pro-
visorium* to this House in a form which shall make
it the protector and promoter alike of the great
interests involved and of the honor of our father-
land." After a pause, turning toward the government benches: " But in any case, gentlemen of the
Majority, make sure of this: henceforth, as before,
you will find us at our post. The Germans of Austria
will neither surrender nor die !"

Then burst a storm of applause which rose and
fell, rose and fell, burst out again and again and
again, explosion after explosion, hurricane after
hurricane, with no apparent promise of ever coming
to an end; and meantime the whole Left was surging
and weltering about the champion, all bent upon
wringing his hand and congratulating him and glori-
fying him.

Finally he got away, and went home and ate five
loaves and twelve baskets of fishes, read the morning
papers, slept three hours, took a short drive, then
returned to the House and sat out the rest of the
thirty-three-hour session.

To merely *stand up* in one spot twelve hours on
a stretch is a feat which very few men could achieve;
to add to the task the utterance of a hundred thousand
words would be beyond the possibilities of the most
of those few; to superimpose the requirement that
the words should be put into the form of a compact,

coherent, and symmetrical oration would probably
rule out the rest of the few, bar Dr. Lecher.

III. CURIOUS PARLIAMENTARY ETIQUETTE

In consequence of Dr. Lecher's twelve-hour speech
and the other obstructions furnished by the Minority,
the famous thirty-three-hour sitting of the House
accomplished nothing. The government side had
made a supreme effort, assisting itself with all the
helps at hand, both lawful and unlawful, yet had
failed to get the *Ausgleich* into the hands of a committee. This was a severe defeat. The Right was
mortified, the Left jubilant.

Parliament was adjourned for a week — to let the
members cool off, perhaps — a sacrifice of precious
time, for but two months remained in which to carry
the all-important *Ausgleich* to a consummation.

If I have reported the behavior of the House in-
telligibly, the reader has been surprised at it, and has
wondered whence these law-makers come and what
they are made of; and he has probably supposed
that the conduct exhibited at the Long Sitting was
far out of the common, and due to special excitement and irritation. As to the make-up of the
House, it is this: the deputies come from all the
walks of life and from all the grades of society.
There are princes, counts, barons, priests, peasants,
mechanics, laborers, lawyers, judges, physicians,
professors, merchants, bankers, shopkeepers. They
are religious men, they are earnest, sincere, de-

o*₋*₋*

voted, and they hate the Jews. The title of
Doctor is so common in the House that one may
almost say that the deputy who does not bear it is
by that reason conspicuous. I am assured that it is
not a self-granted title, and not an honorary one, but
an *earned* one; that in Austria it is very seldom conferred as a mere compliment; that in Austria the
degrees of Doctor of Music, Doctor of Philosophy,
and so on, are not conferred by the seats of learning;
and so, when an Austrian is called Doctor it means
that he is either a lawyer or a physician, and that
he is not a self-educated man, but is college-bred,
and has been diplomaed for merit.

That answers the question of the constitution of
the House. Now as to the House's curious manners.
The manners exhibited by this convention of Doctors
were not at that time being tried as a wholly new experiment. I will go back to a previous sitting in
order to show that the deputies had already had some
practice.

There had been an incident. The dignity of the
House had been wounded by improprieties indulged
in in its presence by a couple of the members. This
matter was placed in the hands of a committee to
determine where the guilt lay, and the degree of it,
and also to suggest the punishment. The chairman
of the committee brought in his report. By this it
appeared that, in the course of a speech, Deputy
Schrammel said that religion had no proper place
in the public schools — it was a private matter.

Whereupon Deputy Gregorig shouted, " How about
free love !"

To this, Deputy Iro flung out this retort : " Soda-
water at the Wimberger !"

This appeared to deeply offend Deputy Gregorig,
who shouted back at Iro, " You cowardly blatherskite, say that again !"

The committee had sat three hours. Gregorig
had apologized; Iro had explained. Iro explained
that he didn't say anything about soda-water at the
Wimberger. He explained in writing, and was very
explicit : " I declare *upon my word of honor* that I
did not say the words attributed to me."

Unhappily for his word of honor it was proved by
the official stenographers and by the testimony of
several deputies that he *did* say them.

The committee did not officially know why the
apparently inconsequential reference to soda-water
at the Wimberger should move Deputy Gregorig to
call the utterer of it a cowardly blatherskite; still,
after proper deliberation, it was of the opinion that
the House ought to formally censure the whole business. This verdict seems to have been regarded as
sharply severe. I think so because Deputy Dr.
Lueger, Bürgermeister of Vienna, felt it a duty to
soften the blow to his friend Gregorig by showing
that the soda-water remark was not so innocuous as
it might look; that indeed Gregorig's tough retort
was justifiable — and he proceeded to explain why.
He read a number of scandalous post-cards which

he intimated had proceeded from Iro, as indicated
by the handwriting, though they were anonymous.
Some of them were posted to Gregorig at his place
of business, and could have been read by all his
subordinates; the others were posted *to Gregorig's
wife*. Lueger did not say — but everybody knew
— that the cards referred to a matter of town gossip
which made Mr. Gregorig a chief actor in a tavern
scene where siphon squirting played a prominent and
humorous part, and wherein women had a share.

There were several of the cards; more than several,
in fact; no fewer than five were sent in one day.
Dr. Lueger read some of them, and described others.
Some of them had pictures on them; one a picture
of a hog with a monstrous snout, and beside it
a squirting soda-siphon; below it some sarcastic
doggerel.

Gregorig deals in shirts, cravats, etc. One of the
cards bore these words: " Much respected Deputy
and collar-sewer — or *stealer*."

Another: " Hurrah for the Christian-Social work
among the women-assemblages! Hurrah for the
soda-squirter!" Comment by Dr. Lueger: " I
cannot venture to read the rest of that one, nor
the signature, either."

Another: "Would you mind telling me if . . ."
Comment by Dr. Lueger: " The rest of it is
not properly readable."

To Deputy Gregorig's wife: " Much respected
Madam Gregorig, — The undersigned desires **an**

invitation to the next soda-squirt." Comment by
Dr. Lueger: " Neither the rest of the card nor the
signature can I venture to read to the House, so
vulgar are they."

The purpose of this card — to expose Gregorig
to his family — was repeated in others of these
anonymous missives.

The House, by vote, censured the two improper
deputies.

This may have had a modifying effect upon the
phraseology of the membership for awhile, and upon
its general exuberance also, but it was not for long.
As has been seen, it had become lively once more
on the night of the Long Sitting. At the next
sitting after the long one there was certainly no lack
of liveliness. The President was persistently ignoring the Rules of the House in the interest of the
government side, and the Minority were in an
unappeasable fury about it. The ceaseless din
and uproar, the shouting and stamping and desk-
banging, were deafening, but through it all burst
voices now and then that made themselves heard.
Some of the remarks were of a very candid sort,
and I believe that if they had been uttered in
our House of Representatives they would have attracted attention. I will insert some samples here.
Not in their order, but selected on their merits:

Dr. Mayreder (to the President). " You have
lied ! You conceded the floor to me; make it good,
or you have lied !"

Mr. Glöckner (to the President). "Leave! Get out!"

Wolf (indicating the President). "There sits a man to whom a certain title belongs!"

Unto Wolf, who is continuously reading, in a powerful voice, from a newspaper, arrive these personal remarks from the Majority: "Oh, shut your mouth!" "Put him out!" "Out with him!" Wolf stops reading a moment to shout at Dr. Lueger who has the floor, but cannot get a hearing, "Please Betrayer of the People, begin!"

Dr. Lueger. "Meine Herren —" ["Oho!" and groans.]

Wolf. "*That's* the holy light of the Christian Socialists!"

Mr. Kletzenbauer (Christian Socialist). "Damnation! are you ever going to quiet down?"

Wolf discharges a galling remark at Mr. Wohlmeyer.

Wohlmeyer (responding). "You Jew, you!"

There is a moment's lull, and Dr. Lueger begins his speech. Graceful, handsome man, with winning manners and attractive bearing, a bright and easy speaker, and is said to know how to trim his political sails to catch any favoring wind that blows. He manages to say a few words, then the tempest overwhelms him again.

Wolf stops reading his paper a moment to say a drastic thing about Lueger and his Christian-Social pieties, which sets the C. S.'s in a sort of frenzy.

Mr. Vielohlawek. " You leave the Christian
ocialists alone, you word-of-honor-breaker! Ob-
truct all you want to, but you leave *them* alone!
ou've no business in this House; you belong in a
in-mill!"

Mr. Prochazka. " In a lunatic-asylum, you
ean!"

Vielohlawek. " It's a pity that such a man should
e leader of the Germans; he disgraces the German
ame!"

Dr. Scheicher. " It's a shame that the like of him
hould insult us."

Strohbach (to Wolf). "Contemptible cub — we
ill bounce thee out of this!" [It is inferable that
he " thee " is not intended to indicate affection this
me, but to re-enforce and emphasize Mr. Stroh-
ach's scorn.]

Dr. Scheicher. " His insults are of no consequence.
e wants his ears boxed."

Dr. Lueger (to Wolf). " You'd better worry a
fle over your Iro's word of honor. You are
having like a street arab."

Dr. Scheicher. " It's infamous!"

Dr. Lueger. "And *these* shameless creatures are
e leaders of the German People's Party!"

Meantime Wolf goes whooping along with his
wspaper-readings in great contentment.

Dr. Pattai. " Shut up! Shut up! Shut *up!* You
ven't the floor!"

Strohbach. " The miserable cub!"

Dr. Lueger (to Wolf, raising his voice strenuous
above the storm). "You are a wholly honorl
street brat!" [A voice, "Fire the rapscallion out
But Wolf's soul goes marching noisily on, just t
same.]

Schönerer (vast and muscular, and endowed w
the most powerful voice in the Reichsrath; con
ploughing down through the standing crowds, re
and choking with anger; halts before Deputy Wo
meyer, grabs a rule and smashes it with a blow up
a desk, threatens Wohlmeyer's face with his fi
and bellows out some personalities, and a promise
"Only you wait — we'll teach you!" [A whi
wind of offensive retorts assails him from the ba
of meek and humble Christian Socialists compact
around their leader, that distinguished religious e
pert, Dr. Lueger, Bürgermeister of Vienna. C
breath comes in excited gasps now, and we a
full of hope. We imagine that we are back fi
years ago in the Arkansas Legislature, and
think we know what is going to happen, and a
glad we came, and glad we are up in the galle
out of the way, where we can see the wh
thing and yet not have to supply any of
material for the inquest. However, as it tur
out, our confidence is abused, our hopes are m
placed.]

Dr. Pattai (wildly excited). "You quiet down,
we shall turn ourselves loose! There will be a cuffi
of ears!"

Prochazka (in a fury). "No — *not* ear-boxing,
t genuine *blows!* "

Vielohlawek. "I would rather take my hat off to
[ew than to Wolf!"

Strohbach (to Wolf). " Jew-flunky! Here we
ve been fighting the Jews for ten years, and now
u are helping them to power again. How much
you get for it?"

Holansky. " What he wants is a strait-jacket!"

Wolf continues his readings. It is a market re-
rt now.

Remark flung across the House to Schönerer:
*Die Grossmutter auf dem Misthaufen erzeugt
rden!* "

It will be judicious not to translate that. Its flavor
pretty high, in any case, but it becomes particularly
mey when you remember that the first gallery was
ll stocked with ladies.

Apparently it was a great hit. It fetched thunders
joyous enthusiasm out of the Christian Socialists,
d in their rapture they flung biting epithets with
steful liberality at specially detested members of
 Opposition; among others, this one at Schönerer:
Bordell in der Krugerstrasse ! " Then they added
ese words, which they whooped, howled, and also
n sang, in a deep-voiced chorus: " *Schmul Leeb
hn ! Schmul Leeb Kohn ! Schmul Leeb Kohn !* "
d made it splendidly audible above the banging of
sk-boards and the rest of the roaring cyclone of
ndish noises. [A gallery witticism comes flitting

by from mouth to mouth around the great curve
" The swan-song of Austrian representative gov
ernment!" You can note its progress by th
applausive smiles and nods it gets as it skim
along.]

Kletzenbauer. " Holofernes, where is Judith?"
[Storm of laughter.]

Gregorig (the shirt-merchant). " This Wol
Theater is costing 6,000 florins!"

Wolf (with sweetness). " Notice him, gentlemen
it is Mr. Gregorig." [Laughter.]

Vielohlawek (to Wolf). " You Judas!"

Schneider. " Brothel-Knight!"

Chorus of Voices. " East-German offal-tub!"

And so the war of epithets crashes along, wit
never-diminishing energy, for a couple of hours.

The ladies in the gallery were learning. That w
well; for by-and-by ladies will form a part of tl
membership of all the legislatures in the world;
soon as they can prove competency they will l
admitted. At present, men only are competent
legislate; therefore they look down upon wome
and would feel degraded if they had to have the
for colleagues in their high calling.

Wolf is yelling another market report now.

Gessman. "Shut up, infamous louse-brat!"

During a momentary lull Dr. Lueger gets a heari
for three sentences of his speech. They dema
and require that the President shall suppress the fo
noisiest members of the Opposition.

Wolf (with a that-settles-it toss of the head).
The shifty trickster of Vienna has spoken!''
Iro belonged to Schönerer's party.   The word-of-
onor incident has given it a new name.   Gregorig
a Christian Socialist, and hero of the post-cards
d the Wimberger soda-squirting incident.   He
ands vast and conspicuous, and conceited and self-
tisfied, and roosterish and inconsequential, at
ueger's elbow, and is proud and cocky to be in
ch great company.   He looks very well indeed;
ally majestic, and aware of it.   He crows out his
tle empty remark, now and then, and looks as
eased as if he had been delivered of the *Ausgleich*.
deed, he does look notably fine.   He wears almost
e only dress vest on the floor; it exposes a con-
ental spread of white shirt-front; his hands are
osed at ease in the lips of his trousers pockets; his
ad is tilted back complacently; he is attitudinizing;
is playing to the gallery.   However, they are all
ing that.   It is curious to see.   Men who only
te, and can't make speeches, and don't know how
invent witty ejaculations, wander about the vacated
rts of the floor, and stop in a good place and strike
itudes — attitudes suggestive of weighty thought,
ostly — and glance furtively up at the galleries to
 how it works; or a couple will come together
d shake hands in an artificial way, and laugh a gay
nufactured laugh, and do some constrained and
f-conscious attitudinizing; and *they* steal glances
 the galleries to see if they are getting notice.

16E

It is like a scene on the stage — by-play by mi
actors at the back while the stars do the great w
at the front.   Even Count Badeni attitudinizes
a moment;   strikes a reflective Napoleonic attit
of fine picturesqueness—but soon thinks better
it and desists.   There are two who do not attitud
ize—poor harried and insulted President Abraha
owicz, who seems wholly miserable, and can find
way to put in the dreary time but by swinging
bell and by discharging occasional remarks wh
nobody can hear;   and a resigned and patient pri
who sits lonely in a great vacancy on Majo
territory and munches an apple.

Schönerer uplifts his fog-horn of a voice
shakes the roof with an insult discharged at
Majority.

Dr. Lueger. " The Honorless Party would be
keep still here !''

Gregorig (the echo, swelling out his shirt-fro
'' Yes, keep quiet, pimp !''

Schönerer (to Lueger).   ''Political mountebank

Prochazka (to Schönerer).   '' Drunken clown !'

During the final hour of the sitting many ha
phrases were distributed through the proceedin
Among them were these — and they are strikin
good ones:

Blatherskite !
Blackguard !
Scoundrel !
Brothel-daddy !

This last was the contribution of Dr. Gessman,
d gave great satisfaction. And deservedly. It
:ms to me that it was one of the most sparkling
ngs that was said during the whole evening.

At half-past two in the morning the House ad-
rned. The victory was with the Opposition.
·; not quite that. The effective part of it was
tched away from them by an unlawful exercise
Presidential force — another contribution toward
ving the mistreated Minority out of their minds.

At other sittings of the parliament, gentlemen of
Opposition, shaking their fists toward the Presi-
t, addressed him as " Polish Dog." At one
ing an angry deputy turned upon a colleague
 shouted,

' — — — — — — !"

ou must try to imagine what it was. If I should
·r it even in the original it would probably not get
 the Magazine editor's blue pencil; to offer a
 slation would be to waste my ink, of course.
 s remark was frankly printed in its entirety by
 of the Vienna dailies, but the others disguised
 toughest half of it with stars.

f the reader will go back over this chapter and
 er its array of extraordinary epithets into a bunch
 examine them, he will marvel at two things:
· this convention of gentlemen could consent to
 such gross terms; and why the users were
wed to get out of the place alive. There is no
 to understand this strange situation. If every

man in the House were a professional blackguard
and had his home in a sailor boarding-house, or
could still not understand it; for although that sort
do use such terms, they never *take* them. These men
are not professional blackguards; they are mainly
gentlemen, and educated; yet they use the terms
and take them, too. They really seem to attach a
consequence to them. One cannot say that they are
like schoolboys; for that is only almost true, not
entirely. Schoolboys blackguard each other fiercely
and by the hour, and one would think that nothing
would ever come of it but noise; but that would
be a mistake. Up to a certain limit the result would
be noise only, but that limit overstepped, trouble
would follow right away. There are certain phrases
—phrases of a peculiar character—phrases of the
nature of that reference to Schönerer's grandmother
for instance, which not even the most spiritless school-
boy in the English-speaking world would allow to
pass unavenged. One difference between schoolboys and the law-makers of the Reichsrath seems to
be that the law-makers have no limit, no danger-line.
Apparently they may call each other what they please,
and go home unmutilated.

Now, in fact, they did have a scuffle on two
occasions, but it was not on account of names
called. There has been no scuffle where *that* was
the cause.

It is not to be inferred that the House lacks a sense
of honor because it lacks delicacy. That would be

error. Iro was caught in a lie, and it profoundly
sgraced him. The House cut him, turned its back
on him. He resigned his seat; otherwise he would
ve been expelled. But it was lenient with Gregorig,
10 had called Iro a cowardly blatherskite in debate.
merely went through the form of mildly censuring
n. That did not trouble Gregorig.

The Viennese say of themselves that they are an
sy-going, pleasure-loving community, making the
st of life, and not taking it very seriously. Never-
eless, they are grieved about the ways of their parlia-
ent, and say quite frankly that they are ashamed.
ey claim that the low condition of the parliament's
unners is new, not old. A gentleman who was at
e head of the government twenty years ago con-
ms this, and says that in his time the parliament
s orderly and well-behaved. An English gentle-
un of long residence here endorses this, and says
at a low order of politicians originated the present
ms of questionable speech on the stump some
ars ago, and imported them into the parliament.*
>wever, some day there will be a Minister of
iquette and a sergeant-at-arms, and then things
l go better. I mean if parliament and the Con-
:ution survive the present storm.

---

* In that gracious bygone time when a mild and good-tempered
it was the atmosphere of our House, when the manner of our speak-
was studiously formal and academic, and the storms and explosions
:o-day were wholly unknown," etc.— *Translation of the opening
ark of an editorial in this morning's Neue Freie Presse, December
16**.*

IV. THE HISTORIC CLIMAX.

During the whole of November things went from
bad to worse. The all-important *Ausgleich* remained
hard aground, and could not be sparred off. Badeni's
government could not withdraw the Language Ordi-
nance and keep its majority, and the Opposition
could not be placated on easier terms. One night
while the customary pandemonium was crashing
and thundering along at its best, a fight broke out.
It was a surging, struggling, shoulder-to-shoulder
scramble. A great many blows were struck. Twice
Schönerer lifted one of the heavy ministerial fauteuils
—some say with one hand—and threatened members
of the Majority with it, but it was wrenched away
from him; a member hammered Wolf over the head
with the President's bell, and another member choked
him; a professor was flung down and belabored with
fists and choked; he held up an open penknife as a
defence against the blows; it was snatched from him
and flung to a distance; it hit a peaceful Christian
Socialist who wasn't doing anything, and brought
blood from his hand. This was the only blood
drawn. The men who got hammered and choked
looked sound and well next day. The fists and the
bell were not properly handled, or better results would
have been apparent. I am quite sure that the fighters
were not in earnest.

On Thanksgiving day the sitting was a history-
making one. On that day the harried, bedeviled
and despairing government went insane. In order

free itself from the thraldom of the Opposition it
committed this curiously juvenile crime: it moved an
important change of the Rules of the House, forbade
debate upon the motion, put it to a stand-up vote
instead of ayes and noes, and then gravely claimed
that it had been adopted; whereas, to even the dullest
witness — if I without immodesty may pretend to
that place — it was plain that nothing legitimately
be called a vote had been taken at all

I think that Saltpeter never uttered a truer thing
than when he said, "Whom the gods would destroy
they first make mad."

Evidently the government's mind was tottering
when this bald insult to the House was the best way
could contrive for getting out of the frying-pan.

The episode would have been funny if the matter
stake had been a trifle; but in the circumstances
was pathetic. The usual storm was raging in the
ouse. As usual, many of the Majority and the
most of the Minority were standing up — to have a
better chance to exchange epithets and make other
noises. Into this storm Count Falkenhayn entered,
with his paper in his hand; and at once there was a
rush to get near him and hear him read his motion.

a moment he was walled in by listeners. The
several clauses of his motion were loudly applauded
these allies, and as loudly disapplauded — if I
ay invent a word — by such of the Opposition as
uld hear his voice. When he took his seat the
esident promptly put the motion — persons desiring

to vote in the affirmative, *stand up!* The Hou
was already standing up; had been standing for
hour; and before a third of it had found out wh
the President had been saying, he had proclaim
the adoption of the motion! And only a few hea
that. In fact, when that House is legislating y
can't tell it from artillery-practice.

You will realize what a happy idea it was
side-track the lawful ayes and noes and substitu
a stand-up vote by this fact: that a little lat
when a deputation of deputies waited upon t
President and asked him if he was actually w
ing to claim that that measure had been passe
he answered, "Yes—and *unanimously.*" It sho
that in effect the whole house was on its f
when that trick was sprung.

The "Lex Falkenhayn," thus strangely bo
gave the President power to suspend for three da
any deputy who should continue to be disorde
after being called to order twice, and it also plac
at his disposal such force as might be necessary
make the suspension effective. So the House ha
sergeant-at-arms at last, and a more formidable o
as to power, than any other legislature in Christ
dom had ever possessed. The Lex Falkenhayn a
gave the House itself authority to suspend memb
for *thirty* days.

On these terms the *Ausgleich* could be put throu
in an hour — apparently. The Opposition wo
have to sit meek and quiet, and stop obstructing,

turned into the street, deputy after deputy, leaving
e Majority an unvexed field for its work.

Certainly the thing looked well.   The government
s out of the frying-pan at last.   It congratulated
elf, and was almost girlishly happy.   Its stock rose
ddenly from less than nothing to a premium.   It
nfessed to itself, with pride, that its Lex Falkenhayn
s a master-stroke — a work of genius.

However, there were doubters; men who were
ubled, and believed that a grave mistake had been
de.   It might be that the Opposition was crushed,
d profitably for the country, too; but the *manner*
it — the *manner* of it!   That was the serious part.
could have far-reaching results; results whose
avity might transcend all guessing.   It might be
initial step toward a return to government by
ce, a restoration of the irresponsible methods of
solete times.

There were no vacant seats in the galleries next
y.   In fact, standing-room outside the building
s at a premium.   There were crowds there, and a
ttering array of helmeted and brass-buttoned
lice, on foot and on horseback, to keep them from
ting too much excited.   No one could guess what
s going to happen, but every one felt that *some-
ng* was going to happen, and hoped he might have
hance to see it, or at least get the news of it while
vas fresh.

At noon the House was empty — for I do not
nt myself.   Half an hour later the two galleries

were solidly packed, the floor still empty. Anothe
half-hour later Wolf entered and passed to his place
then other deputies began to stream in, among ther
many forms and faces grown familiar of late. B
one o'clock the membership was present in full force
A band of Socialists stood grouped against th
ministerial desks, in the shadow of the Presidenti:
tribune. It was observable that these official strong
holds were now protected against rushes by bolte
gates, and that these were in ward of servant
wearing the House's livery. Also the removabl
desk-boards had been taken away, and nothing le:
for disorderly members to slat with.

There was a pervading, anxious hush — at lea:
what stood very well for a hush in that house.
was believed by many that the Opposition was cowec
and that there would be no more obstruction, n
more noise. That was an error.

Presently the President entered by the distant doc
to the right, followed by Vice-President Fuchs, an
the two took their way down past the Polish bench
toward the tribune. Instantly the customary stor:
of noises burst out, and rose higher and higher, an
wilder and wilder, and really seemed to surpass an
thing that had gone before it in that place. Th
President took his seat, and begged for order, but n
one could hear him. His lips moved — one coul
see that; he bowed his body forward appealingl
and spread his great hand eloquently over his brea
— one could see that; but as concerned his uttere

words, he probably could not hear them himself. Below him was that crowd of two dozen Socialists glaring up at him, shaking their fists at him, roaring imprecations and insulting epithets at him. This went on for some time. Suddenly the Socialists burst through the gates and stormed up through the ministerial benches, and a man in a red cravat reached up and snatched the documents that lay on the President's desk and flung them abroad. The next moment he and his allies were struggling and fighting with the half-dozen uniformed servants who were there to protect the new gates. Meantime a detail of Socialists had swarmed up the side steps and over-flowed the President and the Vice, and were crowd-ing and shouldering and shoving them out of the place. They crowded them out, and down the steps and across the House, past the Polish benches; and all about them swarmed hostile Poles and Czechs, who resisted them. One could see fists go up and come down, with other signs and shows of a heady fight; then the President and the Vice disappeared through the door of entrance, and the victorious Socialists turned and marched back, mounted the tribune, flung the President's bell and his remaining papers abroad, and then stood there in a compact little crowd, eleven strong, and held the place as if it were a fortress. Their friends on the floor were in a frenzy of triumph, and manifested it in their deafening way. The whole House was on its feet, amazed and wondering.

It was an astonishing situation, and imposing dramatic. Nobody had looked for this. The un expected had happened. What next? But there *can* be no next; the play is over; the grand clima is reached; the possibilities are exhausted: rin down the curtain.

Not yet. That distant door opens again. An now we see what history will be talking of fi centuries hence: a uniformed and helmeted battalic of bronzed and stalwart men marching in double fi down the floor of the House — a free parliame profaned by an invasion of brute force

It was an odious spectacle — odious and awfu For one moment it was an unbelievable thing — thing beyond all credibility; it must be a delusion, dream, a nightmare. But no, it was real — pitifu real, shamefully real, hideously real. These six policemen had been soldiers, and they went at th work with the cold unsentimentality of their trad They ascended the steps of the tribune, laid th hands upon the inviolable persons of the represe atives of a nation, and dragged and tugged a hauled them down the steps and out at the door; th ranged themselves in stately military array in fr of the ministerial *estrade*, and so stood.

It was a tremendous episode. The memory of will outlast all the thrones that exist to-day. In whole history of free parliaments the like of it h been seen but three times before. It takes its i posing place among the world's unforgettable thin

I think that in my lifetime I have not twice seen abiding history made before my eyes, but I know that I have seen it once.

Some of the results of this wild freak followed instantly. The Badeni government came down with a crash; there was a popular outbreak or two in Vienna; there were three or four days of furious rioting in Prague, followed by the establishing there of martial law; the Jews and Germans were harried and plundered, and their houses destroyed; in other Bohemian towns there was rioting — in some cases the Germans being the rioters, in others the Czechs — and in all cases the Jew had to roast, no matter which side he was on. We are well along in December now;* the new Minister-President has not been able to patch up a peace among the warring factions of the parliament, therefore there is no use in calling it together again for the present; public opinion believes that parliamentary government and the Constitution are actually threatened with extinction, and that the permanency of the monarchy itself is a not absolutely certain thing!

Yes, the Lex Falkenhayn was a great invention, and did what was claimed for it — it got the government out of the frying-pan.

---

* It is the 9th.— M. T.

CONCERNING THE JEWS

SOME months ago I published a magazine artic
descriptive of a remarkable scene in tl
Imperial Parliament in Vienna. Since then I ha·
received from Jews in America several letters of i
quiry. They were difficult letters to answer, f·
they were not very definite. But at last I received
definite one. It is from a lawyer, and he really asl
the questions which the other writers probably b·
lieved they were asking. By help of this text I w·
do the best I can to publicly answer this co
respondent, and also the others — at the same tin
apologizing for having failed to reply privatel·
The lawyer's letter reads as follows:

I have read "Stirring Times in Austria." One point in particul·
is of vital import to not a few thousand people, including myself, beii
a point about which I have often wanted to address a question to sor
disinterested person. The show of military force in the Austrian Parli·
ment, which precipitated the riots, was not introduced by any Jew. I
Jew was a member of that body. No Jewish question was involved
the Ausgleich or in the language proposition. No Jew was insulti
anybody. In short, no Jew was doing any mischief toward anybo·
whatsoever. In fact, the Jews were the only ones of the nineteen d
ferent races in Austria which did not have a party — they are absolute
non-participants. Yet in your article you say that in the rioting whi·
followed, all classes of people were unanimous only on one thing, vi·

n being against the Jews. Now will you kindly tell me why, in your
udgment, the Jews have thus ever been, and are even now, in these
lays of supposed intelligence, the butt of baseless, vicious animosities?
 dare say that for centuries there has been no more quiet, undisturbing,
nd well-behaving citizens, as a class, than that same Jew.   It seems to
me that ignorance and fanaticism cannot alone account for these horri-
le and unjust persecutions.

Tell me, therefore, from your vantage-point of cold view, what in
our mind is the cause. Can American Jews do anything to correct it
ither in America or abroad? Will it ever come to an end? Will a
ew be permitted to live honestly, decently, and peaceably like the rest
f mankind? What has become of the golden rule?

I will begin by saying that if I thought myself
prejudiced against the Jew, I should hold it fairest
o leave this subject to a person not crippled in that
vay.   But I think I have no such prejudice.   A few
ears ago a Jew observed to me that there was no
ncourteous reference to his people in my books,
nd asked how it happened.   It happened because
he disposition was lacking.   I am quite sure that
bar one) I have no race prejudices, and I think I
ave no color prejudices nor caste prejudices nor
reed prejudices.   Indeed, I know it.   I can stand
ny society.   All that I care to know is that a man
s a human being — that is enough for me; he can't
e any worse.   I have no special regard for Satan;
ut I can at least claim that I have no prejudice
gainst him.   It may even be that I lean a little his
vay, on account of his not having a fair show.   All
eligions issue bibles against him, and say the most
njurious things about him, but we never hear *his*
ide.   We have none but the evidence for the prose-

cution, and yet we have rendered the verdict. To my mind, this is irregular. It is un-English; it is un-American; it is French. Without this precedent Dreyfus could not have been condemned. Of course Satan has some kind of a case, it goes without saying. It may be a poor one, but that is nothing; that can be said about any of us. As soon as I can get at the facts I will undertake his rehabilitation myself, if I can find an unpolitic publisher. It is a thing which we ought to be willing to do for any one who is under a cloud. We may not pay him reverence, for that would be indiscreet, but we can at least respect his talents. A person who has for untold centuries maintained the imposing position of spiritual head of four-fifths of the human race, and political head of the whole of it, must be granted the possession of executive abilities of the loftiest order. In his large presence the other popes and politicians shrink to midges for the microscope. I would like to see him. I would rather see him and shake him by the tail than any other member of the European Concert. In the present paper I shall allow myself to use the word Jew as if it stood for both religion and race. It is handy; and besides, that is what the term means to the general world.

In the above letter one notes these points:

1.   The Jew is a well-behaved citizen.

2.   Can ignorance and fanaticism *alone* account for his unjust treatment ?

3.   Can Jews do anything to improve the situation?

4. The Jews have no party; they are non-participants.

5. Will the persecution ever come to an end?

6. What has become of the golden rule?

Point No. 1. — We must grant proposition No. 1, for several sufficient reasons. The Jew is not a disturber of the peace of any country. Even his enemies will concede that. He is not a loafer, he is not a sot, he is not noisy, he is not a brawler nor a rioter, he is not quarrelsome. In the statistics of crime his presence is conspicuously rare — in all countries. With murder and other crimes of violence he has but little to do: he is a stranger to the hangman. In the police court's daily long roll of " assaults " and " drunk and disorderlies " his name seldom appears. That the Jewish home is a home in the truest sense is a fact which no one will dispute. The family is knitted together by the strongest affections; its members show each other every due respect; and reverence for the elders is an inviolate law of the house. The Jew is not a burden on the charities of the state nor of the city; these could cease from their functions without affecting him. When he is well enough, he works; when he is incapacitated, his own people take care of him. And not in a poor and stingy way, but with a fine and large benevolence. His race is entitled to be called the most benevolent of all the races of men. A Jewish beggar is not impossible, perhaps; such a thing may exist, but there are few

17E

men that can say they have seen that spectacle. Th
Jew has been staged in many uncomplimentar
forms, but, so far as I know, no dramatist has don
him the injustice to stage him as a beggar. When
ever a Jew has real need to beg, his people save hir
from the necessity of doing it. The charitable in
stitutions of the Jews are supported by Jewis
money, and amply. The Jews make no noise abou
it; it is done quietly; they do not nag and peste
and harass us for contributions; they give us peace
and set us an example — an example which we hav
not found ourselves able to follow; for by nature w
are not free givers, and have to be patiently an
persistently hunted down in the interest of the un
fortunate.

These facts are all on the credit side of the prop
osition that the Jew is a good and orderly citizen
Summed up, they certify that he is quiet, peaceable
industrious, unaddicted to high crimes and brut
dispositions; that his family life is commendable
that he is not a burden upon public charities; th
he is not a beggar; that in benevolence he is abov
the reach of competition. These are the ver
quintessentials of good citizenship. If you can ad
that he is as honest as the average of his neighbor
— But I think that question is affirmativel
answered by the fact that he is a successful busines
man. The basis of successful business is honesty
a business cannot thrive where the parties to
cannot trust each other. In the matter of numbe

he Jew counts for little in the overwhelming
opulation of New York; but that his honesty
ounts for much is guaranteed by the fact that the
immense wholesale business of Broadway, from the
Battery to Union Square, is substantially in his
ands.

I suppose that the most picturesque example in
history of a trader's trust in his fellow-trader was
he where it was not Christian trusting Christian, but
Christian trusting Jew. That Hessian Duke who
used to sell his subjects to George III. to fight
George Washington with got rich at it; and by-and-
by, when the wars engendered by the French
Revolution made his throne too warm for him, he
was obliged to fly the country. He was in a hurry,
and had to leave his earnings behind — $9,000,000.
He had to risk the money with some one without
security. He did not select a Christian, but a Jew
—a Jew of only modest means, but of high
character; a character so high that it left him lone-
some —Rothschild of Frankfort. Thirty years later,
when Europe had become quiet and safe again, the
Duke came back from overseas, and the Jew returned the loan, with interest added.*

---

* Here is another piece of picturesque history; and it reminds us
that shabbiness and dishonesty are not the monopoly of any race or
creed, but are merely human:

"Congress passed a bill to pay $379.56 to Moses Pendergrass, of Lib-
ertyville, Missouri. The story of the reason of this liberality is patheti-
cally interesting, and shows the sort of pickle that an honest man may
get into who undertakes to do an honest job of work for Uncle Sam.

The Jew has his other side. He has some discreditable ways, though he has not a monopoly of them, because he cannot get entirely rid of vexatious Christian competition. We have seen that he seldom transgresses the laws against crimes of violence.

In 1886 Moses Pendergrass put in a bid for the contract to carry the mail on the route from Knob Lick to Libertyville and Coffman, thirty miles a day, from July 1, 1887, for one year. He got the postmaster at Knob Lick to write the letter for him, and while Moses intended that his bid should be $400, his scribe carelessly made it $4. Moses got the contract, and did not find out about the mistake until the end of the first quarter, when he got his first pay. When he found at what rate he was working he was sorely cast down, and opened communication with the Post Office Department. The department informed him that he must either carry out his contract or throw it up, and that if he threw it up his bondsmen would have to pay the government $1,459.85 damages. So Moses carried out his contract, walked thirty miles every week-day for a year, and carried the mail, and received for his labor $4 — or, to be accurate, $6.84; for, the route being extended after his bid was accepted, the pay was proportionately increased. Now, after ten years a bill was finally passed to pay to Moses the difference between what he earned in that unlucky year and what he received."

The *Sun*, which tells the above story, says that bills were introduced in three or four Congresses for Moses's relief, and that committees repeatedly investigated his claim.

It took six Congresses, containing in their persons the compressed virtues of 70,000,000 of people, and cautiously and carefully giving expression to those virtues in the fear of God and the next election, eleven years to find out some way to cheat a fellow-Christian out of about $1 on his honestly executed contract, and out of nearly $300 due him on its enlarged terms. And they succeeded. During the same time they paid out $1,000,000,000 in pensions — a third of it unearned and undeserved. This indicates a splendid all-around competency in theft, for it starts with farthings, and works its industries all the way up to ship loads. It may be possible that the Jews can beat this, but the man that bets on it is taking chances.

Indeed, his dealings with courts are almost restricted to matters connected with commerce. He has a reputation for various small forms of cheating, and for practicing oppressive usury, and for burning himself out to get the insurance, and arranging for cunning contracts which leave him an exit but lock the other man in, and for smart evasions which find him safe and comfortable just within the strict letter of the law, when court and jury know very well that he has violated the spirit of it. He is a frequent and faithful and capable officer in the civil service, but he is charged with an unpatriotic disinclination to stand by the flag as a soldier — like the Christian Quaker.

Now if you offset these discreditable features by the creditable ones summarized in a preceding paragraph beginning with the words, "These facts are all on the credit side," and strike a balance, what must the verdict be? This, I think: that, the merits and demerits being fairly weighed and measured on both sides, the Christian can claim no superiority over the Jew in the matter of good citizenship.

Yet, in all countries, from the dawn of history, the Jew has been persistently and implacably hated, and with frequency persecuted.

Point No. 2.—"Can fanaticism *alone* account for this?"

Years ago I used to think that it was responsible for nearly all of it, but latterly I have come to think that this was an error. Indeed, it is now my conviction that it is responsible for hardly any of it.

17*₊*₊

In this connection I call to mind Genesis, chapter xlvii.

We have all thoughtfully — or unthoughtfully — read the pathetic story of the years of plenty and the years of famine in Egypt, and how Joseph, with that opportunity, made a corner in broken hearts, and the crusts of the poor, and human liberty — a corner whereby he took a nation's money all away, to the last penny; took a nation's live-stock all away, to the last hoof; took a nation's land away, to the last acre; then took the nation itself, buying it for bread, man by man, woman by woman, child by child, till all were slaves; a corner which took everything, left nothing; a corner so stupendous that, by comparison with it, the most gigantic corners in subsequent history are but baby things, for it dealt in hundreds of millions of bushels, and its profits were reckonable by hundreds of millions of dollars, and it was a disaster so crushing that its effects have not wholly disappeared from Egypt to-day, more than three thousand years after the event.

Is it presumable that the eye of Egypt was upon Joseph, the foreign Jew, all this time? I think it likely. Was it friendly? We must doubt it. Was Joseph establishing a character for his race which would survive long in Egypt ? And in time would his name come to be familiarly used to express that character — like Shylock's ? It is hardly to be doubted. Let us remember that this was *centuries before the crucifixion*.

I wish to come down eighteen hundred years later and refer to a remark made by one of the Latin historians. I read it in a translation many years ago, and it comes back to me now with force. It was alluding to a time when people were still living who could have seen the Saviour in the flesh. Christianity was so new that the people of Rome had hardly heard of it, and had but confused notions of what it was. The substance of the remark was this: Some Christians were persecuted in Rome through error, they being " *mistaken for Jews.*"

The meaning seems plain. These pagans had nothing against Christians, but they were quite ready to persecute Jews. For some reason or other they hated a Jew before they even knew what a Christian was. May I not assume, then, that the persecution of Jews is a thing which *antedates* Christianity and was not born of Christianity? I think so. What was the origin of the feeling?

When I was a boy, in the back settlements of the Mississippi Valley, where a gracious and beautiful Sunday-school simplicity and unpracticality prevailed, the " Yankee " (citizen of the New England States) was hated with a splendid energy. But religion had nothing to do with it. In a trade, the Yankee was held to be about five times the match of the Westerner. His shrewdness, his insight, his judgment, his knowledge, his enterprise, and his formidable cleverness in applying these forces were frankly confessed, and most competently cursed.

Q*₊*₊

In the cotton States, after the war, the simple and
ignorant negroes made the crops for the white
planter on shares.   The Jew came down in force, set
up shop on the plantation, supplied all the negro's
wants on credit, and at the end of the season was
proprietor of the negro's share of the present crop
and of part of his share of the next one.   Before
long, the whites detested the Jew, and it is doubtful
if the negro loved him.

The Jew is being legislated out of Russia.   The
reason is not concealed.   The movement was in-
stituted because the Christian peasant and villager
stood no chance against his commercial abilities.
He was always ready to lend money on a crop, and
sell vodka and other necessaries of life on credit
while the crop was growing.   When settlement day
came he owned the crop; and next year or year
after he owned the farm, like Joseph.

In the dull and ignorant England of John's time
everybody got into debt to the Jew.   He gathered
all lucrative enterprises into his hands; he was the
king of commerce; he was ready to be helpful in all
profitable ways; he even financed crusades for the
rescue of the Sepulchre.   To wipe out his account
with the nation and restore business to its natural
and incompetent channels he had to be banished the
realm.

For the like reasons Spain had to banish him
four hundred years ago, and Austria about a couple
of centuries later.

In all the ages Christian Europe has been obliged
to curtail his activities.   If he entered upon a
mechanical trade, the Christian had to retire from it.
If he set up as a doctor, he was the best one, and
he took the business.   If he exploited agriculture,
the other farmers had to get at something else.
Since there was no way to successfully compete
with him in any vocation, the law had to step in
and save the Christian from the poorhouse.   Trade
after trade was taken away from the Jew by statute
till practically none was left.   He was forbidden to
engage in agriculture; he was forbidden to practice
law; he was forbidden to practice medicine, except
among Jews; he was forbidden the handicrafts.
Even the seats of learning and the schools of science
had to be closed against this tremendous antagonist.
Still, almost bereft of employments, he found ways
to make money, even ways to get rich.   Also ways
to invest his takings well, for usury was not denied
him.   In the hard conditions suggested, the Jew
without brains could not survive, and the Jew with
brains had to keep them in good training and well
sharpened up, or starve.   Ages of restriction to the
one tool which the law was not able to take from
him — his brain — have made that tool singularly
competent; ages of compulsory disuse of his hands
have atrophied them, and he never uses them now.
This history has a very, very commercial look, a
most sordid and practical commercial look, the business aspect of a Chinese cheap-labor crusade.

Religious prejudices may account for one part of it,
but not for the other nine.

Protestants have persecuted Catholics, but they
did not take their livelihoods away from them. The
Catholics have persecuted the Protestants with
bloody and awful bitterness, but they never closed
agriculture and the handicrafts against them. Why
was that ? That has the candid look of genuine
religious persecution, not a trade-union boycott in a
religious disguise.

The Jews are harried and obstructed in Austria
and Germany, and lately in France; but England
and America give them an open field and yet
survive. Scotland offers them an unembarrassed
field too, but there are not many takers. There are
a few Jews in Glasgow, and one in Aberdeen; but
that is because they can't earn enough to get away.
The Scotch pay themselves that compliment, but it
is authentic.

I feel convinced that the Crucifixion has not much
to do with the world's attitude toward the Jew; that
the reasons for it are older than that event, as suggested by Egypt's experience and by Rome's regret
for having persecuted an unknown quantity called a
Christian, under the mistaken impression that she
was merely persecuting a Jew. *Merely* a Jew — a
skinned eel who was used to it, presumably. I am
persuaded that in Russia, Austria, and Germany
nine-tenths of the hostility to the Jew comes from
the average Christian's inability to compete success-

fully with the average Jew in business — in either straight business or the questionable sort.

In Berlin, a few years ago, I read a speech which frankly urged the expulsion of the Jews from Germany; and the agitator's *reason* was as frank as his proposition. It was this: *that eighty-five per cent.* of the successful lawyers of Berlin were Jews, and that about the same percentage of the great and lucrative businesses of all sorts in Germany were in the hands of the Jewish race! Isn't it an amazing confession? It was but another way of saying that in a population of 48,000,000, of whom only 500,-000 were registered as Jews, eighty-five per cent. of the brains and honesty of the whole was lodged in the Jews. I must insist upon the honesty — it is an essential of successful business, taken by and large. Of course it does not rule out rascals entirely, even among Christians, but it is a good working rule, nevertheless. The speaker's figures may have been inexact, but *the motive of persecution* stands out as clear as day.

The man claimed that in Berlin the banks, the newspapers, the theaters, the great mercantile, shipping, mining, and manufacturing interests, the big army and city contracts, the tramways, and pretty much all other properties of high value, and *also* the small businesses — were in the hands of the Jews. He said the Jew was pushing the Christian to the wall all along the line; that it was all a Christian could do to scrape together a living; and that the Jew *must* be banished, and soon — there was no other way of saving the Christian. Here in Vienna, last autumn, an agitator said that all these disastrous details were true of Austria-Hungary also; and in fierce language he demanded the expulsion of the Jews. When politicians come out without a blush and read the baby act in this frank way, *unrebuked*, it is a very good indication that they have a market back of them, and know where to fish for votes.

You note the crucial point of the mentioned agitation; the argument is that the Christian cannot *compete* with the Jew, and that hence his very bread is in peril. To human beings this is a much more hate-inspiring thing than is any detail connected with religion. With most people, of a necessity, bread and meat take first rank, religion second. I am convinced that the persecution of the Jew is not due in any large degree to religious prejudice.

No, the Jew is a money-getter; and in getting his money he is a very serious obstruction to less capable neighbors who are on the same quest. I think that that is the trouble. In estimating worldly values the Jew is not shallow, but deep. With precocious wisdom he found out in the morning of time that some men worship rank, some worship heroes, some worship power, some worship God, and that over these ideals they dispute and cannot unite — but that they all worship money; so he made it the end and aim of his life to get it. He

was at it in Egypt thirty-six centuries ago; he was
at it in Rome when that Christian got persecuted by
mistake for him; he has been at it ever since.   The
cost to him has been heavy; his success has made
the whole human race his enemy — but it has paid,
for it has brought him envy, and that is the only
thing which men will sell both soul and body to get.
He long ago observed that a millionaire commands
respect, a two-millionaire homage, a multi-millionaire
the deepest deeps of adoration.   We all know that
feeling; we have seen it express itself.   We have
noticed that when the average man mentions the
name of a multi-millionaire he does it with that
mixture in his voice of awe and reverence and lust
which burns in a Frenchman's eye when it falls on
another man's centime.

Point No. 4. — "The Jews have no party; they
are non-participants."

Perhaps you have let the secret out and given
yourself away.   It seems hardly a credit to the race
that it is able to say that; or to you, sir, that you
can say it without remorse; more, that you should
offer it as a plea against maltreatment, injustice, and
oppression.   Who gives the Jew the right, who
gives any race the right, to sit still, in a free
country, and let somebody else look after its safety?
The oppressed Jew was entitled to all pity in the
former times under brutal autocracies, for he was
weak and friendless, and had no way to help his
case.   But he has ways now, and he has had them

for a century, but I do not see that he has tried t
make serious use of them. When the Revolutio
set him free in France it was an act of grace — th
grace of other people; he does not appear in it a
a helper. I do not know that he helped when Eng
land set him free. Among the Twelve Sane Men o
France who have stepped forward with great Zola a
their head to fight (and win, I hope and believe*
the battle for the most infamously misused Jew o
modern times, do you find a great or rich o
illustrious Jew helping? In the United States h
was created free in the beginning — he did not nee
to help, of course. In Austria, and Germany, an
France he has a vote, but of what considerable us
is it to him? He doesn't seem to know how t
apply it to the best effect. With all his splendi
capacities and all his fat wealth he is to-day no
politically important in any country. In America
as early as 1854, the ignorant Irish hod-carrier, wh
had a spirit of his own and a way of exposing it t
the weather, made it apparent to all that he must b
politically reckoned with; yet fifteen years befor
that we hardly knew what an Irishman looked like
As an intelligent force, and numerically, he ha
always been away down, but he has governed th
country just the same. It was because he wa
organized. It made his vote valuable — in fact
essential.

You will say the Jew is everywhere numerically

* The article was written in the summer of 1898.—ED.

feeble. That is nothing to the point — with the
Irishman's history for an object-lesson. But I am
coming to your numerical feebleness presently. In
all parliamentary countries you could no doubt elect
Jews to the legislatures — and even *one* member in
such a body is sometimes a force which counts.
How deeply have you concerned yourselves about
this in Austria, France, and Germany? Or even in
America for that matter? You remark that the Jews
were not to blame for the riots in this Reichsrath
here, and you add with satisfaction that there wasn't
one in that body. That is not strictly correct; if it
were, would it not be in order for you to explain it
and apologize for it, not try to make a merit of it?
But I think that the Jew was by no means in as large
force there as he ought to have been, with his
chances. Austria opens the suffrage to him on fairly
liberal terms, and it must surely be his own fault
that he is so much in the background politically.

As to your numerical weakness. I mentioned
some figures awhile ago — 500,000 — as the Jewish
population of Germany. I will add some more —
000,000 in Russia, 5,000,000 in Austria, 250,000
the United States. I take them from memory; I
had them in the Encyclopædia Britannica about ten
years ago. Still, I am entirely sure of them. If
those statistics are correct, my argument is not as
strong as it ought to be as concerns America, but it
still has strength. It is plenty strong enough as
concerns Austria, for ten years ago 5,000,000 was

nine per cent. of the empire's population. The Irish would govern the Kingdom of Heaven if they had a strength there like that.

I have some suspicions; I got them at second hand, but they have remained with me these ten or twelve years. When I read in the E. B. that the Jewish population of the United States was 250,000, I wrote the editor, and explained to him that I was personally acquainted with more Jews than that in my country, and that his figures were without doubt a misprint for 25,000,000. I also added that I was personally acquainted with *that* many there; but that was only to raise his confidence in me, for it was not true. His answer miscarried, and I never got it; but I went around talking about the matter, and people told me they had reason to suspect that for business reasons many Jews whose dealings were mainly with the Christians did not report themselves as Jews in the census. It looked plausible; it looks plausible yet. Look at the city of New York; and look at Boston, and Philadelphia, and New Orleans, and Chicago, and Cincinnati, and San Francisco — how your race swarms in those places! — and everywhere else in America, down to the least little village. Read the signs on the marts of commerce and on the shops: Goldstein (gold stone), Edelstein (precious stone), Blumenthal (flower-vale), Rosenthal (rose-vale), Veilchenduft (violet odor), Singvogel (song-bird), Rosenzweig (rose branch), and all the amazing list of beautiful and enviable names

which Prussia and Austria glorified you with so long
ago. It is another instance of Europe's coarse and
cruel persecution of your race; not that it was
coarse and cruel to outfit it with pretty and poetical
names like those, but that it was coarse and cruel to
make it *pay* for them or else take such hideous and
often indecent names that to-day their owners never
use them; or, if they do, only on official papers.
And it was the many, not the few, who got the
odious names, they being too poor to bribe the
officials to grant them better ones.

Now why was the race renamed? I have been told
that in Prussia it was given to using fictitious names,
and often changing them, so as to beat the tax-
gatherer, escape military service, and so on; and
that finally the idea was hit upon of furnishing all
the inmates of a house with *one and the same sur-
name*, and then holding the house responsible right
long for those inmates, and accountable for any
disappearances that might occur; it made the Jews
keep track of *each other*, for self-interest's sake, and
saved the government the trouble.*

---

* In Austria the renaming was merely done because the Jews in
the newly acquired regions had no surnames, but were mostly named
Abraham and Moses, and therefore the tax-gatherer could not tell
other from which, and was likely to lose his reason over the matter.
The renaming was put into the hands of the War Department, and a
charming mess the graceless young lieutenants made of it. To them a
Jew was of no sort of consequence, and they labeled the race in a way
to make the angels weep. As an example take these two! *Abraham
Bellyache* and *Schmul Godbedamned.—Culled from " Namens Stu-
dien," by Karl Emil Franzos.*

18E

If that explanation of how the Jews of Prussi
came to be renamed is correct, if it is true that the
fictitiously registered themselves to gain certain ad
vantages, it may possibly be true that in Americ
they refrain from registering themselves as Jews t
fend off the damaging prejudices of the Christia
customer. I have no way of knowing whether th
notion is well founded or not. There may be oth
and better ways of explaining why only that poo
little 250,000 of our Jews got into the Encyclopædi;
I may, of course, be mistaken, but I am strongl
of the opinion that we have an immense Jewis
population in America.

Point No. 3. — "Can Jews do anything to in
prove the situation?"

I think so. If I may make a suggestion witho
seeming to be trying to teach my grandmother ho
to suck eggs, I will offer it. In our days we hav
learned the value of combination. We apply
everywhere — in railway systems, in trusts, in trac
unions, in Salvation Armies, in minor politics,
major politics, in European Concerts. Whatev
our strength may be, big or little, we *organize* i
We have found out that that is the only way to g
the most out of it that is in it. We know the wea
ness of individual sticks, and the strength of tl
concentrated fagot. Suppose you try a scheme li
this, for instance. In England and America p
every Jew on the census-book *as* a Jew (in case y
have not been doing that). Get up volunte

egiments composed of Jews solely, and, when the
rum beats, fall in and go to the front, so as to re-
ove the reproach that you have few Massénas
mong you, and that you feed on a country but
on't like to fight for it. Next, in politics, organize
our strength, band together, and deliver the casting
ote where you can, and where you can't, compel as
ood terms as possible. You huddle to yourselves
ready in all countries, but you huddle to no
fficient purpose, politically speaking. You do not
em to be organized, except for your charities.
iere you are omnipotent; there you compel your
e of recognition — you do not have to beg for it.
shows what you can do when you band together
r a definite purpose.

And then from America and England you can
courage your race in Austria, France, and Ger-
.ny, and materially help it. It was a pathetic tale
it was told by a poor Jew in Galicia a fortnight
o during the riots, after he had been raided by
Christian peasantry and despoiled of everything
had. He said his vote was of no value to him,
I he wished he could be excused from casting it,
indeed casting it was a sure *damage* to him, since
matter which party he voted for, the other party
ild come straight and take its revenge out of him.
e per cent. of the population of the empire,
se Jews, and apparently they cannot put a
ik into any candidate's platform! If you will
I our Irish lads over here I think they will

organize your race and change the aspect of the Reichsrath.

You seem to think that the Jews take no hand in politics here, that they are "absolutely non-participants." I am assured by men competent to speak that this is a very large error, that the Jews are exceedingly active in politics all over the empire, but that they scatter their work and their votes among the numerous parties, and thus lose the advantages to be had by concentration. I think that in America they scatter too, but you know more about that than I do.

Speaking of concentration, Dr. Herzl has a clear insight into the value of that. Have you heard of his plan? He wishes to gather the Jews of the world together in Palestine, with a government of their own — under the suzerainty of the Sultan, I suppose. At the convention of Berne, last year, there were delegates from everywhere, and the proposal was received with decided favor. I am not the Sultan, and I am not objecting; but if that concentration of the cunningest brains in the world was going to be made in a free country (bar Scotland), I think it would be politic to stop it. It will not be well to let that race find out its strength. If the horses knew theirs, we should not ride any more.

Point No. 5. — "Will the persecution of the Jews ever come to an end?"

On the score of religion, I think it has already come to an end. On the score of race prejudice

and trade, I have the idea that it will continue.
That is, here and there in spots about the world,
where a barbarous ignorance and a sort of mere
animal civilization prevail; but I do not think that
elsewhere the Jew need now stand in any fear of
being robbed and raided. Among the high civil-
izations he seems to be very comfortably situated
indeed, and to have more than his proportionate
share of the prosperities going. It has that look in
Vienna. I suppose the race prejudice cannot be
removed; but he can stand that; it is no particular
matter. By his make and ways he is substantially
a foreigner wherever he may be, and even the angels
dislike a foreigner. I am using this word foreigner
in the German sense — *stranger*. Nearly all of us
have an antipathy to a stranger, even of our own
nationality. We pile gripsacks in a vacant seat to
keep him from getting it; and a dog goes further,
and does as a savage would — challenges him on the
spot. The German dictionary seems to make no
distinction between a stranger and a foreigner; in its
view a stranger *is* a foreigner — a sound position, I
think. You will always be by ways and habits and
predilections substantially strangers — foreigners —
wherever you are, and that will probably keep the
race prejudice against you alive.

But you were the favorites of Heaven originally,
and your manifold and unfair prosperities convince
me that you have crowded back into that snug place
again. Here is an incident that is significant. Last

18*.*.*

week in Vienna a hail-storm struck the prodigious
Central Cemetery and made wasteful destruction
there. In the Christian part of it, according to the
official figures, 621 window panes were broken; more
than 900 singing-birds were killed; five great trees
and many small ones were torn to shreds and the
shreds scattered far and wide by the wind; the orna-
mental plants and other decorations of the graves
were ruined, and more than a hundred tomb-lanterns
shattered; and it took the cemetery's whole force
of 300 laborers more than three days to clear away
the storm's wreckage. In the report occurs this
remark — and in its italics you can hear it grit its
Christian teeth: ". . . . lediglich die *israelitisch*
Abtheilung des Friedhofes vom Hagelwetter *ganz
lich verschont* worden war." Not a hailstone hit the
Jewish reservation! Such nepotism makes me tired

Point No. 6. — " What has become of the golden
rule?"

It exists, it continues to sparkle, and is well taken
care of. It is Exhibit A in the Church's assets, and
we pull it out every Sunday and give it an airing
But you are not permitted to try to smuggle it into
this discussion, where it is irrelevant and would no
feel at home. It is strictly religious furniture, like
an acolyte, or a contribution-plate, or any of those
things. It has never been intruded into business
and Jewish persecution is not a religious passion,
is a business passion.

To conclude. — If the statistics are right, the Jew

constitute but *one per cent.* of the human race. It suggests a nebulous dim puff of star dust lost in the blaze of the Milky Way. Properly the Jew ought hardly to be heard of; but he is heard of, has always been heard of. He is as prominent on the planet as any other people, and his commercial importance is extravagantly out of proportion to the smallness of his bulk. His contributions to the world's list of great names in literature, science, art, music, finance, medicine, and abstruse learning are also away out of proportion to the weakness of his numbers. He has made a marvelous fight in this world, in all the ages; and has done it with his hands tied behind him. He could be vain of himself, and be excused for it. The Egyptian, the Babylonian, and the Persian rose, filled the planet with sound and splendor, then faded to dream-stuff and passed away; the Greek and the Roman followed, and made a vast noise, and they are gone; other peoples have sprung up and held their torch high for a time, but it burned out, and they sit in twilight now, or have vanished. The Jew saw them all, beat them all, and is now what he always was, exhibiting no decadence, no infirmities of age, no weakening of his parts, no slowing of his energies, no dulling of his alert and aggressive mind. All things are mortal but the Jew; all other forces pass, but he remains. What is the secret of his immortality?

R*₊*₊

FROM THE "LONDON TIMES" OF 1904

I

Correspondence of the "London Times."

CHICAGO, April 1, 1904.

I RESUME by cable-telephone where I left of
yesterday. For many hours, now, this vast city
— along with the rest of the globe, of course — ha
talked of nothing but the extraordinary episod
mentioned in my last report. In accordance with
your instructions, I will now trace the romance from
its beginnings down to the culmination of yesterday
— or to-day; call it which you like. By an odd
chance, I was a personal actor in a part of thi
drama myself. The opening scene plays in Vienna
Date, one o'clock in the morning, March 31, 1898
I had spent the evening at a social entertainment
About midnight I went away, in company with
the military attachés of the British, Italian, an
American embassies, to finish with a late smoke
This function had been appointed to take place i
the house of Lieutenant Hillyer, the third attach
mentioned in the above list. When we arrived ther
we found several visitors in the room: youn
Szczepanik;* Mr. K., his financial backer; Mr. W

---

* Pronounced (approximately) Ze*pan*nik.

(276)

the latter's secretary; and Lieutenant Clayton of the United States army. War was at that time threatening between Spain and our country, and Lieutenant Clayton had been sent to Europe on military business. I was well acquainted with young Szczepanik and his two friends, and I knew Mr. Clayton slightly. I had met him at West Point years before, when he was a cadet. It was when General Merritt was superintendent. He had the reputation of being an able officer, and also of being quick-tempered and plain-spoken.

This smoking-party had been gathered together partly for business. This business was to consider the availability of the telelectroscope for military service. It sounds oddly enough now, but it is nevertheless true that at that time the invention was not taken seriously by any one except its inventor. Even his financial supporter regarded it merely as a curious and interesting toy. Indeed, he was so convinced of this that he had actually postponed its use by the general world to the end of the dying century by granting a two years' exclusive lease of it to a syndicate, whose intent was to exploit it at the Paris World's Fair.

When we entered the smoking-room we found Lieutenant Clayton and Szczepanik engaged in a warm talk over the telelectroscope in the German tongue. Clayton was saying:

"Well, you know *my* opinion of it, anyway!" and he brought his fist down with emphasis upon the table.

" And I do not value it," retorted the young inventor, with provoking calmness of tone and manner.

Clayton turned to Mr. K., and said:

" *I* cannot see why you are wasting money on
this toy. In my opinion, the day will never come
when it will do a farthing's worth of real service for
any human being."

" That may be; yes, that may be; still, I have
put the money in it, and am content. I think,
myself, that it is only a toy; but Szczepanik claims
more for it, and I know him well enough to believe
that he can see farther than I can — either with his
telelectroscope or without it."

The soft answer did not cool Clayton down; it
seemed only to irritate him the more; and he repeated and emphasized his conviction that the invention would never do any man a farthing's worth
of real service. He even made it a " brass " farthing,
this time. Then he laid an English farthing on the
table, and added:

" Take that, Mr. K., and put it away; and if ever
the telelectroscope does any man an actual service,
— mind, a *real* service, — please mail it to me as a
reminder, and I will take back what I have been
saying. Will you?"

" I will ;" and Mr. K. put the coin in his pocket.

Mr. Clayton now turned toward Szczepanik, and
began with a taunt — a taunt which did not reach a
finish; Szczepanik interrupted it with a hardy retort,
and followed this with a blow. There was a brisk

fight for a moment or two; then the attachés separated the men.

The scene now changes to Chicago. Time, the autumn of 1901. As soon as the Paris contract released the telelectroscope, it was delivered to public use, and was soon connected with the telephonic systems of the whole world. The improved "limitless-distance" telephone was presently introduced, and the daily doings of the globe made visible to everybody, and audibly discussable, too, by witnesses separated by any number of leagues.

By and by Szczepanik arrived in Chicago. Clayton (now captain) was serving in that military department at the time. The two men resumed the Viennese quarrel of 1898. On three different occasions they quarreled, and were separated by witnesses. Then came an interval of two months, during which time Szczepanik was not seen by any of his friends, and it was at first supposed that he had gone off on a sight-seeing tour and would soon be heard from. But no; no word came from him. Then it was supposed that he had returned to Europe. Still, time drifted on, and he was not heard from. Nobody was troubled, for he was like most inventors and other kinds of poets, and went and came in a capricious way, and often without notice.

Now comes the tragedy. On the 29th of December, in a dark and unused compartment of the cellar under Captain Clayton's house, a corpse was discovered by one of Clayton's maid-servants. It was easily identified as Szczepanik's. The man had died by violence. Clayton was arrested, indicted, and brought to trial, charged with this murder. The evidence against him was perfect in every detail, and absolutely unassailable. Clayton admitted this himself. He said that a reasonable man could not examine this testimony with a dispassionate mind and not be convinced by it; yet the man would be in error, nevertheless. Clayton swore that he did not commit the murder, and that he had had nothing to do with it.

As your readers will remember, he was condemned to death. He had numerous and powerful friends, and they worked hard to save him, for none of them doubted the truth of his assertion. I did what little I could to help, for I had long since become a close friend of his, and thought I knew that it was not in his character to inveigle an enemy into a corner and assassinate him. During 1902 and 1903 he was several times reprieved by the governor; he was reprieved once more in the beginning of the present year, and the execution-day postponed to March 31st.

The governor's situation has been embarrassing, from the day of the condemnation, because of the fact that Clayton's wife is the governor's niece. The marriage took place in 1899, when Clayton was thirty-four and the girl twenty-three, and has been a happy one. There is one child, a little girl three

years old. Pity for the poor mother and child
kept the mouths of grumblers closed at first; but
this could not last forever,— for in America politics
has a hand in everything,— and by and by the
governor's political opponents began to call attention to his delay in allowing the law to take its
course. These hints have grown more and more
frequent of late, and more and more pronounced.
As a natural result, his own party grew nervous.
Its leaders began to visit Springfield and hold long
private conferences with him. He was now between
two fires. On the one hand, his niece was imploring
him to pardon her husband; on the other were the
leaders, insisting that he stand to his plain duty as
chief magistrate of the State, and place no further
bar to Clayton's execution. Duty won in the
struggle, and the governor gave his word that he
would not again respite the condemned man. This
was two weeks ago. Mrs. Clayton now said:

"Now that you have given your word, my last
hope is gone, for I know you will never go back
from it. But you have done the best you could for
John, and I have no reproaches for you. You love
him, and you love me, and we both know that if you
could honorably save him, you would do it. I will
go to him now, and be what help I can to him, and
get what comfort I may out of the few days that are
left to us before the night comes which will have no
end for me in life. You will be with me that day?
You will not let me bear it alone?"

" I will take you to him myself, poor child, and
I will be near you to the last."

By the governor's command, Clayton was now
allowed every indulgence he might ask for which
could interest his mind and soften the hardships of
his imprisonment. His wife and child spent the
days with him; I was his companion by night. He
was removed from the narrow cell which he had
occupied during such a dreary stretch of time, and
given the chief warden's roomy and comfortable
quarters. His mind was always busy with the
catastrophe of his life, and with the slaughtered
inventor, and he now took the fancy that he would
like to have the telelectroscope and divert his mind
with it. He had his wish. The connection was
made with the international telephone-station, and
day by day, and night by night, he called up one
corner of the globe after another, and looked upon
its life, and studied its strange sights, and spoke
with its people, and realized that by grace of this
marvelous instrument he was almost as free as the
birds of the air, although a prisoner under lock
and bars. He seldom spoke, and I never interrupted him when he was absorbed in this amusement. I sat in his parlor and read and smoked, and
the nights were very quiet and reposefully sociable
and I found them pleasant. Now and then I would
hear him say, " Give me Yedo "; next, " Give me
Hong-Kong "; next, " Give me Melbourne." And
I smoked on, and read in comfort, while he wandered

about the remote under-world, where the sun was shining in the sky, and the people were at their daily work. Sometimes the talk that came from those far regions through the microphone attachment interested me, and I listened.

Yesterday — I keep calling it yesterday, which is quite natural, for certain reasons — the instrument remained unused, and that, also, was natural, for it was the eve of the execution-day. It was spent in tears and lamentations and farewells. The governor and the wife and child remained until a quarter past eleven at night, and the scenes I witnessed were pitiful to see. The execution was to take place at four in the morning. A little after eleven a sound of hammering broke out upon the still night, and there was a glare of light, and the child cried out, "What is that, papa?" and ran to the window before she could be stopped, and clapped her small hands, and said: "Oh, come and see, mama — such a pretty thing they are making!" The mother knew — and fainted. It was the gallows!

She was carried away to her lodging, poor woman, and Clayton and I were alone — alone, and thinking, brooding, dreaming. We might have been statues, we sat so motionless and still. It was a wild night, for winter was come again for a moment, after the habit of this region in the early spring. The sky was starless and black, and a strong wind was blowing from the lake. The silence in the room was so deep that all outside sounds seemed exag-

gerated by contrast with it. These sounds were
fitting ones; they harmonized with the situation and
the conditions: the boom and thunder of sudden
storm-gusts among the roofs and chimneys, then the
dying down into moanings and wailings about the
eaves and angles; now and then a gnashing and
lashing rush of sleet along the window-panes; and
always the muffled and uncanny hammering of the
gallows-builders in the courtyard. After an age of
this, another sound — far off, and coming smothered
and faint through the riot of the tempest — a bell
tolling twelve! Another age, and it tolled again.
By and by, again. A dreary, long interval after
this, then the spectral sound floated to us once more
— one, two, three; and this time we caught our
breath: sixty minutes of life left!

Clayton rose, and stood by the window, and
looked up into the black sky, and listened to the
thrashing sleet and the piping wind; then he said:
" That a dying man's last of earth should be — this !"
After a little he said: " I must see the sun again —
the sun !" and the next moment he was feverishly
calling: " China! Give me China — Peking !"

I was strangely stirred, and said to myself: " To
think that it is a mere human being who does this
unimaginable miracle — turns winter into summer,
night into day, storm into calm, gives the freedom
of the great globe to a prisoner in his cell, and the
sun in his naked splendor to a man dying in
Egyptian darkness !"

I was listening.

"What light! what brilliancy! what radiance! . . . This is Peking?"

"Yes."

"The time?"

"Mid-afternoon."

"What is the great crowd for, and in such gorgeous costumes? What masses and masses of rich color and barbaric magnificence! And how they flash and glow and burn in the flooding sunlight! What *is* the occasion of it all?"

"The coronation of our new emperor — the Czar."

"But I thought that that was to take place yesterday."

"This *is* yesterday — to you."

"Certainly it is. But my mind is confused, these days; there are reasons for it. . . Is this the beginning of the procession?"

"Oh, no; it began to move an hour ago."

"Is there much more of it still to come?"

"Two hours of it. Why do you sigh?"

"Because I should like to see it all."

"And why can't you?"

"I have to go — presently."

"You have an engagement?"

After a pause, softly: "Yes." After another pause: "Who are these in the splendid pavilion?"

"The imperial family, and visiting royalties from here and there and yonder in the earth."

19E

" And who are those in the adjoining pavilions to
the right and left?"

" Ambassadors and their families and suites to the
right; unofficial foreigners to the left."

" If you will be so good, I —"

Boom! That distant bell again, tolling the half-
hour faintly through the tempest of wind and sleet.
The door opened, and the governor and the mother
and child entered — the woman in widow's weeds!
She fell upon her husband's breast in a passion of
sobs, and I — I could not stay; I could not bear it.
I went into the bedchamber, and closed the door.
I sat there waiting — waiting — waiting, and listening to the rattling sashes and the blustering of the
storm. After what seemed a long, long time, I
heard a rustle and movement in the parlor, and
knew that the clergyman and the sheriff and the
guard were come. There was some low-voiced
talking; then a hush; then a prayer, with a sound
of sobbing; presently, footfalls — the departure for
the gallows; then the child's happy voice: " Don'
cry *now*, mama, when we've got papa again, and
taking him home."

The door closed; they were gone. I was ashamed.
I was the only friend of the dying man that had no
spirit, no courage. I stepped into the room, and
said I would be a man and would follow. But we
are made as we are made, and we cannot help it.
did not go.

I fidgeted about the room nervously, and presently

went to the window, and softly raised it, — drawn
by that dread fascination which the terrible and the
awful exert,— and looked down upon the courtyard.
By the garish light of the electric lamps I saw the
little group of privileged witnesses, the wife crying
on her uncle's breast, the condemned man standing
on the scaffold with the halter around his neck, his
arms strapped to his body, the black cap on his
head, the sheriff at his side with his hand on the
drop, the clergyman in front of him with bare head
and his book in his hand.

" *I am the resurrection and the life —*"
I turned away. I could not listen; I could not
look. I did not know whither to go or what to do.
Mechanically, and without knowing it, I put my eye
to that strange instrument, and there was Peking
and the Czar's procession ! The next moment I was
leaning out of the window, gasping, suffocating,
trying to speak, but dumb from the very imminence
of the necessity of speaking. The preacher could
speak, but I, who had such need of words —

"*And may God have mercy upon your soul.
Amen.*"
The sheriff drew down the black cap, and laid his
hand upon the lever. I got my voice.

" Stop, for God's sake ! The man is innocent.
Come here and see Szczepanik face to face !"
Hardly three minutes later the governor had my
place at the window, and was saying:

" Strike off his bonds and set him free !"

Three minutes later all were in the parlor again.
The reader will imagine the scene; I have no need
to describe it. It was a sort of mad orgy of joy.

A messenger carried word to Szczepanik in the
pavilion, and one could see the distressed amaze-
ment dawn in his face as he listened to the tale.
Then he came to his end of the line, and talked with
Clayton and the governor and the others; and the
wife poured out her gratitude upon him for saving
her husband's life, and in her deep thankfulness she
kissed him at twelve thousand miles' range.

The telelectrophonoscopes of the globe were put
to service now, and for many hours the kings and
queens of many realms (with here and there a re-
porter) talked with Szczepanik, and praised him,
and the few scientific societies which had not already
made him an honorary member conferred that grace
upon him.

How had he come to disappear from among us?
It was easily explained. He had not grown used to
being a world-famous person, and had been forced
to break away from the lionizing that was robbing
him of all privacy and repose. So he grew a beard,
put on colored glasses, disguised himself a little in
other ways, then took a fictitious name, and went
off to wander about the earth in peace.

Such is the tale of the drama which began with
an inconsequential quarrel in Vienna in the spring
of 1898, and came near ending as a tragedy in the
spring of 1904.   MARK TWAIN.

II

Correspondence of the " London Times."

CHICAGO, April 5, 1904.

TO-DAY, by a clipper of the Electric Line, and the latter's Electric Railway connections, ar-rived an envelope from Vienna, for Captain Clay-on, containing an English farthing. The receiver of it was a good deal moved. He called up Vienna, and stood face to face with Mr. K., and said:

" I do not need to say anything; you can see it all in my face. My wife has the farthing. Do not be afraid — she will not throw it away."   M. T.

III

Correspondence of the " London Times."

CHICAGO, April 23, 1904.

NOW that the after developments of the Clayton case have run their course and reached a finish, I will sum them up. Clayton's romantic escape from a shameful death steeped all this region in an enchantment of wonder and joy — during the proverbial nine days. Then the sobering process followed, and men began to take thought, and to say: " But *a man was killed,* and Clayton killed him." Others replied: " That is true: we have been overlooking that important detail; we have been led away by excitement."

The feeling soon became general that Clayton ought to be tried again. Measures were taken

19*.*.*

accordingly, and the proper representations conveyed to Washington; for in America, under the new paragraph added to the Constitution in 1899, second trials are not State affairs, but national, and must be tried by the most august body in the land — the Supreme Court of the United States. The justices were, therefore, summoned to sit in Chicago. The session was held day before yesterday, and was opened with the usual impressive formalities, the nine judges appearing in their black robes, and the new chief justice (Lemaitre) presiding. In opening the case, the chief justice said:

"It is my opinion that this matter is quite simple. The prisoner at the bar was charged with murdering the man Szczepanik; he was tried for murdering the man Szczepanik; he was fairly tried, and justly condemned and sentenced to death for murdering the man Szczepanik. It turns out that the man Szczepanik was not murdered at all. By the decision of the French courts in the Dreyfus matter, it is established beyond cavil or question that the decisions of courts are permanent and cannot be revised. We are obliged to respect and adopt this precedent. It is upon precedents that the enduring edifice of jurisprudence is reared. The prisoner at the bar has been fairly and righteously condemned to death for the murder of the man Szczepanik, and, in my opinion, there is but one course to pursue in the matter: he must be hanged."

Mr. Justice Crawford said:

"But, your Excellency, he was pardoned on the scaffold for that."

"The pardon is not valid, and cannot stand, because he was pardoned for killing a man whom he had not killed. A man cannot be pardoned for a crime which he has not committed; it would be an absurdity."

"But, your Excellency, he did kill a man."

"That is an extraneous detail; we have nothing to do with it. The court cannot take up this crime until the prisoner has expiated the other one."

Mr. Justice Halleck said:

"If we order his execution, your Excellency, we shall bring about a miscarriage of justice; for the governor will pardon him again."

"He will not have the power. He cannot pardon a man for a crime which he has not committed. As I observed before, it would be an absurdity."

After a consultation, Mr. Justice Wadsworth said:

"Several of us have arrived at the conclusion, your Excellency, that it would be an error to hang the prisoner for killing Szczepanik, but only for killing the other man, since it is proven that he did not kill Szczepanik."

"On the contrary, it is proven that he *did* kill Szczepanik. By the French precedent, it is plain that we must abide by the finding of the court."

"But Szczepanik is still alive."

"So is Dreyfus."

In the end it was found impossible to ignore or

s*₊*₊

get around the French precedent.   There could be
but one result: Clayton was delivered over to the
executioner.   It made an immense excitement; the
State rose as one man and clamored for Clayton's
pardon and re-trial.   The governor issued the
pardon, but the Supreme Court was in duty bound
to annul it, and did so, and poor Clayton was
hanged yesterday.   The city is draped in black, and,
indeed, the like may be said of the State.   All
America is vocal with scorn of " French justice,"
and of the malignant little soldiers who invented it
and inflicted it upon the other Christian lands.

AT THE APPETITE CURE

THIS establishment's name is Hochberghaus. It is in Bohemia, a short day's journey from Vienna, and being in the Austrian empire is, of course, a health resort. The empire is made up of health resorts; it distributes health to the whole world. Its waters are all medicinal. They are bottled and sent throughout the earth; the natives themselves drink beer. This is self-sacrifice, apparently — but outlanders who have drunk Vienna beer have another idea about it. Particularly the Pilsener which one gets in a small cellar up an obscure back lane in the First Bezirk — the name has escaped me, but the place is easily found: You inquire for the Greek church; and when you get to it, go right along by — the next house is that little beer-mill. It is remote from all traffic and all noise; it is always Sunday there. There are two small rooms, with low ceilings supported by massive arches; the arches and ceilings are whitewashed, otherwise the rooms would pass for cells in the dungeons of a bastile. The furniture is plain and cheap, there is no ornamentation anywhere; yet it is a heaven for the self-sacrificers, for the beer there is incomparable; there is nothing like it elsewhere in the world.　In the first room you will find twelve or fifteen ladies and gentlemen of civilian quality; in the other one a dozen generals and ambassadors.　One may live in Vienna many months and not hear of this place; but having once heard of it and sampled it the sampler will afterward infest it.

However, this is all incidental — a mere passing note of gratitude for blessings received — it has nothing to do with my subject.　My subject is health resorts.　All unhealthy people ought to domicile themselves in Vienna, and use that as a base, making flights from time to time to the outlying resorts, according to need.　A flight to Marienbad to get rid of fat; a flight to Carlsbad to get rid of rheumatism; a flight to Kaltenleutgeben to take the water cure and get rid of the rest of the diseases.　It is all so handy.　You can stand in Vienna and toss a biscuit into Kaltenleutgeben, with a twelve-inch gun.　You can run out thither at any time of the day; you go by the phenomenally slow trains, and yet inside of an hour you have exchanged the glare and swelter of the city for wooded hills, and shady forest paths, and soft cool airs, and the music of birds, and the repose and peace of paradise.

And there are plenty of other health resorts at your service and convenient to get at from Vienna; charming places, all of them; Vienna sits in the center of a beautiful world of mountains with now

and then a lake and forests; in fact, no other city
is so fortunately situated.

There are abundance of health resorts, as I have
said. Among them this place — Hochberghaus. It
stands solitary on the top of a densely wooded
mountain, and is a building of great size. It is
called the Appetite Anstallt, and people who have
lost their appetites come here to get them restored.
When I arrived I was taken by Professor Haimberger
to his consulting-room and questioned:

" It is six o'clock. When did you eat last? "

" At noon."

" What did you eat?"

" Next to nothing."

" What was on the table?"

" The usual things."

" Chops, chickens, vegetables, and so on?"

" Yes; but don't mention them — I can't bear
it."

" Are you tired of them?"

" Oh, utterly. I wish I might never hear of them
again."

" The mere sight of food offends you, does it? "

" More, it revolts me."

The doctor considered awhile, then got out a long
menu and ran his eye slowly down it.

" I think," said he, " that what you need to eat
is — but here, choose for yourself."

I glanced at the list, and my stomach threw a
handspring. Of all the barbarous layouts that were

ever contrived, this was the most atrocious.   At the
top   stood   " tough, underdone, overdue tripe,
garnished with garlic " ;   half-way down the bill stood
" young   cat;   old   cat;   scrambled   cat " ;   at the
bottom stood " sailor-boots, softened with tallow —
served raw."   The wide intervals of the bill were
packed with dishes calculated to insult a cannibal.
I said :

" Doctor, it is not fair to joke over so serious a
case as mine.   I came here to get an appetite, not to
throw away the remnant that's left."

He said gravely : " I am not joking, why should
I joke ?"

" But I can't eat these horrors."

" Why not?"

He said it with a naïveté that was admirable,
whether it was real or assumed.

" Why not?   Because — why, doctor, for months
I have seldom been able to endure anything more
substantial than omelettes and custards.   These unspeakable dishes of yours —"

" Oh, you will come to like them.   They are very
good.   And you *must* eat them.   It is the rule of
the place, and is strict.   I cannot permit any departure from it."

I said smiling : " Well, then, doctor, you will have
to permit the departure of the patient.   I am
going."

He looked hurt, and said in a way which changed
the aspect of things :

" I am sure you would not do me that injustice. accepted you in good faith — you will not shame 1at confidence. This appetite-cure is my whole ving. If you should go forth from it with the sort f appetite which you now have, it could become 1own, and you can see, yourself, that people would 1y my cure failed in your case and hence can fail 1 other cases. You will not go; you will not do 1e this hurt."

I apologized and said I would stay.

" That is right. I was sure you would not go; would take the food from my family's mouths."

" Would they mind that? Do they eat these fiend- h things?"

" They? My family?" His eyes were full of 2ntle wonder. "Of course not."

" Oh, they don't! Do you?"

" Certainly not."

" I see. It's another case of a physician who 2esn't take his own medicine."

" I don't need it. It is six hours since you 1nched. Will you have supper now — or later?"

" I am not hungry, but now is as good a time as 1y, and I would like to be done with it and have it ff my mind. It is about my usual time, and regularity commanded by all the authorities. Yes, I will try 2 nibble a little now — I wish a light horsewhipping ould answer instead."

The professor handed me that odious menu.

" Choose — or will you have it later?"

" Oh, dear me, show me to my room; I forgot your hard rule."

" Wait just a moment before you finally decide. There is another rule. If you choose now, the order will be filled at once; but if you wait, you will have to await my pleasure. You cannot get a dish from that entire bill until I consent."

" All right. Show me to my room, and send the cook to bed; there is not going to be any hurry."

The professor took me up one flight of stairs and showed me into a most inviting and comfortable apartment consisting of parlor, bedchamber, and bathroom.

The front windows looked out over a far-reaching spread of green glades and valleys, and tumbled hills clothed with forests — a noble solitude unvexed by the fussy world. In the parlor were many shelves filled with books. The professor said he would now leave me to myself; and added:

" Smoke and read as much as you please, drink all the water you like. When you get hungry, ring and give your order, and I will decide whether it shall be filled or not. Yours is a stubborn, bad case, and I think the first fourteen dishes in the bill are each and all too delicate for its needs. I ask you as a favor to restrain yourself and not call for them."

" Restrain myself, is it? Give yourself no uneasiness. You are going to save money by me. The idea of coaxing a sick man's appetite back with this buzzard-fare is clear insanity."

I said it with bitterness, for I felt outraged by this
calm, cold talk over these heartless new engines of
assassination. The doctor looked grieved, but not
offended. He laid the bill of fare on the commode
at my bed's head, " so that it would be handy,"
and said:

" Yours is not the worst case I have encountered,
by any means; still it is a bad one and requires
robust treatment; therefore I shall be gratified if you
will restrain yourself and skip down to No. 15 and
begin with that."

Then he left me and I began to undress, for I was
dog-tired and very sleepy. I slept fifteen hours and
woke up finely refreshed at ten the next morning.
Vienna coffee! It was the first thing I thought of —
that unapproachable luxury — that sumptuous coffee-
house coffee, compared with which all other European
coffee and all American hotel coffee is mere fluid
poverty. I rang, and ordered it; also Vienna bread,
that delicious invention. The servant spoke through
the wicket in the door and said — but you know what
he said. He referred me to the bill of fare. I
allowed him to go — I had no further use for him.

After the bath I dressed and started for a walk,
and got as far as the door. It was locked on the
outside. I rang and the servant came and explained
that it was another rule. The seclusion of the patient
was required until after the first meal. I had not
been particularly anxious to get out before; but it
was different now. Being locked in makes a person

wishful to get out. I soon began to find it difficul
to put in the time. At two o'clock I had bee
twenty-six hours without food. I had been growing
hungry for some time; I recognized that I wa
not only hungry now, but hungry with a stron
adjective in front of it. Yet I was not hungr
enough to face the bill of fare.

I must put in the time somehow. I would rea
and smoke. I did it; hour by hour. The book
were all of one breed — shipwrecks; people lost i
deserts; people shut up in caved-in mines; peopl
starving in besieged cities. I read about all th
revolting dishes that ever famishing men had staye
their hunger with. During the first hours these thing
nauseated me; hours followed in which they did no
so affect me; still other hours followed in which
found myself smacking my lips over some tolerabl
infernal messes. When I had been without foo
forty-five hours I ran eagerly to the bell and ordere
the second dish in the bill, which was a sort c
dumplings containing a compost made of caviar an
tar.

It was refused me. During the next fifteen hour
I visited the bell every now and then and ordered
dish that was further down the list. Always a re
fusal. But I was conquering prejudice after pre
udice, right along; I was making sure progress;
was creeping up on No. 15 with deadly certainty
and my heart beat faster and faster, my hopes ros
higher and higher.

At last when food had not passed my lips for sixty hours, victory was mine, and I ordered No. 5:

" Soft-boiled spring chicken — in the egg; six dozen, hot and fragrant!"

In fifteen minutes it was there; and the doctor along with it, rubbing his hands with joy. He said with great excitement:

" It's a cure, it's a cure! I knew I could do it. Dear sir, my grand system never fails — never. You've got your appetite back — you know you have; say it and make me happy."

" Bring on your carrion — I can eat anything in the bill!"

" Oh, this is noble, this is splendid — but I knew I could do it, the system never fails. How are the birds?"

" Never was anything so delicious in the world; and yet as a rule I don't care for game. But don't interrupt me, don't — I can't spare my mouth, I really can't."

Then the doctor said:

" The cure is perfect. There is no more doubt or danger. Let the poultry alone; I can trust you with a beefsteak, now."

The beefsteak came — as much as a basketful of — with potatoes, and Vienna bread and coffee; and I ate a meal then that was worth all the costly preparation I had made for it. And dripped tears of gratitude into the gravy all the time — gratitude

20E

to the doctor for putting a little plain common sense
into me when I had been empty of it so many, many
years.

II

Thirty years ago Haimberger went off on a long
voyage in a sailing-ship. There were fifteen passengers on board. The table-fare was of the regula-
tion pattern of the day: At 7 in the morning, a cup
of bad coffee in bed; at 9, breakfast: bad coffee
with condensed milk; soggy rolls, crackers, salt fish;
at 1 P. M., luncheon: cold tongue, cold ham, cold
corned beef, soggy cold rolls, crackers; 5 P. M.,
dinner: thick pea soup, salt fish, hot corned beef
and sauerkraut, boiled pork and beans, pudding;
9 till 11 P. M., supper: tea, with condensed
milk, cold tongue, cold ham, pickles, sea biscuit,
pickled oysters, pickled pig's feet, grilled bones,
golden buck.

At the end of the first week eating had ceased;
nibbling had taken its place. The passengers came
to the table, but it was partly to put in the time, and
partly because the wisdom of the ages commanded
them to be regular in their meals. They were tired
of the coarse and monotonous fare, and took no
interest in it, had no appetite for it. All day
and every day they roamed the ship half hungry,
plagued by their gnawing stomachs, moody, untalk-
ative, miserable. Among them were three confirmed
dyspeptics. These became shadows in the course
of three weeks. There was also a bedridden invalid;

e lived on boiled rice; he could not look at the
egular dishes.

Now came shipwreck and life in open boats,
ith the usual paucity of food. Provisions ran lower
nd lower. The appetites improved, then. When
othing was left but raw ham and the ration of that
as down to two ounces a day per person, the
ppetites were perfect. At the end of fifteen days
ne dyspeptics, the invalid and the most delicate
ldies in the party were chewing sailor-boots in
cstasy, and only complaining because the supply of
nem was limited. Yet these were the same people
ho couldn't endure the ship's tedious corned beef
nd sauerkraut and other crudities. They were
escued by an English vessel. Within ten days the
hole fifteen were in as good condition as they had
een when the shipwreck occurred.

"They had suffered no damage by their adven-
ire," said the professor. "Do you note that?"

"Yes."

"Do you note it well?"

"Yes — I think I do."

"But you don't. You hesitate. You don't
se to the importance of it. I will say it again
- with emphasis —*not one of them suffered any
amage.*"

"Now I begin to see. Yes, it was indeed re-
aarkable."

"Nothing of the kind. It was perfectly natural.
here was no reason why they should suffer damage.

They were undergoing Nature's Appetite Cure, th
best and wisest in the world."

" Is that where you got your idea?"

" That is where I got it."

" It taught those people a valuable lesson."

" What makes you think that?"

" Why shouldn't I? You seem to think it taugl
you one."

" That is nothing to the point. I am not
fool."

" I see. Were they fools?"

" They were human beings."

" Is it the same thing?"

" Why do you ask? You know it yourself. A
regards his health — and the rest of the things
the average man is what his environment and l
superstitions have made him; and their function
to make him an ass. He can't add up three or fo
new circumstances together and perceive what th
mean; it is beyond him. He is not capable
observing for himself. He has to get everythi
at second-hand. If what are miscalled the lo
animals were as silly as man is, they would all per
from the earth in a year."

" Those passengers learned no lesson, then?"

" Not a sign of it. They went to their regu
meals in the English ship, and pretty soon they w
nibbling again — nibbling, appetiteless, disgus
with the food, moody, miserable, half hungry, tl
outraged stomachs cursing and swearing and whin

nd supplicating all day long. And in vain, for they
ere the stomachs of fools."

" Then as I understand it, your scheme is —"

" Quite simple. Don't eat till you are hungry.
f the food fails to taste good, fails to satisfy you,
ejoice you, comfort you, don't eat again until
ou are *very* hungry. Then it will rejoice you —
nd do you good, too."

" And I observe no regularity, as to hours?"

" When you are conquering a bad appetite — no.
.fter it is conquered, regularity is no harm, so long
s the appetite remains good. As soon as the
ppetite wavers, apply the corrective again — which
 starvation, long or short according to the needs of
ıe case."

" The best diet, I suppose — I mean the whole-
•mest ——"

" All diets are wholesome. Some are wholesomer
.an others, but all the ordinary diets are wholesome
ıough for the people who use them. Whether the
•od be fine or coarse, it will taste good and it will
ıurish if a watch be kept upon the appetite and a
tle starvation introduced every time it weakens.
ansen was used to fine fare, but when his meals
ere restricted to bear-meat months at a time he
ıffered no damage and no discomfort, because his
•petite was kept at par through the difficulty of
ıtting his bear-meat regularly."

" But doctors arrange carefully considered and
:licate diets for invalids."

20*٭٭

" They can't help it. The invalid is full of in
herited superstitions and won't starve himself. H
believes it would certainly kill him."

" It would weaken him, wouldn't it?"

" Nothing to hurt. Look at the invalids in ou
shipwreck. They lived fifteen days on pinches o
raw ham, a suck at sailor-boots, and genera
starvation. It weakened them, but it didn't hur
them. It put them in fine shape to eat heartily o
hearty food and build themselves up to a conditio
of robust health. But they did not perceive that
they lost their opportunity; they remained invalids
it served them right. Do you know the tricks tha
the health-resort doctors play?"

" What is it?"

" My   system   disguised — covert   starvatior
Grape-cure, bath-cure, mud-cure — it is all the sam
The grape and the bath and the mud make a sho
and do a trifle of the work — the real work is dor
by the surreptitious starvation. The patient a
customed to four meals and late hours — at bo
ends of the day — now consider what he has to
at a health resort. He gets up at 6 in the mornin
Eats one egg. Tramps up and down a promenac
two hours with the other fools. Eats a butterfl
Slowly drinks a glass of filtered sewage that sme
like a buzzard's breath. Promenades another tv
hours, but alone; if you speak to him he sa
anxiously, ' My water ! — I am walking off n
water ! — please don't interrupt,' and goes stumpi

HE EATS A BUTTERFLY

long again. Eats a candied rose-leaf. Lies at rest
in the silence and solitude of his room for hours;
mustn't speak, mustn't read, mustn't smoke. The
doctor comes and feels of his heart, now, and his
pulse, and thumps his breast and his back and his
stomach, and listens for results through a penny
flageolet; then orders the man's bath — half a degree,
Réaumur, cooler than yesterday. After the bath,
another egg. A glass of sewage at 3 or 4 in the
afternoon, and promenade solemnly with the other
freaks. Dinner at 6 — half a doughnut and a cup
of tea. Walk again. Half-past 8, supper — more
butterfly; at 9, to bed. Six weeks of this régime
— think of it. It starves a man out and puts him in
splendid condition. It would have the same effect
in London, New York, Jericho — anywhere.''

" How long does it take to put a person in condition here?''

" It ought to take but a day or two; but in fact
it takes from one to six weeks, according to the
character and mentality of the patient.''

" How is that?''

" Do you see that crowd of women playing foot-
ball, and boxing, and jumping fences yonder? They
have been here six or seven weeks. They were
spectral poor weaklings when they came. They
were accustomed to nibbling at dainties and delicacies
at set hours four times a day, and they had no
appetite for anything. I questioned them, and then
locked them into their rooms, the frailest ones to

T*₊*₊

starve nine or ten hours, the others twelve or fifteen.
Before long they began to beg; and indeed they
suffered a good deal. They complained of nausea,
headache, and so on. It was good to see them eat
when the time was up. They could not remember
when the devouring of a meal had afforded them
such rapture — that was their word. Now, then,
that ought to have ended their cure, but it didn't.
They were free to go to any meals in the house, an
they chose their accustomed four. Within a day o
two I had to interfere. Their appetites wer
weakening. I made them knock out a meal. Tha
set them up again. Then they resumed the four.
begged them to learn to knock out a meal themselves
without waiting for me. Up to a fortnight ago the
couldn't; they really hadn't manhood enough; b
they were gaining it, and now I think they are safe
They drop out a meal every now and then of the
own accord. They are in fine condition now, an
they might safely go home, I think, but their co
fidence is not quite perfect yet, so they are waitin
awhile."

" Other cases are different?"

" Oh, yes. Sometimes a man learns the who
trick in a week. Learns to regulate his appetite a
keep it in perfect order. Learns to drop out a me
with frequency and not mind it."

" But why drop the entire meal out? Why not
part of it?"

" It's a poor device, and inadequate. If t

tomach doesn't call vigorously — with a shout, as
ou may say — it is better not to pester it but just
ive it a real rest.   Some people can eat more meals
han others, and still thrive.   There are all sorts of
eople, and all sorts of appetites.   I will show you
 man presently who was accustomed to nibble at
ight meals a day.   It was beyond the proper gait
f his appetite by two.   I have got him down to
ix a day, now, and he is all right, and enjoys life.
How many meals do you effect per day?"

   " Formerly — for twenty-two years — a meal and
 half; during the past two years, two and a half:
offee and a roll at 9, luncheon at 1, dinner at 7:30
r 8."

   " Formerly a meal and a half — that is, coffee
nd a roll at 9, dinner in the evening, nothing
etween — is that it?"

   " Yes."

   " Why did you add a meal?"

   " It was the family's idea.   They were uneasy.
hey thought I was killing myself."

   " You found a meal and a half per day enough,
ll through the twenty-two years?"

   " Plenty."

   " Your present poor condition is due to the extra
eal.   Drop it out.   You are trying to eat oftener
an your stomach demands.   You don't gain, you
se.   You eat less food now, in a day, on two and a
 half meals, than you formerly ate on one and a
alf."

" True — a good deal less; for in those old days my dinner was a very sizable thing."

" Put yourself on a single meal a day, now — dinner — for a few days, till you secure a good, sound, regular, trustworthy appetite, then take to your one and a half permanently, and don't listen to the family any more. When you have any ordinary ailment, particularly of a feverish sort, eat nothing at all during twenty-four hours. That will cure it. It will cure the stubbornest cold in the head, too. No cold in the head can survive twenty-four hours on modified starvation."

" I know it. I have proved it many a time."

IN MEMORIAM

OLIVIA SUSAN CLEMENS

DIED AUGUST 18, 1896; AGED 24

IN a fair valley — oh, how long ago, how long ago!
  Where all the broad expanse was clothed in vines
And fruitful fields and meadows starred with flowers,
And clear streams wandered at their idle will,
And still lakes slept, their burnished surfaces
A dream of painted clouds, and soft airs
Went whispering with odorous breath,
And all was peace — in that fair vale,
Shut from the troubled world, a nameless hamlet
    drowsed.

Hard by, apart, a temple stood;
And strangers from the outer world
Passing, noted it with tired eyes,
And seeing, saw it not:
A glimpse of its fair form — an answering momen-
    tary thrill —
And they passed on, careless and unaware.

They could not know the cunning of its make;
They could not know the secret shut up in its heart;
Only the dwellers of the hamlet knew:

They knew that what seemed brass was gold;
What marble seemed, was ivory;
The glories that enriched the milky surfaces —
The trailing vines, and interwoven flowers,
And tropic birds awing, clothed all in tinted fire —
They knew for what they were, not what they
 seemed:
Encrustings all of gems, not perishable splendors of
 the brush.
They knew the secret spot where one must stand —
They knew the surest hour, the proper slant of
 sun —
To gather in, unmarred, undimmed,
The vision of the fane in all its fairy grace,
A fainting dream against the opal sky.
 And more than this. They knew
That in the temple's inmost place a spirit dwelt,
Made all of light!
 For glimpses of it they had caught
Beyond the curtains when the priests
That served the altar came and went.

All loved that light and held it dear
That had this partial grace;
But the adoring priests alone who lived
By day and night submerged in its immortal glow
Knew all its power and depth, and could appraise
 the loss
If it should fade and fail and come no more.

 All this was long ago — so long ago!

The light burned on; and they that worship'd it,
And they that caught its flash at intervals and held
   it dear,
Contented lived in its secure possession.   Ah,
How long ago it was!
                    And then when they
Were nothing fearing, and God's peace was in the
   air,
And none was prophesying harm —
The vast disaster fell:
Where stood the temple when the sun went down,
Was vacant desert when it rose again!

   Ah, yes! 'Tis ages since it chanced!
                         So long ago it was,
That from the memory of the hamlet-folk the Light
   has passed —
They scarce believing, now, that once it was,
Or, if believing, yet not missing it,
And reconciled to have it gone.

   Not so the priests!   Oh, not so
The stricken ones that served it day and night,
Adoring it, abiding in the healing of its peace:
They stand, yet, where erst they stood
Speechless in that dim morning long ago;
And still they gaze, as then they gazed,
And murmur, " It will come again;
It knows our pain — it knows — it knows —
Ah, surely it will come again."

                                        S. L. C.

LAKE LUCERNE, August 18, 1897.

MARK TWAIN

A BIOGRAPHICAL SKETCH

By SAMUEL E. MOFFETT

IN 1835 the creation of the Western empire of America had just begun. In the whole region west of the Mississippi, which now contains 21,-000,000 people — nearly twice the entire population of the United States at that time — there were less than half a million white inhabitants. There were only two states beyond the great river, Louisiana and Missouri. There were only two considerable groups of population, one about New Orleans, the other about St. Louis. If we omit New Orleans, which is east of the river, there was only one place in all that vast domain with any pretension to be called a city. That was St. Louis, and that metropolis, the wonder and pride of all the Western country, had no more than 10,000 inhabitants.

It was in this frontier region, on the extreme fringe of settlement " that just divides the desert from the sown," that Samuel Langhorne Clemens was born, November 30, 1835, in the hamlet of Florida, Missouri. His parents had come there to be in the

thick of the Western boom, and by a fate for
which no lack of foresight on their part was to
blame, they found themselves in a place which
succeeded in accumulating 125 inhabitants in the
next sixty years.   When we read of the westward sweep of population and wealth in the United
States, it seems as if those who were in the van
of that movement must have been inevitably carried on to fortune.   But that was a tide full of
eddies and back currents, and Mark Twain's parents
possessed a faculty for finding them that appears
nothing less than miraculous.   The whole Western
empire was before them where to choose.   They
could have bought the entire site of Chicago for a
pair of boots.   They could have taken up a farm
within the present city limits of St. Louis.   What
they actually did was to live for a time in Columbia,
Kentucky, with a small property in land, and six
inherited slaves, then to move to Jamestown, on the
Cumberland plateau of Tennessee, a place that was
then no farther removed from the currents of the
world's life than Uganda, but which no resident of
that or any other part of Central Africa would now
regard as a serious competitor, and next to migrate
to Missouri, passing St. Louis and settling first in
Florida, and afterward in Hannibal.   But when the
whole map was blank the promise of fortune glowed
as rosily in these regions as anywhere else.   Florida
had great expectations when Jackson was President.
When John Marshall Clemens took up 80,000 acres

of land in Tennessee, he thought he had established his children as territorial magnates. That phantom vision of wealth furnished later one of the motives of " The Gilded Age." It conferred no other benefit.

If Samuel Clemens missed a fortune he inherited good blood. On both sides his family had been settled in the South since early colonial times. His father, John Marshall Clemens, of Virginia, was a descendant of Gregory Clemens, who became one of the judges that condemned Charles I. to death, was excepted from the amnesty after the Restoration in consequence, and lost his head. A cousin of John M. Clemens, Jeremiah Clemens, represented Alabama in the United States Senate from 1849 to 1853.

Through his mother, Jane Lampton (Lambton), the boy was descended from the Lambtons of Durham, whose modern English representatives still possess the lands held by their ancestors of the same name since the twelfth century. Some of her forbears on the maternal side, the Montgomerys, went with Daniel Boone to Kentucky, and were in the thick of the romantic and tragic events that accompanied the settlement of the " Dark and Bloody Ground," and she herself was born there twenty-nine years after the first log cabin was built within the limits of the present commonwealth. She was one of the earliest, prettiest, and brightest of the many belles that have given Kentucky such an enviable reputation as a nursery of fair women, and her vivacity and wit left no doubt in the minds of her friends concerning the source of her son's genius.

John Marshall Clemens, who had been trained for the bar in Virginia, served for some years as a magistrate at Hannibal, holding for a time the position of county judge.   With his death, in March, 1847, Mark Twain's formal education came to an end, and his education in real life began.   He had always been a delicate boy, and his father, in consequence, had been lenient in the matter of enforcing attendance at school, although he had been profoundly anxious that his children should be well educated.   His wish was fulfilled, although not in the way he had expected. It is a fortunate thing for literature that Mark Twain was never ground into smooth uniformity under the scholastic emery wheel.   He has made the world his university, and in men, and books, and strange places, and all the phases of an infinitely varied life, has built an education broad and deep, on the foundations of an undisturbed individuality.

His high school was a village printing-office, where his elder brother Orion was conducting a newspaper. The thirteen-year-old boy served in all capacities, and in the occasional absences of his chief he reveled in personal journalism, with original illustrations hacked on wooden blocks with a jackknife, to an extent that riveted the town's attention, " but not its admiration," as his brother plaintively confessed. The editor spoke with feeling, for he had to take the consequences of these exploits on his return.

From his earliest childhood young Clemens had
been of an adventurous disposition. Before he was
thirteen, he had been extracted three times from the
Mississippi, and six times from Bear Creek, in a substantially drowned condition, but his mother, with
the high confidence in his future that never deserted
her, merely remarked: " People who are born to be
hanged are safe in the water." By 1853 the Hannibal tether had become too short for him. He
disappeared from home and wandered from one
Eastern printing-office to another. He saw the
World's Fair at New York, and other marvels,
and supported himself by setting type. At the
end of this *Wanderjahr* financial stress drove him
back to his family. He lived at St. Louis, Mus-
catine, and Keokuk until 1857, when he induced
the great Horace Bixby to teach him the mystery
of steamboat piloting. The charm of all this
warm, indolent existence in the sleepy river towns
has colored his whole subsequent life. In " Tom
Sawyer," " Huckleberry Finn," " Life on the
Mississippi," and " Pudd'nhead Wilson," every
phase of that vanished estate is lovingly dwelt upon.

Native character will always make itself felt, but
one may wonder whether Mark Twain's humor would
have developed in quite so sympathetic and buoyant
a vein if he had been brought up in Ecclefechan
instead of in Hannibal, and whether Carlyle might
not have been a little more human if he had spent his
boyhood in Hannibal instead of in Ecclefechan.

A Mississippi pilot in the later fifties was a
personage of imposing grandeur. He was a miracle
of attainments; he was the absolute master of his
boat while it was under way, and just before his
fall he commanded a salary precisely equal to that
earned at that time by the Vice-President of the
United States or a Justice of the Supreme Court.
The best proof of the superlative majesty and desira-
bility of his position is the fact that Samuel Clemens
deliberately subjected himself to the incredible labor
necessary to attain it — a labor compared with which
the efforts needed to acquire the degree of Doctor of
Philosophy at a University are as light as a summer course of modern novels. To appreciate the
full meaning of a pilot's marvelous education, one
must read the whole of "Life on the Mississippi,"
but this extract may give a partial idea of a
single feature of that training — the cultivation of
the memory:

"First of all, there is one faculty which a pilot
must incessantly cultivate until he has brought it to
absolute perfection. Nothing short of perfection
will do. That faculty is memory. He cannot stop
with merely thinking a thing is so and so; he must
know it; for this is eminently one of the exact sci-
ences. With what scorn a pilot was looked upon, in
the old times, if he ever ventured to deal in that
feeble phrase ' I think,' instead of the vigorous one
' know!' One cannot easily realize what a tremendous thing it is to know every trivial detail of

twelve hundred miles of river, and know it with absolute exactness. If you will take the longest street in New York, and travel up and down it, conning its features patiently until you know every house, and window, and door, and lamp-post, and big and little sign by heart, and know them so accurately that you can instantly name the one you are abreast of when you are set down at random in that street in the middle of an inky black night, you will then have a tolerable notion of the amount and the exactness of a pilot's knowledge who carries the Mississippi River in his head. And then, if you will go on until you know every street crossing, the character, size, and position of the crossing-stones, and the varying depth of mud in each of those numberless places, you will have some idea of what the pilot must know in order to keep a Mississippi steamer out of trouble. Next, if you will take half of the signs in that long street and *change their places* once a month, and still manage to know their new positions accurately on dark nights, and keep up with these repeated changes without making any mistakes, you will understand what is required of a pilot's peerless memory by the fickle Mississippi.

" I think a pilot's memory is about the most wonderful thing in the world. To know the Old and New Testaments by heart, and be able to recite them glibly, forward or backward, or begin at random anywhere in the book and recite both ways, and never trip or make a mistake, is no extravagant mass of knowledge, and no marvelous facility, compared to a pilot's massed knowledge of the Mississippi, and his marvelous facility in handling it. . .

" And how easily and comfortably the pilot's memory does its work; how placidly effortless is its way; how *unconsciously* it lays up its vast stores, hour by hour, day by day, and never loses or mislays a single valuable package of them all! Take an instance. Let a leadsman say: ' Half twain! half twain! half twain! half twain! half twain!' until it becomes as monotonous as the ticking of a clock; let conversation be going on all the time, and the pilot be doing his share of the talking, and no longer consciously listening to the leadsman; and in the midst of this endless string of half twains let a single ' quarter twain!' be interjected, without emphasis, and then the half twain cry go on again, just as before: two or three weeks later that pilot can describe with precision the boat's position in the river when that quarter twain was uttered, and give you such a lot of head marks, stern marks, and side marks to guide you that you ought to be able to take the boat there and put her in that same spot again yourself! The cry of ' Quarter twain ' did not really take his mind from his talk, but his trained faculties instantly photographed the bearings, noted the change of depth, and laid up the important details for future reference without requiring any assistance from him in the matter."

21*.*.

Young Clemens went through all that appalling training, stored away in his head the bewildering mass of knowledge a pilot's duties required, received the license that was the diploma of the river university, entered into regular employment, and regarded himself as established for life, when the outbreak of the Civil War wiped out his occupation at a stroke, and made his weary apprenticeship a useless labor. The commercial navigation of the lower Mississippi was stopped by a line of fire, and black, squat gunboats, their sloping sides plated with railroad iron, took the place of the gorgeous white side-wheelers, whose pilots had been the envied aristocrats of the river towns. Clemens was in New Orleans when Louisiana seceded, and started North the next day. The boat ran a blockade every day of her trip, and on the last night of the voyage the batteries at the Jefferson barracks, just below St. Louis, fired two shots through her chimneys.

Brought up in a slaveholding atmosphere, Mark Twain naturally sympathized at first with the South. In June he joined the Confederates in Ralls County, Missouri, as a Second Lieutenant under General Tom Harris. His military career lasted for two weeks. Narrowly missing the distinction of being captured by Colonel Ulysses S. Grant, he resigned, explaining that he had become " incapacitated by fatigue " through persistent retreating. In his subsequent writings he has always treated his brief experience of warfare as a burlesque episode, although the official

reports and correspondence of the Confederate com-
manders speak very respectfully of the work of the
raw countrymen of the Harris Brigade. The elder
Clemens brother, Orion, was *persona grata* to the
Administration of President Lincoln, and received in
consequence an appointment as the first Secretary of
the new Territory of Nevada. He offered his speedily
reconstructed junior the position of private secretary
to himself, " with nothing to do and no salary."
The two crossed the plains in the overland coach in
eighteen days — almost precisely the time it will take
to go from New York to Vladivostok when the
Trans-Siberian Railway is finished.

A year of variegated fortune hunting among the
silver mines of the Humboldt and Esmeralda regions
followed. Occasional letters written during this time
to the leading newspaper of the Territory, the Virginia
City *Territorial Enterprise*, attracted the attention
of the proprietor, Mr. J. T. Goodman, a man of
keen and unerring literary instinct, and he offered
the writer the position of local editor on his staff.
With the duties of this place were combined those
of legislative correspondent at Carson City, the
capital. The work of young Clemens created a sensation among the lawmakers. He wrote a weekly
letter, spined with barbed personalities. It appeared every Sunday, and on Mondays the legislative business was obstructed with the complaints of
members who rose to questions of privilege, and expressed their opinion of the correspondent with

T*.*.

acerbity. This encouraged him to give his letters more individuality by signing them. For this purpose he adopted the old Mississippi leadsman's call for two fathoms (twelve feet)—"Mark Twain."

At that particular period dueling was a passing fashion on the Comstock. The refinements of Parisian civilization had not penetrated there, and a Washoe duel seldom left more than one survivor. The weapons were always Colt's navy revolvers— distance, fifteen paces; fire and advance; six shots allowed. Mark Twain became involved in a quarrel with Mr. Laird, the editor of the Virginia *Union*, and the situation seemed to call for a duel. Neither combatant was an expert with the pistol, but Mark Twain was fortunate enough to have a second who was. The men were practicing in adjacent gorges, Mr. Laird doing fairly well, and his opponent hitting everything but the mark. A small bird lit on a sage bush thirty yards away, and Mark Twain's second fired and knocked off its head. At that moment the enemy came over the ridge, saw the dead bird, observed the distance, and learned from Gillis, the humorist's second, that the feat had been performed by Mark Twain, for whom such an exploit was nothing remarkable. They withdrew for consultation, and then offered a formal apology, after which peace was restored, leaving Mark Twain with the honors of war.

However, this incident was the means of effecting another change in his life. There was a new law which prescribed two years' imprisonment for any one who should send, carry, or accept a challenge. The fame of the proposed duel had reached the capital, eighteen miles away, and the governor wrathfully gave orders for the arrest of all concerned, announcing his intention of making an example that would be remembered. A friend of the duelists heard of their danger, outrode the officers of the law, and hurried the parties over the border into California.

Mark Twain found a berth as city editor of the San Francisco *Morning Call*, but he was not adapted to routine newspaper work, and in a couple of years he made another bid for fortune in the mines. He tried the "pocket mines" of California, this time, at Jackass Gulch, in Calaveras County, but was fortunate enough to find no pockets. Thus he escaped the hypnotic fascination that has kept some intermittently successful pocket miners willing prisoners in Sierra cabins for life, and in three months he was back in San Francisco, penniless, but in the line of literary promotion. He wrote letters for the Virginia *Enterprise* for a time, but tiring of that, welcomed an assignment to visit Hawaii for the Sacramento *Union*, and write about the sugar interests. It was in Honolulu that he accomplished one of his greatest feats of "straight newspaper work." The clipper *Hornet* had been burned on "the line," and when the skeleton survivors arrived, after a passage of forty-three days in an open boat on ten days' provisions, Mark Twain gathered their stories, worked all day and all night, and threw a complete account of the horror aboard a schooner that had already cast off. It was the only full account that reached California, and it was not only a clean " scoop " of unusual magnitude, but an admirable piece of literary art. The *Union* testified its appreciation by paying the correspondent ten times the current rates for it.

After six months in the Islands, Mark Twain returned to California, and made his first venture upon the lecture platform. He was warmly received, and delivered several lectures with profit. In 1867 he went East by way of the Isthmus, and joined the Quaker City excursion to Europe and the Holy Land, as correspondent of the *Alta California*, of San Francisco. During this tour of five or six months the party visited the principal ports of the Mediterranean and the Black Sea. From this trip grew " The Innocents Abroad," the creator of Mark Twain's reputation as a literary force of the first order. " The Celebrated Jumping Frog of Calaveras County " had preceded it, but " The Innocents " gave the author his first introduction to international literature. A hundred thousand copies were sold the first year, and as many more later.

Four years of lecturing followed — distasteful, but profitable. Mark Twain always shrank from the public exhibition of himself on the platform, but he was a popular favorite there from the first. He was one of a little group, including Henry Ward Beecher

and two or three others, for whom every lyceum committee in the country was bidding, and whose capture
at any price insured the success of a lecture course.

The Quaker City excursion had a more important
result than the production of " The Innocents
Abroad." Through her brother, who was one of
the party, Mr. Clemens became acquainted with
Miss Olivia L. Langdon, the daughter of Jervis
Langdon, of Elmira, New York, and this acquaintance led, in February, 1870, to one of the most ideal
marriages in literary history.

Four children came of this union. The eldest,
Langdon, a son, was born in November, 1870, and
died in 1872. The second, Susan Olivia, a daughter,
was born in the latter year, and lived only twenty-
four years, but long enough to develop extraordinary
mental gifts and every grace of character. Two
other daughters, Clara Langdon and Jean, were born
in 1874 and 1880, respectively, and still live (1899).

Mark Twain's first home as a man of family was
in Buffalo, in a house given to the bride by her father
as a wedding present. He bought a third interest
in a daily newspaper, the Buffalo *Express*, and
joined its staff. But his time for jogging in harness
was past. It was his last attempt at regular newspaper work, and a year of it was enough. He had
become assured of a market for anything he might
produce, and he could choose his own place and
time for writing.

There was a tempting literary colony at Hartford;

the place was steeped in an atmosphere of antique
peace and beauty, and the Clemens family were
captivated by its charm. They moved there in
October, 1871, and soon built a house which was
one of the earliest fruits of the artistic revolt against
the mid-century Philistinism of domestic architecture
in America. For years it was an object of wonder
to the simple-minded tourist. The facts that its
rooms were arranged for the convenience of those
who were to occupy them, and that its windows,
gables, and porches were distributed with an eye to
the beauty, comfort, and picturesqueness of that
particular house, instead of following the traditional
lines laid down by the carpenters and contractors
who designed most of the dwellings of the period,
distracted the critics, and gave rise to grave dis-
cussions in the newspapers throughout the country
of " Mark Twain's practical joke."

The years that followed brought a steady literary
development. " Roughing It," which was written
in 1872, and scored a success hardly second to that
of " The Innocents," was, like that, simply a
humorous narrative of personal experiences, variegated by brilliant splashes of description; but with
" The Gilded Age," which was produced in the same
year, in collaboration with Mr. Charles Dudley
Warner, the humorist began to evolve into the
philosopher. " Tom Sawyer," appearing in 1876,
was a veritable manual of boy nature, and its sequel,
" Huckleberry Finn," which was published nine years

later, was not only an advanced treatise in the same
science, but a most moving study of the workings
of the untutored human soul, in boy and man.
" The Prince and the Pauper," 1882, " A Connecti-
cut Yankee at King Arthur's Court " (1890), and
" Pudd'nhead Wilson " (first published serially in
1893-94), were all alive with a comprehensive and
passionate sympathy to which their humor was quite
subordinate, although Mark Twain never wrote, and
probably never will write, a book that could be read
without laughter. His humor is as irrepressible as
Lincoln's, and like that, it bubbles out on the most
solemn occasions; but still, again like Lincoln's, it
has a way of seeming, in spite of the surface in-
congruity, to belong there. But it was in the
" Personal Recollections of Joan of Arc," whose
anonymous serial publication in 1894-95 betrayed
some critics of reputation into the absurdity of
attributing it to other authors, notwithstanding the
characteristic evidences of its paternity that obtruded
themselves on every page, that Mark Twain became
most distinctly a prophet of humanity. Here, at
last, was a book with nothing ephemeral about it —
one that will reach the elemental human heart as well
among the flying machines of the next century, as it
does among the automobiles of to-day, or as it would
have done among the stage coaches of a hundred
years ago.

And side by side with this spiritual growth had
come a growth in knowledge and in culture. The

Mark Twain of " The Innocents," keen-eyed, quick
of understanding, and full of fresh, eager interest in
all Europe had to show, but frankly avowing that he
" did not know what in the mischief the Renaissance
was," had developed into an accomplished scholar
and a man of the world for whom the globe had few
surprises left.　The Mark Twain of 1895 might con-
ceivably have written " The Innocents Abroad,"
although it would have required an effort to put himself in the necessary frame of mind, but the Mark
Twain of 1869 could no more have written " Joan
of Arc " than he could have deciphered the Maya
hieroglyphics.

In 1873 the family spent some months in England
and Scotland, and Mr. Clemens lectured for a few
weeks in London.　Another European journey
followed in 1878.

" A Tramp Abroad " was the result of this
tour, which lasted eighteen months.　" The Prince
and the Pauper," " Life on the Mississippi," and
" Huckleberry Finn " appeared in quick succes-
sion in 1882, 1883, and 1885.　Considerably more
amusing than anything the humorist ever wrote was
the fact that the trustees of some village libraries in
New England solemnly voted that " Huckleberry
Finn," whose power of moral uplift has hardly been
surpassed by any book of our time, was too demoral-
izing to be allowed on their shelves.

All this time fortune had been steadily favorable,
and Mark Twain had been spoken of by the press,

sometimes with admiration, as an example of the
financial success possible in literature, and sometimes
with uncharitable envy, as a haughty millionaire,
forgetful of his humble friends. But now began the
series of unfortunate investments that swept away
the accumulations of half a lifetime of hard work,
and left him loaded with debts incurred by other
men. In 1885 he financed the publishing house of
Charles L. Webster & Company in New York. The
firm began business with the prestige of a brilliant
coup. It secured the publication of the Memoirs
of General Grant, which achieved a sale of more
than 600,000 volumes. The first check received
by the Grant heirs was for $200,000, and this was
followed a few months later by one for $150,000.
These are the largest checks ever paid for an author's
work on either side of the Atlantic. Meanwhile,
Mr. Clemens was spending great sums on a type-
setting machine of such seductive ingenuity as to
captivate the imagination of everybody who saw it.
It worked to perfection, but it was too complicated
and expensive for commercial use, and after sinking
a fortune in it between 1886 and 1889, Mark Twain
had to write off the whole investment as a dead loss.

On top of this the publishing house, which had
been supposed to be doing a profitable business,
turned out to have been incapably conducted, and
all the money that came into its hands was lost.
Mark Twain contributed $65,000 in efforts to save
its life, but to no purpose, and when it finally failed,

he found that it had not only absorbed everything he had put in, but had incurred liabilities of $96,000, of which less than one-third was covered by assets.

He could easily have avoided any legal liability for the debts, but as the credit of the company had been based largely upon his name, he felt bound in honor to pay them. In 1895-96 he took his wife and second daughter on a lecturing tour around the world, wrote "Following the Equator," and cleared off the obligations of the house in full.

The years 1897, 1898, and 1899 were spent in England, Switzerland, and Austria. Vienna took the family to its heart, and Mark Twain achieved such a popularity among all classes there as is rarely won by a foreigner anywhere. He saw the manufacture of a good deal of history in that time. It was his fortune, for instance, to be present in the Austrian Reichsrath on the memorable occasion when it was invaded by sixty policemen, and sixteen refractory members were dragged roughly out of the hall. That momentous event in the progress of parliamentary government profoundly impressed him.

Mark Twain, although so characteristically American in every fiber, does not appeal to Americans alone, nor even to the English-speaking race. His work has stood the test of translation into French, German, Russian, Italian, Swedish, Norwegian, and Magyar. That is pretty good evidence that it possesses the universal quality that marks the master.

Another evidence of its fidelity to human nature is the readiness with which it lends itself to dramatization. "The Gilded Age," "Tom Sawyer," "The Prince and the Pauper," and "Pudd'nhead Wilson" have all been successful on the stage.

In the thirty-eight years of his literary activity Mark Twain has seen generation after generation of "American humorists" rise, expand into sudden popularity, and disappear, leaving hardly a memory behind. If he has not written himself out like them, if his place in literature has become every year more assured, it is because his "humor" has been something radically different from theirs. It has been irresistibly laughter-provoking, but its sole end has never been to make people laugh. Its more important purpose has been to make them think and feel. And with the progress of the years Mark Twain's own thoughts have become finer, his own feelings deeper and more responsive. Sympathy with the suffering, hatred of injustice and oppression, and enthusiasm for all that tends to make the world a more tolerable place for mankind to live in, have grown with his accumulating knowledge of life as it is. That is why Mark Twain has become a classic, not only at home, but in all lands whose people read and think about the common joys and sorrows of humanity.